the shadow over santa susana

BLACK MAGIC, MIND CONTROL, AND THE MANSON FAMILY MYTHOS

ADAM GORIGHTLY

CREATION

the shadow over santa susana

by
Adam Gorightly

ISBN 978-1-84068-151-2
Published 2009 by Creation Books
www.creationbooks.com

Design by Tears Corporation
A Butcherbest Production

Author's acknowledgements
Special thanks to:
Scott Moody for his perseverance in pulling this project together.
Mark Turner for editorial assistance and fact-checking.

CONTENTS

The pass where the Devil you can see
Flying along in sight for all to see
On the edge of infinity
Santa Susana is the pass where you look to be
Santa Susana is the pass where you look for me
12 in the night love or fight
Anyway is right if you come out in the night
It's so out of sight in Devil's Canyon

–Lyrics seized during the Barker Ranch raid

Foreword

Charles Manson, and the mythos surrounding him, his followers, and their bloody deeds, has loomed large in my consciousness since the summer of 1969. Back then, I was eight years old, and living with my family on the West Side of Los Angeles. That August I was just aware enough of the adult world's darker doings to realize that something terrible had happened to some famous and not-so-famous people living in the Southland, and that "crazy hippies" were behind it. Eventually said crazy hippies were put on trial for the Tate-LaBianca killing, and I remember being both frightened and fascinated by press photos and news clips of the hirsute, wild-eyed Manson and his female followers.

As I grew older, I devoured books, articles, and TV shows about the Manson murders. Like so many other people, I was fascinated by the story of the backwoods ex-con who slithered into San Francisco's Summer of Love like the Serpent of Eden, seducing young girls with acid and erotic domination, and programming them to be murderous drones in his plan to start a cataclysmic race war.

Sure, there were far deadlier and more deranged murderers around – in the post-Sixties era, California alone produced several lone-wolf serial killers who bested the entire Manson Family's total death count several times over. And the hippie cult's slaughter at the Tate and LaBianca residences didn't nearly measure up to the (self-inflicted) carnage wrought by Jim Jones and Marshall Applewhite's sects in the years after Helter Skelter.

But there was something special about Charles Manson and his "Family" that has held public attention like no other criminal case in the forty years since those terrible nights in Los Angeles. Part of the allure, of course, was the perfectly-mixed stew of sensational elements in the case: mass murder, sex, drugs, movie stars, hippies, occultism, outlaw bikers, cowboys, and the *Day-of-the-Locust*-on-acid atmosphere of late-Sixties L.A.'s entertainment and cultural underworlds.

And of course, there is Manson himself. A diminutive, unlettered son of the White rural underclass who had spent most of his pre-Family life in institutional lockups, Charlie missed out on most of the social programming of the adult world and postwar American culture, and consequently became something of a cipher, and a human mirror that reflected both his followers' and outsiders' desires and fears. To the Family, he was variously Jesus and Satan, a tender lover and a stern father, a religious prophet and a gang leader. To the world at large, he's been variously an embodiment of the dark forces lurking beneath the Sixties' love-and-peace ideals; a symbol of the American penal system's assorted failures; and a walking warning-sign to spiritual seekers tempted to give their all to a self-proclaimed guru.

Yet there remains a final element in the Manson Family story that gnaws at one's consciousness like no other true-crime case. It's hard to read either of the canonical books on the case – Vincent Bugliosi's *Helter Skelter*, or Ed Sanders' *The Family* – and not feel that big pieces of the story are missing, that there's much more to the bizarre and bloody dealings of the Clan Manson than either author reveals. Bugliosi himself believed that there was more motivation to the killings beyond the acid-addled "Helter Skelter" doomsday-scenario he played to the jury and the press, and admitted that he didn't bother to follow up many intriguing leads in his (understandable) rush to put Manson and his girls permanently behind bars. Counterculture writer Sanders tried to follow some of those leads, and ran up against stony silence, death threats, and lawsuits. (*The Family* was bowdlerized after its first edition because one well-connected cult that Sanders connected to Manson threatened the publisher with legal retribution.)

And this is where Adam Gorightly comes in. Forty years after the bloody nights on Cielo and Waverly Drives, this self-confessed "crackpot historian" has fearlessly assembled all the known facts, rumors, speculations, and theories surrounding the Manson Mythos, and put together an epic narrative that follows the whole bizarre tale, from the out-of-wedlock birth of "No-Name Maddox" in 1934, to our own era of postmodern paranoia.

Gorightly dares to look behind the official story of the *Acid-Crazed-Hippie-Cult*, and what he finds is both troubling and fascinating. He questions how a known career criminal and ostensible parolee like Manson could have spent two years servicing and abusing a personal harem of under-aged women, pestering well-connected music- and movie-industry figures, and running a variety of felonious moneymaking activities, without earning an immediate trip back to the Federal lockup. He examines unsolved disappearances and murders of dozens of people associated with the Family, and muses on their possible fates. And he uncovers disturbing information about Manson and his followers' connections to sinister occult groups, mind-control experiments, perverted Hollywood stars, major drug dealing operations, Satanic cult murders, and even the less-savory activities of military-intelligence agents and other professional spooks.

The book is, at one level, a straightforward and detailed recounting of the Helter Skelter murder case. It's also an alternatively serious and fanciful inquiry into the many unanswered questions surrounding Manson, his followers, and their many questionable activities and connections outside the Tate-LaBianca homicides. And it's a meditation on the symbolic aspects of the Manson mythos, and how the now-septuagenarian lifer, the mass media, and the popular imagination have conspired to create a folk demon of far greater potency and staying power than the that ascribed to more bloodthirsty criminals, or more destructive cults. Until some future author can dig more deeply into the Manson mysteries and myths, *The Shadow over Santa Susana* will stand as the definitive story of this most intriguing, bizarre and enigmatic phenomenon.

Mike Marinacci
Author, *Mysterious California*; and co-author, *Weird California*
San Francisco, CA
January 2009

CHAPTER 1
"No Name Maddox"

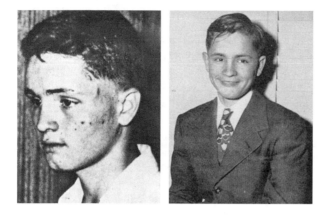

From the moment of his birth – November 11th, 1934, in Cincinnati, Ohio – Charles Manson's place in society was firmly fixed as an outcast, just as later in prison, he carved an X into his forehead, a symbol that he'd X-ed himself out of society.

As the hospital record stated, upon the occasion of his illegitimate birth, the child in question – who later became known as the "most dangerous man alive!" – was christened unceremoniously "no name Maddox." Charlie was a bastard, and later identified the person who fathered him as "a young drugstore cowboy" named Colonel Scott. Manson's mother, Ada Kathleen Maddox (she used Kathleen as her first name), later married an older man, William Manson, who hung around long enough to give Charlie his surname.

Kathleen Maddox was not unlike the many young wayward women Charlie later accepted into his Family. Manson himself once compared her to a hippie, while others have described her as a teenaged alcoholic prostitute. Kathleen left home in her early teens and learned to live by her wits on the streets, giving birth to Manson at sixteen, then abandoning him when she came to realize the responsibilities associated with parenthood. On one occasion, it has been reported, Kathleen traded Charlie to a barmaid for a pitcher of beer.

In 1939, Kathleen was arrested when she and her brother robbed a West Virginia service station, knocking out the attendant with a coke bottle. For this offense, Kathleen was sentenced to five years in the state pen. Thus began a shuttling process for Charlie indicative of his youth, and a foreshadowing of his future – being handed from one relative to another; from one prison to the next.

During the time Kathleen was behind bars, Manson was caught in a revolving door of relatives, orphanages and reformatories. At first, Charlie was sent to his grandmother in West Virginia, the very same repressive and religiously strict environment his own mother had fled. But due to his grandmother's ill health, a few weeks later Charlie was shipped to McMechen, West Virginia to live with Kathleen's sister Glenna, and his uncle Bill.

Charlie's uncle Bill was a strict disciplinarian. One time he threatened to dress Charlie up like a girl if he didn't shape up. Apparently, Charlie didn't take this threat seriously, because when he started school, Uncle Bill followed through with his promise. This incident did nothing but help toughen up little Charlie, as he ended up kicking ass on everyone who made fun of him in his frilly pink outfit. This result must have pleased Uncle Bill, Charlie later recalled, because from then on he let him wear boy's clothing.

Anecdotal tales from Charlie's youth paint the picture of Manson as someone who was either headed toward greatness, infamy, or a combination of both. One Christmas Day, the neighborhood kids took relish rubbing in the fact that they'd gotten all these great gifts, knowing full well that Charlie was poor, and had received very little. Resenting how the kids chided him, Charlie inflicted his youthful wrath upon the gloating brats when he decided to round up all the neighbor's Christmas toys, cart them home and –with a pile of kindling – started a fire that consumed all of the presents. As a result, the children's parents called the local sheriff, and – although he wasn't taken to jail – this proved to be Charlie's first official brush with the law. At the time, he was just seven years old.

After her release from prison, Kathleen and Charlie were re-united. In this setting, Charlie learned to live by his wits and fend for himself, as his mom often abandoned him several days at a time. The childhood background provided to Charlie was an endless string of bars, flophouses and all night movie joints. As always, Charlie was out of place, an unwanted child that his mom was unwilling to take responsibility for. At times, she would promise to change her ways, but the prospect of a good time always lured her back to the nightlife. During his mom's many absences, Charlie passed his time developing his common thievery skills. Due to these activities, Manson was eventually caught and sent away to reform school.

Manson's first step on the path toward prospective rehabilitation was the Gibault School for Boys in Terre Haute, Indiana, which he entered in 1947, and subsequently fled in 1948. Afterwards, Charlie was sent to a juvenile center in Indianapolis, from which he escaped the very next day.

Thus began the revolving reformatory door, which Manson was in and out of over the next few years. By the time he was in his early teens, Charlie was living on his own and working odd jobs, often supplementing whatever income he could generate by thievery. Again, this inevitably brought him to the attention of the authorities. However, the next time Manson was brought before the court, the attending Judge decided to take pity on the lad, arranging for him to be sent to the prestigious Boy's Town U.S.A. An Indianapolis newspaper at this time carried a photo of young Charles Milles Manson – decked out in suit and tie – being admitted into Boy's Town, which carried the corny caption: "Boy leaves 'sinful' home for a new life in Boy's Town." Charlie's "new life" lasted all of three days, when he ran away from the school. Later in 1948, Charlie was committed to the Indiana Boy's School in Plainfield. Later in life, he referred to Plainfield as "Pains-ville", and described it as a seriously fucked-up joint filled with sadomasochist perverts masquerading as authority.

Manson's troubles at Plainfield began when he got on the bad side of a guard who, on a regular basis, beat him up. This same guard would often masturbate while at the same time directing the older boys thump on Manson. The boys would torture Charlie until he'd cry out in pain, and it was at this point that the pervert guard was able to achieve orgasm. According to Manson, this same guard also incited the older boys to gang rape him. Throughout this period, Charlie was severely whipped as a form of discipline. To this day he still bears the scars on his back; a testament to the state-sanctioned violence that help create Manson's lunatic legacy.

On parole, at age seventeen, Charlie raped a younger boy. By the time he was eighteen, Manson was listed as "dangerous, with homosexual and assaultive tendencies." In February 1951, he led a gang of youths in an escape from Plainfield, high-tailing it for California. For transportation, they stole cars, robbing service stations along the way to keep their tanks gassed. This spree of automotive thievery came to a sudden halt outside of Beaver, Utah, when the wayward lads hit a roadblock intended for some bank robbers.

Charlie's next stop was the National Training School for Boys in Washington, D.C., where he was examined by the staff psychiatrist, a Dr. Block. During their session, Manson ingratiated himself with Dr. Block, using those innate abilities which later in life served him well; the uncanny aptitude to fit into whatever role was most advantageous to manipulate others, whether they were parole officers, psychiatrists, or young wayward women looking for a daddy.

Manson has been described more than once by those who knew him best as a chameleon; someone who could change his skin at a moment's notice to fit a changing environment. This, and Manson's ability to get others to buy into his "trip", were perhaps his two most influential abilities;

the power of persuasion and control. Although Dr. Block observed that Manson was a "slick institutionalized youth" who knew how to work the system, his report on Charlie ended with the summation that, "...one is left with the feeling that behind all this lies an extremely sensitive boy who has not yet given up in terms of securing some kind of love and affection from the world."

During the next three months, Manson became Dr. Block's pet project. What the doctor believed would help young Charles most was a positive environment to build up his self-esteem, shattered – as it was – by the rejection he had experienced from his mother. In short, Dr. Block recommended that Charlie be given the transfer he desired.

In November, shortly after his seventeenth birthday, Charlie was visited by his aunt Glenna, who told the authorities she'd be willing to supply her nephew a home and employment upon release. So things were looking up for Charlie, who was due for parole in February 1952. But for some reason, a self-destructive bent reared itself in the form of an act of forced sodomy Charlie performed on another lad at the institution.

Charlie's next stop was the Federal Reformatory in Petersburg, Virginia, where he arrived on January 18th, 1952. By August, Charlie had committed eight disciplinary offenses, three of which were violently sexual in nature. Later that year, he was transferred to the Federal Reformatory at Chillicothe, Ohio, where legend has it Manson encountered a lad named Toby who possessed strange powers and was "definitely satanic."

As Charlie recalled, "(Toby) could hypnotize by suggestion. He could have you turn into stone, your hands; you could hold them together in front of you and you could have four people, even six others, divided at each side of you and pulling on each arm and they couldn't separate; couldn't break your hands apart."

Manson became fascinated by the vast powers of the mind. Through Toby, he glimpsed the infinite reservoirs residing within, waiting to be tapped for prospective good or ill. Also at Chillicothe, Charlie became an apprentice of the legendary Mafioso, Frank Costello, who provided yet another dubious role model. Once again, Charlie was most likely taking notes on not only how to succeed in the criminal world, but how to do so in a grand and charismatic fashion. Costello was an inmate who commanded great respect; just the type of personality Charlie himself longed to cultivate; that of someone who was equally feared and respected in the straight and criminal worlds.

During the next two years at Chillicothe, Charlie was able to keep his nose clean, and even received a Meritorious Service Award in January 1954 for his work in the motor pool. Because of this, he was granted parole on May 8th, 1954.

Upon release, Charlie returned to West Virginia where he hooked up with a sixteen-year-old hospital waitress, Rosalie Jean Willis. On April 10, 1956, Charles Manson, Jr. was born. Although sparse information concerning Charlie's namesake is available, one can assume that the burden of bearing such an infamous legacy in some way attributed to junior's early demise in 1983 of an apparent self-inflicted gunshot. However, by then Charlie Jr. had changed his name to Jay White, due to the fact that his mother Rosalie had married a man named White after parting ways with Manson.

‡

For a nineteen-year-old ne'er-do-well – who had spent a large portion of his life institutionalized – adapting to this new world of responsibility proved more than Manson could handle. Fatherhood did nothing to stabilize Charlie's restless spirit. As he later explained, "After awhile I met this girl and she wrapped her pussy around me. She wanted to go to California, so I stole a car and drove to California."

Upon arrival in Los Angeles, Manson was arrested for car theft, the familiar pattern repeating and the revolving door opening again, then closing behind him. He was subsequently convicted and sentenced to Terminal Island Prison in Los Angeles.

In September 1958, Manson was released from Terminal Island on five years parole. When he hit the streets, Charlie decided to try his hand at the pimp trade. His mentor in this new vocation was Frank Peters, a Malibu procurer, who he lived with at the time. Unfortunately, Charlie's new housemate was under surveillance by the F.B.I., who informed Manson's probation officer that Charlie's stable of hookers included a sixteen-year-old named Judy, in addition to "Fat Flo," the daughter of wealthy Pasadena parents. When questioned about these activities, Manson stated that Judy and Fat Flo were just his "girlfriends."

In February 1959, Manson's probation officer was visited by an upset parent, Ralph Samuels. Apparently, Samuels' nineteen-year-old daughter, Jo Anne, had come to Hollywood chasing bright lights and stardom. There her star-struck path crossed that of budding movie mogul Manson, who introduced himself – complete with an official printed business card – as "President, 3-Star-Productions, Nite Club, Radio and TV Productions."

Somehow, Manson was able to con Jo Anne into investing her life savings in his company, which was actually a front for pimping out of the Hollywood Roosevelt Hotel. Adding insult to injury, Charlie allegedly drugged and raped Jo Anne's roommate, Beth Baldwin.

The same afternoon that Ralph Samuels contacted Charlie's parole officer, he paid a visit to Manson's Pasadena apartment. Samuels discovered that Manson had abandoned the seedy pad and was horrified to find semi-nude girlie photos scattered about. A police officer who lived in an adjoining apartment described the former tenant as a "sex maniac" and hinted that Manson might have been taking "beaver shots" for out of state sale.

In June 1959, a nineteen-year-old named Leona informed Manson's parole officer that Charlie'd knocked her up, performing a tearful and gut wrenching plea on his behalf. When Manson appeared in court that September, the probation department petitioned against his probation. At this time, Leona delivered a repeat command performance, confessing her devotion for Charlie, indicating how she would marry Manson if he was set free. This time, however, the performance rang hollow, due to the discovery that Leona had previously lied about being impregnated. It was also discovered that Leona had an arrest record for prostitution under the alias of Candy Stevens. Nevertheless, the judge gave Charlie a ten-year sentence, suspended it and placed him on probation. Manson later married Leona, but possibly just to prevent her from testifying against him. When the marriage was later terminated, divorce papers stated the two had produced a son, Charles Luther Manson. So, it appears, Manson named his first two children Charles.

In December, Charlie was arrested again on two different counts: grand theft auto and the use of stolen credit cards. Subsequently, these charges were dropped for lack of evidence. Just the same, he decided that the heat was getting a little too close for comfort, so he headed east – with Leona and another new prostitute – to Laredo, Texas, where he set up shop catering to the needs of drunken convention-goers.

After the convention season ended, Charlie found a home for his two-girl "stable" in one of Laredo's finer whorehouses. Manson considered setting up shop there on a permanent basis, but these plans proved short-lived when one of his girls got arrested and ratted him out. The last thing Charlie needed was to get busted by the Feds for the Mann Act, so he fled south, across the Mexican border, where he made his home in abandoned adobe huts, associating with hardcore elements of the streets, along the way learning to be a matador and experimenting with magic mushrooms.

Eventually the long arm of the law caught up with Charlie. On April 28th, 1959, a warrant was ordered, and Manson was indicted by a federal grand jury on Mann Act charges for transporting underage women across state lines. On June 1st he was arrested in Laredo and extradited to Los Angeles. On June 23rd, 1960, the court ruled that Manson had violated his parole, ordering him to return to prison to serve out a ten-year sentence.

His next stop: McNeil Island, Washington.

CHAPTER 2
Reflecting Man In A Cage

Manson has described himself as a reflection of the world and of those he's encountered on his dark journey. In interviews, he has frequently described himself as an empty vessel; filled by whoever entered his company, whether in prison, the streets or vast desert landscapes.

"I am only a reflection," is the mantra Charlie has oft repeated. "As you put two people in a cell, so would they reflect and flow on each other like as if water would seek a level. And I have been in a cell with a guy eighty years old, and I listened to everything he said…And he explains to me his whole life, and I look at him and he is one of my fathers. But he is also another one of society's rejects."

Not only was prison Manson's home, but schoolhouse, as well. Behind bars he absorbed his jailhouse mentor's lessons; those societal outcasts whose views on life radiated from the wrong side of the tracks. There began Charlie's self-education, with studies of such arcane subjects as hypnotism, Masonic lore, subliminal motivation, Rosicrucianism and Scientology.

Early on, Charlie became fascinated with the vast powers and untapped reservoirs of the human mind. So naturally — when Scientology came into vogue in the 1950s — he was eager to take in all he could of this new self help movement. Manson's instructor — or "auditor" to use the correct Scientology term — was fellow convict, Lanier Rayner, who had studied under L. Ron Hubbard. At McNeil Island, Rayner conducted Scientology auditing sessions, and in one ten man cell had gathered around him a group of seven students.

Manson later claimed that he achieved the level of "theta clear." The Scientology definition of "clear" is "an individual who can be at cause knowingly and at will over mental matter, energy, space and time…" "Theta clear" designates an "operating thetan" or "OT." According to L. Ron Hubbard, operating thetan was an elevated state of consciousness heretofore unknown to Man, pre-Scientology: "Neither Lord Buddha nor Jesus Christ were OTs according to the evidence. They were a shade just above clear." According to Scientology propaganda, OT's can read people's minds, move objects by thought and materialize objects.

It can be assumed that from his auditing sessions, Charlie attained some knowledge of mind control, as well as techniques later used to program his followers. Manson claimed he picked up on the teachings quickly because his "mind wasn't programmed," and that he had received 150 hours of processing sessions in jail. If Charlie actually attained this higher level of Scientology-awareness, it came at a bargain price, for in the outside world such a degree ranged in the thousands of dollars. From these studies Manson lifted jargon such as *mocking up, cease to exist, come to Now* and *putting up pictures.*

After his 1967 prison release, Manson was said to have met with Los Angeles Scientologists and of having attended the initial dedication of the Scientology Celebrity Center. Scientology literature was also found when the Manson Family was apprehended for the Tate/LaBianca murders. The late author Jim Keith, a former executive Scientologist, informed me that he had heard from inside the Church that Charlie had been a recruiter for Scientology, or what is known as a "body router." Through his exposure to Scientology — as well as hypnotism, the various psychology books he was exposed to, and his own observations of human nature — Manson eventually evolved an eclectic "theology" all his own, which would harmonize perfectly with the new generation of flower children he discovered upon his 1967 prison release.

Subliminal motivation was yet another keen interest Manson cultivated. According to a McNeil Island cellmate, Manson once used the prison radio station to send subliminal messages to other prisoners, who at night were required to hang their headsets on their bedsteads. In this manner, subliminal messages could be transmitted subconsciously during sleep, although not loud enough to attract the attention of the guards. Manson used this method to plant suggestions that everybody should keep applauding for him when he sang at the prison talent contest. As it turned out, Manson ended up winning the contest, receiving a standing ovation for several minutes.

Another father figure entered Charlie's life during this period: Alvin "Creepy" Karpis, former FBI enemy Number One and member of the Ma Barker gang. At McNeil Island, Manson's guitar playing began to take a prominent role in his daily activities. So it must have seemed like destiny that he hooked up with Karpis, himself a talented honky-tonk guitar slinger. To this end, Karpis took Charlie under his wizened wing, giving him guitar lessons and dispensing jailhouse wisdom.

According to Bugliosi's *Helter Skelter*, another "fanatical interest" entered Charlie's life at this time: The Beatles. It was 1964, and those four mop-topped Liverpudian lads had just descended upon America like biblical angels from on high. From his prosecutorial palette, Bugliosi painted his portrait of an envious Manson, who proclaimed to other McNeil Island inmates that if given half a chance, he could be as big, or bigger, than The Beatles.

Another interest consuming Charlie was the study of Masonic lore and hand signals, which he would later flash at judges during Tate/LaBianca court appearances. Manson developed a complex series of hand signals he later used with his Family, one such being the "strip and suck" command. While in the company of outlaw bikers, Charlie often used this to impart sexual favors. Once the signal was given, his women would strip, and then go down on the bikers.

Charlie learned many of these secret signals from Creepy Karpis. During his 1987 Geraldo Rivera interview, much ado was made about mysterious hand-jive mojo Manson performed for the home viewing audience. "I don't break laws, I make laws"," Charlie announced, waving his arms in wild patterns. Occult insiders speculated that these were secret signals Manson was sending to some shadowy satanic underground. In an interview conducted during the Tate/LaBianca murder trial, Charlie shed some light on his knowledge of this silent, Freemasonic language:

> ...Masons have that power. It's a secret that's been handed down since the Pharaohs. The secret wisdom. Jesus knew the symbols. The preacher and the judge got ahold of the symbols and they kept them to themselves. Judge Keene uses all those symbols. He'll make a sign like 'cut him off'. Or like when I get up to speak, he'll make a symbol to one of his marshals, and all of the sudden a whole bunch of people will be let in the court and there will be all this confusion so they can't hear what I'm saying. They use all those Masonic signs to hold power over their people. So I started using the symbols. Every time I got into court, or have my picture taken, I use another masonic sign. Like the three fingers, two fingers outstretched. When the judge sees it, it really freaks him out because he can't say anything. When I see them making these signs in court I flash them back at them...

Ultimately, Charlie has looked upon his years in prison as a positive experience, or so he claims. Prison life took the form of monk-like meditation, as from his cell Manson is able to "project the entire Universe." Upon his late 1960's prison release, Charlie discovered that the world was illusory on both sides of the fence, the grandest illusions being "inside" and "outside." One could be as free in prison, he observed, as a slave to the outside world.

Manson is a chameleon, changing change colors at a moment's notice and reflecting back upon others their own projections. Susan Atkins once described him as someone who changed from one minute to the next, becoming whoever he needed to be, putting on whatever face best suited the situation. Fitting seamlessly into the free-wheeling 60s drug culture, Charlie enabled himself access to young chicks and groovy kicks that the squares in normal society secretly envied, from behind their white picket fences. But to suggest that Manson was a product of the psychedelic 60's is not entirely accurate, and only serves to distort his background growing up as a Bowery Boy street hoodlum, who came of age in the 1950's.

Through his prison studies of psychiatry and hypnotism — coupled with an interest in Scientology — Manson claimed he was able to bring himself out of a state depression, from which he'd been suffering for many years. Also, his growing interest in music was another factor that attributed to this growing self-confidence. These intellectual and artistic pursuits were the ingredients that helped form the Charles Manson we've all come to know. The very same Charlie, who — a short time later — would appear upon the 60s Garden of Eden like an insidious pestilence, wilting those unfortunate flowers unlucky enough to stumble into his serpentine path.

Like the snake who beguiled Adam, such is the pop mythology surrounding Manson; that of a wily reptile with venomous charm, who led his prey (followers) to eventual ruin down a primrose path lined in blood. But can it all be blamed on Charlie? Through their own gullibility, those innocent lambs of the Peace and Love Generation set themselves up for a fleecing, with the likes of Charlie only so happy to provide the shears. But if it hadn't been Manson, there were a crush of other dubious gurus waiting in line, with a hard-on to control others, all dressed in paisley and beads, chanting meaningless mantras and strumming out of tune guitars. Granted, Charlie took it to a another level, but it was the willingness for new experience of the 1960s thrill-seeking generation that helped give birth to the bum trips that followed after, bringing the decade to a cataclysmic close in the form of Kent State, Altamont and the Tate/LaBianca murders. It could be said that Charlie was just speeding things up — Helter-Skelter style — by giving his followers what they really wanted; that he was just a conduit for the dark forces laying in wait behind the peace signs, love beads and wilted flowers. In time, swastikas and buck knifes replaced these benign Summer of Love images, transforming them into a gory hatchet job pulled off by a band of spaced-out zombies.

In June of 1966, Manson was transferred from McNeil Island to Terminal Island in San Pedro, California. At this time, friends remember Charlie as fanatically dedicated to his music. One person who served time with Charlie — and became impressed with his musical abilities — was Phil Kaufman, then serving time on a federal marijuana rap.

In the Terminal Island prison yard, Kaufman encountered Charlie playing guitar one day, and afterwards gave Manson contacts with people involved in the Hollywood music scene. Toward the end of 1967, these contacts would allow Charlie entrance into Universal Studios to record some demos. Kaufman later went on to become a bit of a living legend himself, road-managing some of the biggest names in rock and roll, such as The Rolling Stones, Joe Cocker, Gram Parsons, Emmylou Harris and Frank Zappa, along the way earning the dubious title of "Road Mangler."

Upon his impending March 1967 release, Manson begged the authorities to leave him in prison, insisting that he was not ready to return to the outside, but his plea fell on deaf ears. With some measure of trepidation, Charlie hit the bricks, not really knowing what waited around the corner, in Haight-Ashbury.

It was the Summer of Love in the Garden of Eden.

CHAPTER 3
Stranger In A Strange Land

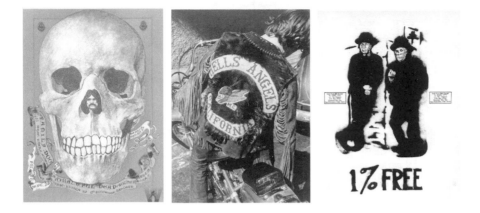

1% FREE

The San Francisco psychedelic scene was a short-lived spectacle; a Roman candle that burned out fast, leaving glorious, yet ruinous trails. Like any other groundbreaking revolution, by the time the mass of society had caught wind of what was blowing by – the tide had passed, pushed by the gales of an ill wind.

By 1967 – the so-called "Summer of Love" – many of the original progenitors of the Haight-Ashbury scene had purposely uprooted themselves from the city. Thus began a back-to-the-land/communal living movement, which, to a great extent, was a relatively short-lived phenomenon in itself. Part of this back-to-the-land movement by the likes of movers and shakers of the San Fran scene (The Grateful Dead, The Hog Farm and Stephen Gaskin, to cite a few) was precipitated by the sudden influx of bikers, hardcore dealers, strung out hypes and assorted con-man gurus who overnight had turned this experimental utopia into a bad scene of bum trips and O.D.'s, overflowing with starry-eyed youth led astray by the enticement of going to San Francisco to wear "flowers in your hair." Thus the fix was in, as the media created a myth while simultaneously ushering in its eventual ruin. Soon the tour buses arrived, filled with squares to gape at the freaks making a spectacle in the street. The Haight had become a hip Disneyland, filled with hawkers, peddling the imitation of a groovy vibration that had passed just as fast as it came. But like moths attracted to flames, the youth continued coming in droves, searching for Utopia in a mounting Tower of Babel.

Haight-Ashbury circa 1967 was an ideal breeding ground for the type of wayward youth that new to the scene and budding guru Manson found easy to attract. As popular legend has it, Charlie – fresh from the slams – landed in San Francisco smack dab in the Summer of Love. Initially, he drifted about town, bumming around, emerging from his institutionalized shell. But his transition back into society proved easier than expected, due mainly to the psychedelic scene unfolding around him, of which Charlie dove into headfirst, feeling an instant connection to all the flower children hanging out in the streets and sleeping in the parks. It was in this social milieu that Manson soon became a familiar figure, fitting seamlessly into a patchwork of social outcasts, for he as well had been an outcast all his life. Manson was adept at interpreting the key elements of people's personalities, determining what responses would put them at ease and make them friends, allies or sexual partners. This ability was another factor that helped him fit so well into the brave new world he discovered upon prison release.

Manson was later quoted in the underground newspaper, *Tuesday's Child*, about how he'd met a boy during this period who introduced him to the Haight. "We slept in the park and we lived in the streets and my hair got a little longer and I started playing music and people liked my music and people smiled at me—I didn't know how to act. It grabbed me up, man, that there were people that were real."

In *Manson in His Own Words*, Charlie described his first acid trip occurring at a Grateful Dead concert when the young fifteen-year-old hippie-boy – mentioned in *Tuesday's Child* – turned him onto the acid at the aforementioned Grateful Dead show. The scene at the concert was all new to Charlie, with strobe lights flashing in myriad colors amid all the strangely garbed people dancing uninhibitedly, with the musicians providing the necessary free-flowing backdrop that swept the dancers up into a primal tribal psychedelic amoeba undulating across the dance floor. Charlie flipped out on this wild scene, and he, too, began dancing to the music.

"The acid, the music and the loss of inhibitions opened up a new world for me. I was experiencing rebirth. Finally, in the middle of one of my dances, I collapsed on the floor." When Charlie awoke the next morning he found himself at a crashpad with several other flower children. This was Manson's first exposure to communal living, and he was taken aback by the positive atmosphere of togetherness and sharing. No one asked him how he'd got there, or what he was doing, they just accepted Charlie as one of their own. With his guitar, singing and songwriting – and homeless state of being – Charlie fit right into the commune scene; a wandering minstrel, soaking up the day-glo/ paisley vibes.

On one occasion, as he was strumming on the steps of Sathar Gate – the entrance to the UC Berkeley campus – then assistant University librarian, Mary Brunner, out walking her dog, happened upon Charlie, who proceeded then to dazzle her with his cosmic croonings and metaphysical singsong rap of love; a funny little man with a giant aura, so it seemed to Mary.

Brunner went bonkers for her new-found paramour, due mainly to the fact that Charlie was the first man who had ever given her such complete and undivided attention. Invariably, she was mush in Manson's manipulative hands, like a clay figure to be formed. Manson moved in with Brunner, who at first was adamant that his affections be shared only with her. This arrangement was short-lived, however, as Charlie soon convinced her to allow other girls into the scene. At first, Brunner was accepting of one additional girl, but told Charlie that was it, she didn't want any more competition. But with each new girl Charlie brought into the fold, two more would follow. Brunner soon relented, as she realized that the only way to remain in Manson's life was as a member of this extended Family, which before long would number eighteen young women, all slavering at the bare feet of their hippie guru.

CHAPTER 4
California Dreamin'

In July 1967 – while hitchhiking through San Jose – Manson was picked-up by a heavy set, balding minister named Deane Moorehouse who invited Manson home for dinner with his family, where they passed the evening discussing the Bible, reciting prayers and singing religious hymns. Afterwards, Charlie was offered a standing invitation to visit whenever he wished, and – because he had so admired the piano that'd accompanied their Christian croonings – Deane promised it to Manson as a gift, which he could pick up whenever he wanted. Another good reason to pay a return visit was to see Deane's fourteen-year-old daughter, Ruth Ann, who Charlie'd been making eyes at during his stay. One day, Charlie returned to claim his piano, and in short order traded it in on a VW Microbus that one of Moorehouse's neighbors had for sale. Thus began a nomadic period for Charlie and the girls, as they took to the road. In due time, Deane's house became a regular waypoint for Manson and his troupe as they traveled up and down the California coast.

During the summer of 1967, Charlie and Mary Brunner traveled to the Mendocino Coast and it was there that Charlie discovered a mix of artists, back-to-the-land enthusiasts, and new age occultists, living together in the vagabond hippie ethic of the day. Communes and occult groups were not uncommon in the surrounding hills and beaches, but there were also those who camouflaged themselves as artists or religious seekers, while behind the scenes using their secluded retreats to grow pot or manufacture hallucinogenic drugs in clandestine drug labs. The time Manson spent in these towns opened his eyes to the possibilities that existed in the world of living free off the land, and doing whatever one pleased. Charlie took it all in, and following the hippie ethic, picked up lots of hitchhikers, shared whatever food he had, smoked plenty of the locally grown grass and grooved behind 'shrooms, fucking whoever happened along the way.

Since parolees were required to show means of support, Manson sought work during this period in the "entertainment field" and actually played a few gigs at San Francisco clubs. But music for Charlie was more than just a simple diversion to keep his parole officer, Roger Smith, off his back. Charlie explained to Smith that he had record studio contacts in Los Angeles, and received permission to head south for a spell to see what lady luck might have to offer in those star-studded Hollywood hills.

During this trip, Charlie wandered around Venice, checking out the scene, which was in many ways similar to Haight Ashbury, what with all the runaways, dropouts and thrill-seekers. This is where he happened upon Lynette Fromme – a vivacious carrot-top with plentiful freckles – sitting on a street corner. Fromme had just been tossed out of her father's house in Redondo Beach, after a quarrel.

"What's the problem?" were the first words Lynne heard muttered from the mouth of Manson.

"How did you know–" she started to say, taken aback by the intense perceptivity emanating from this strange, elf-like man. Charlie smiled and said, "Up in the Haight, I'm called the Gardener," Charlie explained. "I tend to the flower children."

"A gardener," thought Lynnette. "What do Gardeners do? They... *plant seeds*." Suddenly she felt vulnerable and exposed, at the mercy of this mysterious, somewhat odoriferous man.

"So your father kicked you out," Charlie intuited, imploring Lynne to tell him her problems. With a soothing manner, Charlie listened, taking it all in with an impish twinkle in his eyes. She had been trapped, living in a world behind bars, figurative though they may have been. Charlie could empathize completely, Lynne's life behind mental bars in many ways akin to what'd transpired in his own life, and he reflected this knowing back onto her. They were kindred souls. Both had been prisoners in similar penitentiaries of the mind.

"The way out of the room is *not* through the door," Charlie explained. "Just *don't want out*, and you're free." This revelation hit Lynne like a bolt of lightening, instantly illuminating her mind. It was obvious: if she didn't *want out*, then she wouldn't be aware of *being in*. The truth was – and had always been – right in front of her freckled face. Why had it taken this mysterious elf from outer space (with a strong body odor, to boot) just a few Earth minutes to explain this undeniable truth? And why did this "fancy bum" understand so much? Whatever the reason for his mysterious powers, Lynne was sold. In the wink of an eye, she switched gears, leaving behind one world, and entering another, one from which she would never return.

Manson and his girls soon set up temporary residence in the Haight. Mary Brunner later described this hillside hippie pad as a "luxurious hobo castle" with "Arabian tapestries on the walls." In "our elevated and elegant flophouse" Mary went on to say, occupants passed the time "playing our plays, singing and beating our drums." Charlie described himself at this time as a hostel-keeper for runaways, as he immersed himself in the scene as the new-guru-on-the-block.

Around this time, Charlie hooked up with a dealer named "Joe Brockman", an apparent alias used in John Gilmore's *The Garbage People*. Brockman perceived Charlie as an artist, or even as a "priest." One time, Brockman and Charlie scored a brick of marijuana, and afterwards returned to Manson's pad. Once there, Manson took his place on a Turkish rug, sitting holy lotus-style while rapping metaphysical mumbo-jumbo to Brockman and the girls.

A girl named Marge was present, exuding sensual vibes and arousing a deep desire in Brockman to "do her." Manson, picking up on these vibes, encouraged Brockman to "ball her." Initially, Brockman was hesitant to jump Marge's bones in mixed company, but since everyone was into the trip laid down by Manson – especially Marge – Brockman felt it his civic duty to oblige. During the course of their lovemaking – in an apparent gesture to display his mysterious power over women – Charlie reached out with his hand, his palm covering Marge's eyes and forehead. This caused Marge at first to laugh, and then she began speaking in tongues, as Brockman came at the height of this weirdness, shooting his wad to the sounds of Marge's orgasmic glossolalia.

During this period, Brockman scored some of Owsley's finest, and under its hallucinogenic influence glimpsed what he referred to as Manson's "freaky power." On a wall of Manson's pad was a picture of Jesus, and below it Charlie often sat, sending out heavy vibes.

In this surreal setting Brockman one time came on to a tab of Owsley's acid. Suddenly, as he sat before Charlie, the would-be Messiah – with the picture on the wall and the face of Manson before him – Brockman beheld a merging effect, as the two melded together, Manson and Jesus into One.

Brockman was stunned by the realization that, if one dropped enough acid, then – like a psychedelic alchemist – Charlie could manipulate the elements, turning himself into Jesus at will. Of this incident, Brockman later said, "Charlie as Jesus was branded into my thoughts... But it was a painful thing, too, because I still had my resistance going and I knew I just couldn't sit in that movie for the rest of my life, and I knew I couldn't submit to whatever it was the idea of Charlie as Jesus expected of me. I only knew the man was playing heavy games. Charlie could plant that in a person's head, or create it, the same way a magician creates a bunch of flowers in the air..."

Although in jail most of his adult life, Charlie claimed he'd found a way to "unlock his mind." One major component of this philosophy was living in "the Now." Theoretically, Charlie'd left the past behind and this was this path he urged others to follow: break all ties with whatever had come before; the broken homes, abusive relationships and dysfunctional families. In this manner, his young "initiates" became "born again" in Charlie's philosophy, and then grouped together as a Family, sharing a level of awareness distinctive only to the initiated – the special "chosen ones" who banded around him. Sex was the first step in the initiation process. Drugs helped reinforce the trips Charlie laid down.

"There is no good and no bad," Charlie informed his disciples. "There is no difference between you and me. The truth is, and that's all. It doesn't matter what words you use... the truth is what it is... What's here and now. I go there and I'm not here anymore. And I come back and I'm not there anymore... Just what's here and now is what counts. It's infinite and it's nothing. It's all there is and it doesn't matter what you do. It's all perfect and the way it's supposed to be."

As the Summer of Love wore on, it was evident that not all was total bliss in the Haight. You still had the Diggers (a radical community-action group of improvisation actors) serving free food in Panhandle Park, and the Haight Ashbury Clinic offering free medical care for all the bum-trippers and clap-infected flower children, not to mention free concerts in the park, which continued to attract an ever present stream of hippie kids, or "plump white rabbits" as Ed Sanders referred them, surrounded by "wounded coyotes." So a spirit of sharing was still in the air; a noble experiment whose aim was to an Utopian Society where sex and drugs were the religion of choice. Into this atmosphere the predators had entered in the form of "wounded coyotes", Ed Sanders' metaphor for the pimps and hustlers and who were looking to take advantage of the naive acid-dropping middle class children, the aforementioned "rabbits."

The Haight attracted hardcore criminals who grew long their hair, and affected the flower power trappings. Before long, bikers wanted a piece of the action, as well, and tried to take over the LSD market with strong-arm tactics. Bad dope was sold causing bum trips and bad vibrations, and people started getting ripped off in the parks. Manson – who fancied himself the protector of runaway flower children – decided the time was ripe to get out of town, and take his children with him, to find the promised land.

CHAPTER 5
Sexy Sadie and the Church of Satan

On the evening of April 30th, 1966 – Walpurgisnacht in the occult calendar – the Church of Satan was born. As Church of Satan High Priest, Anton LaVey, later noted: "The Satanic Age started in 1966. That's when God was proclaimed dead, The Sexual Freedom League came into prominence, and the hippies developed into a free sex culture…"

Soon LaVey attracted the attention of such Hollywood stars as Sammy Davis, Jr., Jayne Mansfield and Keenan Wynn. Through these connections, he established inroads into the movie industry, appearing in the film *The Mephisto Waltz* as well as *Invocation of my Demon Brother*, directed by occultist Kenneth Anger. *Invocation of my Demon Brother* also featured future Manson Family murderer, Bobby Beausoleil, portraying the role of Lucifer.

It has been rumored that LaVey appeared in Roman Polanski's *Rosemary's Baby* as the Devil, a role that apparently went unaccredited; a purported appearance that many suggest is nothing more than urban legend. In her book *Witchcraft Past and Present*, Valiente noted that *Rosemary's Baby* was "one of the major influences which have brought about the craze for delving into darker regions of the occult… and was it more than a cruel coincidence that Roman Polanski lost his wife and unborn child in the horrific murders?"

Valiente claimed that the film angered certain Satanic groups for revealing occult secrets and, because of this, Polanski and wife Sharon Tate received death threats following the film's release. Polanski himself admitted as much when later questioned by LAPD's Lt. Earl Deemer:

> Deemer: Did you receive any hate mail after the film [*Rosemary's Baby*]?
> Polanski: Yes, some. And it's possible this could be some type of witchcraft thing, you know. A maniac or something. This execution, this tragedy, indicates to me it must be some kind of nut… I wouldn't be surprised if I were the target. In spite of all this drug thing, I think the police jumped too hastily on this type of lead, you know. Because it is their usual type of lead.…

After the Tate murders, stories began circulating that LaVey and Polanski – during the filming of *Rosemary's Baby* – had a falling out and that LaVey cast a curse on the young director. In response, Polanski supposedly laughed in LaVey's face. Looking for a suitable way to teach his little Polish adversary a lesson, rumor has it LaVey then retaliated in the form of The Manson Family murders, paying back Polanski several-fold for his transgression.

‡

In 1965, eighteen-year-old Susan Atkins (later known as "Sadie" in Charlie's Family) won a San Francisco topless dancing contest, and soon after became the youngest go-go dancer on the North Beach strip. One afternoon, the owner of the club where she worked introduced Atkins to an odd looking fellow garbed in black, with a sinister goatee and extraordinarily pale skin, none other than Anton LaVey, who had made a deal to produce a theatrical version of the witches' sabbat at the club.

After displaying her wares in a dance number performed for LaVey, Atkins was chosen for the role of "The Vampire" in his all-topless review. Three years later, she would confess to licking the blood from the knife used to kill Sharon Tate, when this theatrical vampire fantasy became grim reality. Photos from this period capture Atkins in her vampire role, wearing a long, open black robe which reveal her nude and shapely body, mock blood dripping from her lips.

CHAPTER 6
The Way of the Bus

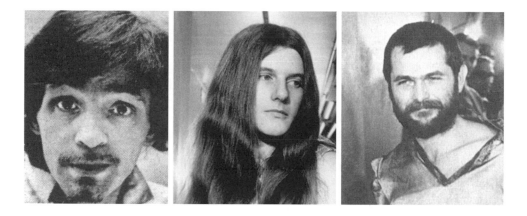

In September 1967, Manson hooked up with eighteen-year-old Patricia "Katie" Krenwinkel, a former campfire girl and Sunday school teacher, who brought with her a religious background to draw upon when taking in the Biblical babble that Charlie later spewed, as she and Manson would later quote Bible passages to one another while under the influence of the divine sacrament, LSD.

Krenwinkel – as her early diaries noted – was the type of girl that the boys seemed to neglect at high school dances. Because of this, it's easy to see why she fell in so readily with the Manson tribe, after spending only four stoned and sex-filled days in Charlie's arms, who initiated her by way of "The Daddy Game", fucking her every which way, while he told her to pretend he was her papa.

Soon after, Krenwinkel quit her insurance company job, leaving her final paycheck un-cashed. And although she had turned her back on "The Establishment", Krenwinkel did not entirely swear-off all worldly goods, as she presented her new family with a Chevron credit card backed by her father, who still loved his daughter enough to pay for her gas. Krenwinkel's father later had this to say about his daughter's sudden sea change: "I am convinced (Manson) was some kind of hypnotist. It was all so spontaneous."

As with most of the Manson girls, it was more the sense of acceptance that led them to this groovy little ex-con guru, who was lover, daddy and personal savior all rolled into one. Sex was secondary in the equation, and only enhanced the sense of freedom the girls found with Charlie – along with the plentiful drugs that opened their brains and bodies to his psycho-sexual probings. As the legend goes, Charlie could supposedly sustain an erection for hours on end, doing one girl after another, able to bring them to near exhaustion – to the point where his sex partner "died" and "lost her ego."

It was claimed by some women that sex with Manson risked the side effect of heart-stoppage. Hearing these notorious tales of Manson and his miraculous "staying power", one wonders if Charlie was not – at one time or another – schooled in the secret mysteries of Tantric Sex, that branch of Hinduism later expanded upon by the likes of no less an enlightened reprobate than Aleister Crowley. Traditionally, Tantric techniques have been employed as a means of becoming one with a deity by identifying the deity in question with a sexual partner.

From the earliest of times, sex orgies have been an integral part of magic ceremonies. By exhausting one's self through prolonged ritual, a sex magician can enter a trance state, thus opening themselves to visions or voices. However, Sex Magick is only one of many vehicles used by spiritual seekers to access altered states. The same effect can be produced by staring for long periods of time into candles or crystal balls. Likewise, overindulgence in drink or drugs – as well as fasting or sleep and sense deprivation – can open up one's consciousness to various "demons" or "spirits." Maybe this is what Charlie was up to – whether conscious of the fact, or not – making "spirits" manifest through manipulations of pranic energy, due to the apparent Tantric practices he employed, thus building up psychic energy in the ethers surrounding the wild Manson Family orgies. Dennis Wilson of The Beach Boys called Manson "The Wizard." Perhaps the actual wizardry Charlie performed was through Sex Magick, as the erect wand he was waving was his *will-to-power*.

Much like Aleister Crowley, Charlie's brand of Tantrism was a bastardization of the holy act. Traditionally, the practice of Tantric sex is an intentional overindulgence in physical excess in order to overcome the physical being; to rise above every pleasure and achieve total identification with natural energy. Crowley, like Manson, stretched the Tantric boundaries, incorporating the Hindu system into his own self styled form of Sex Magick. Crowley, and Manson as well, saw sex as a means of harnessing internal and external power. By unleashing sexual inhibitions, the operator – or Sex Magician – releases vast amounts of energy, ostensibly creating "vibrations" in the surrounding atmosphere that could be directed and used as a form of witchcraft, or magical working. Each new girl accepted into the fold was the happy recipient of an extensive multi-hour lovemaking session, courtesy of Manson. It was Charlie's opinion that it was only after the first three or four hours that sex got really good and magical. At this stage a woman gave up and lost her ego, becoming one with the cosmos.

During acid trips, Charlie would first begin to dance around a bit, with everyone else copying his actions, in a psychedelic conga line. Then he would take his clothes off, and all the rest would follow suit. Once everyone was naked, Charlie would direct the orgy by arranging bodies in various combinations and positions. Manson's instructions were that each of the participants rid themselves of their sexual aversion or hang-up, whatever that might have been – sodomy, rape, fellatio or flagellation – by performing the act in front of the entire group. And so, in this manner, Charlie orchestrated the entire proceedings, and was more often a spectator, than actual participant.

Another famous Manson Family ceremony was to strap Charlie to a cross, following his mock crucifixion with a mass orgy. So, it can be gathered, there was more going on than just mere sexual experimentation. Manson, through these ritual orgies, was indeed stirring up some strange energies.

‡

One of the more obscure artifacts in Mansonophile John Aes-Nihil's collection is *A Psychosexual History of the Manson Family*. About a fourth of *Psychosexual History* is handwritten in red ink, and appears to have been authored by Susan "Sadie" Atkins, or someone pretending to be Atkins. In this regard, the author's voice sounds similar at times to Atkins' style in *Child of Satan, Child of God*, although the events in *Psychosexual History…* differ to those depicted in Atkins' Born Again Christian inspired tome. If Atkins did author *Psychosexual History…*, I doubt at this point she'd cop to it, given the book's slant, which is a pornographic pastiche straight out of the pages of *Penthouse Forum*, featuring Charlie as the ultimate "God of fuck" spurting his spunk in myriad directions, and taking no sexual prisoners. To this end, *Psychosexual History…* lists endless accounts of Spahn Ranch orgies, as well as a chapter featuring George Harrison doing it with John Lennon. Strangely enough, an associate of Aes-Nihil's claims to have 16mm footage of this Lennon-fucking-Harrison film, although he has never let anyone view it.

Psychosexual History… is also Sadie and Charlie's twisted love story, depicted as one of the great romances of the ages. My gut feeling is that Atkins might have indeed authored this inspired mess, although we have no way of knowing for certain. Granted, *Psychosexual History…* is by no stretch of the imagination a work of great literary merit, although it does seem like the sort of self-aggrandizing hokum that Sadie/Susan was once so found of, what with all the sordid sex scenes of her and Charlie reaching cosmic consciousness through shared orgasm, not to mention all the other nonsense strewn about portraying Atkins as a modern day sex goddess, who was led astray by her torrid messiah.

Whatever the case, the person (or persons) responsible for *Psychosexual History...* appear to have had an intimate knowledge concerning the events, locations, and overall timeline of what went down with The Manson Family saga. Granted, this information could have been gleaned from varied sources, including the many books and "oral" history laid down by former Family friends and associates. Nonetheless, the depiction of Manson in *Psychosexual History's* eight hundred and fifty xeroxed pages occasionally resonates with the ring of truth, although at other times it appears to be pure fantasy woven around the myth of "Helter Skelter" and "the God of Fuck."

Within *Psychosexual History...* are accounts of previously uncovered murders, and an alternate version of the Gary Hinman murder. In a passage from *Psychosexual History* – that allegedly took place in Hinman's backyard after a party – Charlie instructed a doped-up Katie Krenwinkel to close her eyes, then pressed his fingertips against her left temple, and began to recite: "You are descending into the level of the divine state of hypnotic slumber. In your slumber, you shall see why we shall have to do something about people like Mr. Hinman, and you shall see what it is we will do." Katie was silent, and her head drooped, as if asleep. Nothing happened to her for the first few minutes, but then her eyes opened wide and she shouted, "Kill!" This awoke Hinman, who had been asleep inside his house, unaware that Charlie and the girls were hanging out in the back yard, frying on acid. He told them to get the fuck out of his yard, and in response Charlie told him ominously that "they would be back."

So was Manson a hypnotist? While in prison he certainly studied the subject, and was conversant enough to engage in discourses with professional hypnotists he later met on the Sunset Strip. If Charlie did, in fact, practice hypnotism on his followers, it was not in the classical method of waving an object in front of someone's eyes, and telling them "you are getting verrrrry sleepy" or having them count backwards until they fell into a trance. Most likely, Charlie employed various elements of hypnotism. It all had to do with the cadence of his voice, the intense look in his eyes, and the rhythmic movements he made with his hands and body. Such methods are utilized in Neuro-Linguistic Programming (NLP). And although Manson probably wasn't aware of the technical name of this discipline – in fact the term, NLP, hadn't even been invented yet – he was no doubt using many of its techniques, such as mirror imaging. As Manson once said: "Certain motions create certain responses in people. I'm learning to control and use these movements."

‡

The fall of 1967, Charlie's Family headed up the Oregon coast and during this period met twenty-five-year-old Bruce Davis, a Scientologist and musician, who joined Manson's ever growing ranks. As Charlie's group was steadily increasing, and as there was not much room to sleep comfortably in the VW bus – let alone have a quality orgy – Manson was able to swing a deal in late October, trading in the VW for an old yellow school bus. Charlie and the girls removed the seats inside the bus to create a communal living area inside and over time added an icebox, sink, stereo, a floating coffee table suspended on wires with hookah pipe, red carpet up to the windows, and a bunch of pillows, peacock feathers, and tapestries.

On the exterior, the bus remained the traditional yellow, which often prompted police to stop Manson's caravan for violating laws governing school buses. Such was the motivation that inspired them to paint the bus jet-black. The plan was to paint "Hollywood Productions" on the side in white letters, but whoever attempted this was spelling challenged, and it came out reading "Holywood Productions." The whole idea was to create the illusion of a roving film crew, thus avoiding the obvious legal entanglements that arise when you have a 33-year-old ex-con with a busload of under-aged girls.

In November 1967, Manson's parole supervision was switched from San Francisco to Los

Angeles, indicating Charlie's intent to change his base of operations from Northern to Southern California. It was around this time that Manson met Susan Atkins. The rest, as they say, is a strange piece of history.

CHAPTER 7
The Birth of Sadie Mae Glutz

Susan climbed the staircase, following the music upstairs, where she discovered – surrounded by a group of fawning females – a strange, charismatic little fellow, playing a beat-up guitar and singing: *The shadow of your smile when you are gone will color all my dreams and light the dawn.*

He sounded like an angel, and when the little man finished his song, Susan asked if she could play his guitar. He handed it to her, and she immediately thought, "I can't play this." But the little man said, "You can play that if you want to." This exchange blew Susan's mind, as she was certain he was *in her head.*

Somebody put a *Doors* record on, and soon the hippie kids were dancing to the pounding, hypnotic beat. Susan joined in, dancing formlessly around the record player, gyrating to the wide-eyed stares of all the hippie dudes groovin' to her moves. Susan totally threw herself into the music. "I'll dance for him," she thought. The little man had placed his guitar on the floor beside the couch, and walked up close and began to dance behind her, his hands on hips, moving her body.

"What's he doing?" Susan wondered, as the little man led her in movements she'd never tried before. Gently, he guided Susan's body through rhythmic and sensual variations. He moved close, putting his arms around her waist, and whispered in her ear, "That's right. That's good. Yes. In reality – in your God-self – there's no repetition. No two moves, no two actions, are the same. Everything is new. Let it be new."

As recounted in *Child of Satan, Child of God*: "Our bodies moved together. Close. Then apart. We moved... he moved me. And we danced. It was all new... It was all new. I was a good dancer, a professional dancer. I had done fantastic things with my long, slim body before the searching eyes of men. But I had never danced like this. I wasn't merely dancing. I *was* dance."

They swung around to look at one another, as their bodies moved to the pounding beat. Suddenly something happened that had no rational explanation. Susan experienced a moment unlike any other, as she and the little man, dancing closer and closer, passed through each other!

As they turned to one another, once again man and woman mirrored each other perfectly in this cosmic dance of souls. He was she, and she was he, and they were all together. Susan stood face to face with the wild little man with the magic hands. He smiled and said, "You are perfect. I've never seen anyone dance like you. It's wonderful. You must always be free." For a few moments, Susan could only smile, as she watched the little man's face. She perceived his features, shifting into many expressions; his eyes were flat, black and hard. "Thank you, " she finally said. "My name is Susan Atkins. Who are you?"

The eye contact was broken, as the little man lowered his head, brushing his hair back with one hand. "I'm Charlie. Charlie Manson."

Charlie then turned and, with a snap of his fingers, said, "Let's go girls." Three girls quickly rose and followed him outside. As Susan later recalled: "Charlie came there that day to speak the truth and release anybody he could, to enlighten anybody he could. This is what I know. This is what I knew."

A couple days later, Charlie visited Susan at her Haight Street pad and told her that he wanted to make love. Without hesitation, they removed each other's clothes and Charlie asked Susan if she'd ever made love with her father. She giggled and said, "No!", and Charlie replied, "Have you ever *thought* of making love with your father." She said, "Yes," and he told her, "All right, when you are making love... picture in your mind that I am your father... You've got to be free of all your inhibitions and your fears. They're weighing you down. They're choking you. You've got to break free."

According to legend, "The Papa Game" was Manson's favorite time proven shtick with a new chick, using new age psycho-babble to imprint on their minds the image of Charlie as the benevolent father figure of free love. Initially, he was gentle. Like opening delicate flowers, he caressed their minds with beautiful words steeped in syrupy psychedelic imagery. Later, Charlie's interactions with his girls often became abusive, and he wasn't above beating them up when he felt they were in need of a good old fashioned ass whuppin' to bring them in line. Some would suggest that Charlie gave them just what they wanted: hard drugs, harder sex and a glorified outlaw attitude masquerading as peace, love & communal hugs. (And sometimes a fist in the face for good measure!) Mind games were the order of the day and Manson was master-gameplayer, using dominance and misogyny as his calling cards, under the guise of new age psychotherapy, tough love and sexual liberation. This system of manipulation kept his women constantly off balance – emotionally and mentally – malleable to the mojo Manson peddled.

Charlie was the avatar of this new philosophy of pull down their pants and fuck 'em hard and fast, blow their minds while they're blowin' you, then slap 'em around a bit to remind them who's boss, all the while preaching freedom and love. Such was Manson's credo, stated of course in his own jangled jargon of missives, malaprops and backward maskings of a disturbed mind: *That all was love and love was all, and in love you could do no wrong.*

In Manson's mind, women possessed no soul; they were simply chattel, there to do the bidding of the Manson Family men, to wait on them hand and foot. And when it was dinner time, the dogs ate before the girls; that was the unwritten law. Yes, the girls were lower on the food chain than canines. Later – as Squeaky Fromme informed officers after the Barker Ranch raid – it got so depraved that Manson even had the girls giving the dogs blow jobs, a prime indicator of how far the whole fucked-up scene had devolved. Apparently, canine fellatio was all a part of Charlie's "ego death" philosophy.

‡

Later that afternoon, as they sat on a sidewalk curb, Charlie suddenly spoke: "Susan, if I postulate what I want, I'll get it, you know."

"What do you mean?"

"It's simple," said Manson. "If I talk about a quarter, for instance—if I think about it, and see it, I'll get it."

Susan said nothing, as she watched the Haight Street freaks pass by, when – without warning – a young man turned around and walked up to Charlie. "Here, brother," he said, "I want to give you something," and put a quarter in his hand.

Charlie looked into Susan's awestruck face with a Christ-like beatitude. He arose and led her to a small fast-food shop and bought a cup of coffee with the quarter he'd received by the grace of whatever mad god ruled the cosmos.

Back on the streets, they walked along in the grace of God: the God who made LSD, free love and lava lamps. Rain was falling down from Heaven; a warm rain, which cleansed their souls. As they started down an incline, Susan's bare feet slipped on the wet pavement, and she fell backward. Swiftly, Charlie grabbed her right arm and held her up and said, "I won't ever let you fall." From that moment onward she was sold; the words gripped her. *"I won't ever let you fall."* That's exactly what Susan yearned for: a protective daddy. She'd been a tough, streetwise, nineteen-year-old chick ready for thrills and kicks, but what she lacked was someone who would never let her down. That's what she saw in Charlie, someone who would lift her up, and never let her hit the ground. He might have been short and sort of funny looking, but there was no denying the little man had strength – inner strength. And Susan knew he would always keep her from falling. She was now reborn in Charlie as Sadie Mae Glutz.

"Come on, " he said. "We're going to L.A."

CHAPTER 8
All Aboard The Black Magic Bus!

Late at night, out on the highway, Charlie and the girls picked up some hippie kids hitching south, somewhere between San Fran and L.A. "Let's have a party," he said, swinging out from behind the driver's seat like a mischievous little elf. They dropped acid, then sat around the floor of the bus, all except Charlie, who positioned himself lotus-style on a huge pile of multi-colored pillows, looking down upon his flock. As they came on to the divine sacrament, he began to rap. "You are all going to die. You all must die."

As Sadie looked at Charlie, his mouth was moving, and his hands formed mystical patterns in the air, yet nothing came out of his mouth, although Sadie could hear his voice, eerie and echoing throughout the body of the bus: "You are all going to die."

"My God!" Sadie thought. "His words are coming out of the sink! He's speaking through the sink."

"You must die to self, " the voice said. "You must die. You must become one."

Suddenly, the bus began shaking so violently that Sadie nearly fell over. She looked over at one of the hippie boys leaning against the wall, and couldn't believe her eyes. The boy had turned to bones; no flesh, hair or clothes. Only a skeleton with bleach-white bones. The others, wide-eyed, stared at him, too.

Then – just as quickly – the boy transformed again into his normal suit of skin. His eyes were filled with terror. Charlie slipped down from his throne of pillows. Yanking the boy to his feet, he punched him in the mouth, knocking the hippie kid down to the floor. The force of the blow appeared superhuman to Sadie. She looked on in amazement, as the kid wailed like a banshee, then scrambled toward the front of the bus and out the door, running into the night.

Inside the bus, insane laughter rose to a horrible pitch. Screeching and cackling, it scraped the nerves of those assembled, unfolding like some twisted nightmare. The laughter was Charlie's, standing in the middle of the bus, with his head thrown back and mouth opened wide. But the laughter, the hideous noise, still emanated from the sink!

Sadie crawled across the bus on her hands and knees, dragging her drained and nearly paralyzed body to Charlie. She clutched frantically at his leg, and held on to it for dear life. "Am I dying?" She screamed. "Oh God, am I dying?"

Suddenly, everything became quiet, as Sadie lay on the floor and Charlie returned to his throne of pillows. After several minutes, Sadie was aware of people moving toward the door. The rest of the hippie kids they'd picked up left without saying a word, disappearing into the darkness.

Sadie walked over to Charlie, and he looked up at her. "Did you see that?" Charlie asked. His voice was almost a whisper, but this time the sound came from his mouth. "My voice came out of the sink."

"Yes," was all Sadie could say.

‡

Charlie and his tribe continued down the coast en route to a Universal Studios recording session that his prison buddy, Phil Kaufman, had set up. On the way they passed through San Jose and picked up Deane Moorehouse's fourteen-year-old daughter, Ruth Ann, adding her to the ever-growing ranks. When Rev. Moorehouse discovered his daughter missing, he flew into a rage, and three days later tracked down Manson near Los Angeles, where he was hanging out at a friend's house. There Moorehouse and a friend burst onto the scene, Deane's friend holding a gun on Charlie, while the agitated preacher tore into this seducer of youth, chastising Charlie for running off with his daughter. Charlie's heavy philosophical reply to Moorehouse was: "I'm just doing to her what you want to do."

Ruth Ann was crying, and when her father asked her what was wrong, she answered: "Daddy, I love Charlie. We made love together and I want to be with him!" To this, a red-faced Moorehouse erupted in another apoplectic fit, ready to rip Charlie to shreds for deflowering his pubescent daughter. Charlie had one of the girls fetch Deane and his friend some sodas, while he calmly took in Moorehouse's tirade. When Moorehouse's temper finally subsided, Charlie said, "Look, Deane, this is between the two of us. Why don't you have your friend put his gun away and go for a walk so you and I can straighten our problem out?"

Deane consented, and had his friend put the gun away and step outside. Charlie then handed the preacher an acid tab. "Here, this will keep your blood pressure down." Deane paused, gave the pill a blank look, and downed it with a sip of soda. Then he started where he'd left off, telling Charlie what his life was going to be like after he was condemned to Hell for "doing" his lovely young daughter. Later – when the acid kicked in – Moorehouse mellowed out, and reconsidered his position. Charlie advised Deane that he might want to get in his friend's car and go home, and Deane agreed. When he came looking for Charlie again a few weeks later, it wasn't on account of his daughter, but because he was in search of more acid. Charlie had revealed to Deane "The Way if the Bus", and The Way was *Psychedelic*. Like many another spiritual searcher from the spaced-out 60's, LSD had opened Moorehouse's mind, but unfortunately the vacuum between his ears was soon to be filled with the ambiguous metaphysical psycho-babble of Charlie Christ.

‡

On September 9th, 1967, Charlie had his first meeting with a Universal Studios record producer, Gary Stromberg, who was initially impressed enough when he heard Manson's music that a recording session was arranged for two days later. In the interim, Stromberg wanted to learn about Charlie's unconventional lifestyle, and all the groovy things he was "into."

The next day, Charlie swung by and picked up Stromberg, introducing him to The Way of the Bus. Once inside the black magic bus, Stromberg's smile was replaced by a look of amazement, as he took in the burning incense and hanging tapestries. For an added touch, the girls placed themselves in comfortable and enticing positions. As soon as Charlie and his would-be benefactor sat down, one of the girls placed a cold drink in their hands, while another brought out munchies. Charlie was handed a lit cigarette, as another one of the girls sensuously massaged his neck and shoulders. This undivided attention, given the two men, made Stromberg feel as if they were kings in a rolling palace filled with ready and willing women servants. Stromberg ended up spending considerable time with Charlie's Family, and by the end of the recording session thought that Manson was one together dude.

Afterward the session, Stromberg thought he could get something out on the market immediately, but unfortunately for Manson, he didn't have the final say in the matter, as the suits at Universal thought more work and arrangement was needed before releasing an album. At this time, a standing offer from Universal was put on the table for another session when Manson had "rounded things out more solid." Tracks recorded at that time are thought to be: "Devil Man", "The More you Love", "Two Pair of Shoes", "Maiden with Green Eyes (Remember Me)", "Swamp Girl", "Bet you Think I Care", "Look at your Game Girl" (first version), "Who to Blame", "True Love you will Find", "My World", "Invisible Tears", "This is Night Life", "Sick City", "Run for Fun", "The House of Tomorrow", "Close to Me", and "She Done Turned me in-Twilight Blues-Your Daddy's Home".

This was not to be Charlie's last association with Universal Studios. Later he worked as a technical advisor to Stromberg and a group of writers on a film script about the return of Jesus Christ. In addition to his role as consultant, Manson extracted a promise from the director to use his music in the soundtrack.

The film's concept revolved around Christ's second coming, this time in the form of a black man. Instead of Rome, the setting for this apocalyptic tale was modern day America's deep south, filled – no less – with nigger hating red-necks as a corollary to the ancient Romans. Later, some would say Charlie took this second coming symbolism to portray his own place in the planet's history, as a misunderstood messiah besieged by modern day scribes and Pharisees preaching hypocrisy. One time – during Charlie's marathon bull sessions with the script writers – he and Squeaky demonstrated an act of Christian humility, as she and Charlie knelt down and exchanged foot kisses; an act Manson used ad nauseam to sway people over to his side, showing he was some kind of peace-loving guru, so humble that he'd bow down and kiss a stranger's smelly feet. Manson later claimed that the issue of Christ being a black man caused a rift in his participation in the film project, as it ran counter to his own view of what a modern day messiah should really be—that is, a Caucasian. (This project may have evolved into the 1971 Sydney Poitier film, *Brother John*.)

Afterwards, rumors surfaced hinting at Manson's commingling with prominent people at Universal Studios. In *Manson In His Own Words*, Charlie described spending several nights at Cary Grant's Universal bungalow, apparently during the star's absence from the lot. At this location, Charlie claimed to have had an affair with a male member of the studio staff. According to Hollywood producer William Belasco, Cary Grant would later re-enter the Manson Family saga in the unlikeliest of places – on the infamous date of August 9th, 1969 – at 10050 Cielo Drive, a short distance from Grant's own mansion. In fact, Grant was no stranger to the Polanski residence, as he had been a former tenant there.

According to Belasco, Grant – perhaps because of his LSD experimentation, or due to his penchant for curious "nocturnal forays" – had befriended a young male. Allegedly Grant and the lad were in the garden at the Polanski residence when a series of blood-curdling screams erupted from the main house. Grant immediately fled the scene in his Rolls, tires screeching in the night. When the next morning came, Grant learned that he'd narrowly escaped. One can only assume – if there is indeed any truth to this account – that Cary Grant's reason for subsequent silence in this matter was to avoid a scandal revolving around homosexual escapades and/or drug involvement.

Another major star – who presumably missed his appointment with Manson Family destiny – was Steve McQueen. McQueen's ex-wife, Neile Adams, claimed that on the night of the Tate murders, Steve had planned to meet his hair-designer pal Jay Sebring at 10050 Cielo Drive, but along the way picked up some hot little chick, got sidetracked and never made it to the house.

In the aftermath of the murders, McQueen was understandably spooked, and in short order assembled a heavy arsenal of guns for protection. McQueen put himself and his family under around-the-clock security, and even went so far as to set up surveillance cameras on his property, which just happened to be located a short distance from 10050 Cielo Drive. Not long afterwards, the "Manson Family Hit List" turned up with McQueen's name on it, along with the names of other top Hollywood celebrities. So not just one, but two major stars – Cary Grant and Steve McQueen – were both almost caught up (presumably) in the carnage. Soon after, McQueen split the country to work on the film, *Le Mans*. Insiders say part of McQueen's impetus for getting out of the country was because he feared for his life.

As regards the above mentioned "Manson Family Hit List", its existence was purportedly brought to the fore when Susan Atkins – up on charges for the Hinman murder – blabbed to one of her jail-house bunkmates that she and her co-defendants had planned to murder a number of show biz personalities; all to be killed with unspeakable methods of torture. Supposedly the list included those who had helped out Manson's Family in the past, but had eventually turned their backs on them. Aside from McQueen – who was to be boiled in oil – the list of intended victims included Elizabeth Taylor, whose breasts would be cut off, and beautiful eyes removed and mailed to her ex-husband, Richard Burton. Burton, in turn, would be castrated. Frank Sinatra and Tom Jones were also on the list. Sinatra's purported fate consisted of being skinned alive while hanging from a meat-hook, while Tom Jones' throat was to be cut while engaged in an act of sexual intercourse with Sadie. Of course, one can put as much stock in all this "Hit List" hooey as they want, in addition to the numerous other lies and half-truths that Susan "Sadie" Atkins spewed during her short stint as media murder sex queen, delivering tabloid carnal knowledge soaked in blood to a hip generation of hardcore gore junkies. Other names of film stars – including phone numbers and addresses – were found in the searches of Spahn Ranch after the murders; names that might have either been actual acquaintances of Charlie's Family, or those possibly marked for death.

‡

For a period of time, Manson claims he had the run of Universal Studios and, while there, associated with several celebrities. Among his acquaintances was a "famous movie actor", who latched on to Charlie right after he first showed up on the Universal lot. Charlie – in *Manson In His Own Words* – refers to this "famous movie actor" as "Mr. B". Well aware that Mr. B's intent was of a sexual nature, Charlie came flat out and asked him, "What is it you want, a dick in your ass or in your mouth?" Mr. B wanted both, and so afterwards Charlie began visiting his dressing room on a regular basis, for fun and profit. With all the deft and aplomb of a letter taken straight out of *Penthouse Forum*, Manson describes the *ménage à trois* between himself, Mr. B and Mr. B's television actress wife, in *Manson In His Own Words*. After each tryst with Mr. B. and his sexy brunette wife, Mr. B. would slip five one-hundred bills into Charlie's pocket.

When possible, Charlie included the girls in his Universal forays, and before long they were on the "let's-get-acquainted lists of many of the not-so-straight idols of the movie world." Charlie and the girls soon found themselves invited to private parties in Beverly Hills, Malibu and other exclusive areas. Admittedly, the Manson bunch had long before unshackled themselves of sexual inhibitions, but whips, chains, torture and the other assorted weirdness to which Charlie and his girls were exposed to at these parties – featuring Hollywood's "Beautiful People" – were far removed from the "innocent" sexual experimentation of which they'd become accustomed. The same can said for the type of drugs used at these parties, as a lot of the movie people they encountered were shooting heroin, smoking opium, and snorting coke, which was vastly different from the pot and acid diet that'd been The Manson Family mainstays.

Until getting mixed-up with this Hollywood set, Charlie noted, "*performances* were not us either." Previously, Charlie and the girls had not been involved in kinky orgies that featured "performances" with whips and chains, but somehow they were drawn into this depraved scene. It's interesting to note that whenever Charlie talks about this S&M scene, there is a certain amount of bitterness in his tone, indicating that something ugly might have gone down during this period; something, perhaps, that even embarrassed or humiliated him. It should be mentioned that Jay Sebring was himself a prominent member of this kinky Hollywood whips and chains crowd, and from this we can only speculate that somewhere along the line he might have crossed paths with – and pissed-off – Manson during the course of some whips and chains "performances."

The Manson Family/Hollywood connections ran deep, and for many years Charlie was reticent to finger the rich and famous that had intersected his star-crossed path. For whatever reason,

Manson decided to lift the lid a little on this "area of silence" when he responded to a request from a gossip tabloid in the mid-70s, *The Hollywood Star*. Among the big names that Charlie dropped were Elvis, Neil Diamond, The Beach Boys, Nancy Sinatra, Jane Fonda, Yul Brynner, Peter Sellers and Peter Falk. When Frank Sinatra caught wind that the publisher of *The Hollywood Star* – Bill Dakota – was calling his daughter Nancy to pump her for info regarding alleged Manson sex orgies, the "Chairman of the Board" threatened to send out some of his boys to break Dakota's knee-caps if the publisher didn't cease and desist with his provocative inquiries.

Manson's infamous tell-all letter recalled Jane Fonda's alleged involvement in a sex tape. Years later, this was followed by John Phillips' biography which recounted swapping partners with Fonda and her husband, as well as another story of Fonda and Sebring having sex in the 10050 Cielo Drive bathroom. As Manson's letter pre-dated these revelations, it lends substance to his *Hollywood Star* allegations.

One persistent rumor surrounding the Tate/LaBianca murders was that Sebring had lured some of Manson's girls into sado-porno films that he and his Hollywood friends were filming, whipping and beating them before the camera, which conceivably precipitated the Tate/LaBianca murders as a form of retribution performed by Charlie's gang. When one delves into the perverse milieu of the late 60's Hollywood scene, it doesn't take an overwhelming leap to entertain the possibility that all of this kinky weirdness might have, in someway, led to the murderous rituals that unfolded.

In this regard, Jay Sebring attended a medieval themed party in Hollywood shortly before the Tate murders which featured a "game." Sebring donned a white hood and allowed other guests to tie a noose around his neck, fastening the end of the rope to a ceiling beam. A death sentence was read and the crowd counted in unison for the moment when the chair would be knocked out from under his legs. Some of the guests, apparently twisted on drugs, actually wanted to kick the chair out from under Jay, but his date – fearing that the doped-up "beautiful people" would actually hang him – screamed out, and Sebring came down off the mock gallows, removed his hood and smiled.

In his autobiography, *Why Me?*, Sammy Davis, Jr. remembered a party he attended in the late 60s, which turned out to be a orgy highlighted by a simulated virgin sacrifice. To his surprise, Davis discovered that the hooded man acting as the "coven" leader was Jay Sebring, who – as Davis described – had always been "a little weird." Sebring had constructed a dungeon in his basement, and tried, albeit unsuccessfully, to entice Davis over to view the "real antique pieces" he had collected, consisting of various torture weapons. Shortly after the party, Davis met Anton LaVey, who warned him not to get involved in the Church of Satan unless he was totally serious about the commitment. Sammy, while not totally serious, joined anyway because he "wanted to have every human experience" possible. In his Vegas nightclub act, Sammy openly flaunted one symbolic red fingernail, and wore a Church of Satan Baphomet pendant around his neck. "The chicks loved it," playboy swinger Sammy noted, a smoke dangling from his lips. At one point, things started getting even too weird for Sammy-baby. "One morning after a 'coven' that wasn't quite fun and games," he recalled, "I got some nail polish remover and took off the red fingernail."

CHAPTER 9
The Spiral Staircase

Before heading to Los Angeles for his Universal recording sessions, Charlie'd met a woman in San Francisco named Gina who, in *Manson In His Own Words*, he remembered as "a trippy broad, about forty-five years old, who experimented with everything" and was "pumped-up" on devil worship. Gina extended an invitation for Charlie to visit her in Los Angeles at an old two-story Gothic mansion she owned in Topanga Canyon which Charlie's Family later nicknamed "The Spiral Staircase" due the circular stairs at the entrance of the residence. Later – during his Universal Studio sessions – Charlie needed a place to park the Family bus for awhile, and so decided to take up Gina on her offer. As Ed Sanders noted, The Spiral Staircase become a "scrounge-lounge" for Manson and his girls over the next few months.

The Spiral Staircase (also known as "The Rattlesnake Pit") was a fabled meeting place of people beautiful and weird, a party house and freak-out pad, home to light shows, acid orgies and occult rituals. According to researcher Salvador Astucia, the Spiral Staircase was once owned by Bela Lugosi and later the popular L.A. rock group, Arthur Lee's *Love*, lived there for a period. In fact, many of the band's publicity stills show them standing on a spiral staircase reportedly taken at their L.A. residence.

In *Manson In His Own Words*, Charlie described himself and the girls – when they first came to The Spiral Staircase – as innocent children, compared to the people they met there. In fact, Charlie specifies this period as a crucial turning point in Manson Family history. Up to this point, their philosophy had always been one of fun and games. But soon it all began spiraling into a madness that "eventually engulfed us in that house."

Charlie described The Spiral Staircase as a "house of transition"; a place where those who walked the straight and narrow could come to by the dark of night and indulge in what they preached against during daylight hours.

At the Spiral Staircase you would find celebrities and prominent sports figures and, on occasion, those who wore the cloth. It was a melding pot of different occult groups and religious practices then being bandied about, much in the same way that different drugs became fashionable for a period of time, then were replaced by the next strange elixir to show up on the market, promising immortal life or, at the very least, a fleeting flash of illumination.

Each time Charlie returned to The Spiral Staircase, he'd see something new and different, and not all of it was *love and flowers*. Animal sacrifices, and the drinking of blood, apparently took place upon the hallowed Spiral Staircase grounds, in conjunction with satanic sex rituals, some located out on the beach near the property, apparently directed by the house's owner, "Gina". It was at The Spiral Staircase that Charlie was exposed to various counterculture gurus, and he no doubt took note of the "heavy" raps laid down, and how they maneuvered and manipulated their followers. Charlie picked up on the way some of these acid fascists maintained control by instilling fear. Later, these lessons would come back to him as a method to employ his own special form of madness, the seeds of which were seemingly planted at The Spiral Staircase.

At a Spiral Staircase light show party, Bobby Beausoleil, a twenty-year-old Santa Barbara musician discovered Charlie and the girls singing together. Beausoleil promptly joined in, playing his guitar along with Charlie's impromptu noodlings.

Charlie felt an immediate musical rapport with Beausoleil, discovering that he could jam and improvise with him in perfect harmony, always anticipating Bobby's next move. On the same note, Bobby was immediately taken with Charlie's improvisational style, and intrigued by his lyrics. Charlie was famous for slipping out of key on his guitar, or stumbling across a chord that would make a trained musician cringe, though more often than not he would recover from his mistake with a new tune that was far more interesting than the one he'd begun. Manson prided himself on the fact that he didn't play in a set meter, and was often "out of time."

Beausoleil attempted recording with Manson several times, but these sessions invariably turned into a fiasco, as Manson was prone to bring along his whole entourage, creating a circus-like atmosphere in the studio. Coupled with this, Manson always presented a challenge for producers due to his refusal to compromise, convinced that the process would in some way "steal his soul" or interfere with his musical muse. Unfortunately, Bobby and Charlie would eventually gain more renown for channeling their energies in a negative direction, in contrast to singing songs of peace and love.

CHAPTER 10
The Dark, Beautiful Sun

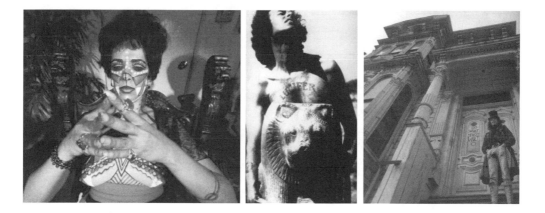

Perhaps he was born under a bad sign, but his last name, Beausoleil means "beautiful sun" in French. An astrologer once described Bobby as a "freedom bound person" with a "sunny magnetism", but added that there was a "darker cast to his aura that leaned on the sinister."

In his teens, Beausoleil experienced strange visions, which came to him in the form of a steel helmeted Nordic maiden, riding through the forest on a great, white horse. "She had shields over her tits and long blonde braids hanging down to her ass...

"It was like I could hear the clanging of the Viking swords, echoing in some great hall...a little later on, I realized it was Valhalla – the great hall where Odin eats the souls of heroes slain in battle. Odin's the god of war, the god of the souls and the god of poetry..." Soon afterwards, Bobby was arrested for robbery, and placed in a reformatory.

"It happened because I was off-balance," he would later explain. "I was disconnected with the act of it, and so consequently I got my ass in a sling. Breaking probation." In reform school, the Viking High Priestess vision came to him nightly. "She'd come to me and I'd ride with her..."

After his reform school release, Beausoleil headed for Hollywood to pursue a music career. Only seventeen, Bobby doctored his driver's license so he would be able to play the clubs. The first band he played with was an early incarnation of Arthur Lee's Love, alleged tenants of The Spiral Staircase. Beausoleil later landed a role in the exploitation film *Mondo Hollywood*, where he appeared as Cupid, addressing his bow. The name Cupid fit Beausoleil well, and it became one of his many nicknames. Oddly enough, *Mondo Hollywood* (also titled *Hippie Hollywood: The Acid Blasting Freaks*) featured two other individuals who would play important roles in later Manson Family developments: Jack Gerard and Jay Sebring.

Jack Gerard made his living by hiring hippies – including several Manson women – through his theatrical agency for porn movies and topless dancing. And, of course, Sebring needs no introduction in his hapless role as a major player in the tragic events that occurred on August 8th and 9th, 1969 at the haunted house on Cielo Drive. In *Mondo Hollywood*, Sebring is shown in a short clip, presiding over his hair salon.

In late 1965, Beausoleil moved to San Francisco and put together a band called The Orkustra. Bobby's original concept was a 15 piece rock orchestra, which eventually evolved into a five member group featuring violin, stand-up bass, percussion, and oboe, with Beausoleil playing guitar, bouzouki, and sitar. "We had a fairly full sound – a unique sound," Beausoleil recalled. "We played the Winterland, Fillmore, Avalon Ballroom, Carousel Ballroom, plus a lot of club gigs." The

Orkustra made history by playing the first Golden Gate Park concert, along with The Grateful Dead. Later – after The Orkustra broke up – the group's violinist, David Laflamme, went on to form one of the more successful bands of the San Francisco music scene, It's A Beautiful Day, while bassist Jamie Leopold joined up with Dan Hicks and His Hot Licks.

The Orkustra became unofficially known as the "Digger's band." Somehow the Diggers – and a group known as the Artist's Liberation Front – convinced a Methodist clergymen to let them put on an event at the Glide Memorial Church touted as "not a happening but a total environmental community." What this event actually turned out to be was the Diggers' covert attempt to promote a full-blown church orgy under the guise of a hip media happening, and – according to accounts – they were somewhat successful in this endeavor.

In the Glide Memorial cathedral a false wall was set-up, concealing The Orkustra and a half dozen belly dancers, as meanwhile, in front of the wall, a poetry reading was in progress. At an appointed time, The Orkustra began playing, as the belly dancers crashed through the wall, surprising the audience. The motive behind this spectacular entrance was to get all those in attendance naked and making love – on stage and in the aisles – in front of God and everyone.

In the midst of this wild scene, an impromptu dance commenced between Beausoleil and a belly dancer, who undulated on a chair before Bobby, as he wailed on guitar. At this juncture, Bobby licked the sweat from the belly dancer's nipples, the stuff of which rock n' roll legends are made. Underground film director Kenneth Anger was so impressed with this display, that after the show he approached Bobby and offered him the title role in a movie project, *Lucifer Rising*. Soon after, Beausoleil moved in with Anger at his home, an old Victorian building that had formerly housed San Francisco's Russian Embassy.

In *The Garbage People*, Beausoleil recounted an acid trip in the Russian Embassy, laying naked on an altar bed, blazing on a tab of Owsley's finest. In the background, Anger chanted incantations from Crowley's *The Book of the Law*, as all around Beausoleil perceived hellfire's swirling and reaching out for his soul. As these fires poured up and over him, a sudden and immense shaft of light drove down, penetrating his chest. And then, in his shattered mind, Bobby died...

"It became everything, and I was like obsessed, experiencing all there was – all the blood and killing, I was being killed. I was swimming in all death and destruction... I could hear the fires around me, raging, I was covered with this cape of blood. There were a million moving things – all death and destruction. It was in my mind, in the environment. The voice of the magician kept on, and each word he said was the crackling of fire...

"I had no fear. There was no fear in me as I went through the most horrible deaths in the world. There was no fear, I knew I was the Devil..."

‡

During this period, Anger and a group called the Brotherhood of Lucifer rented the Straight Theater for $700 and built a satanic altar on the dance floor. The production featured a light show built around slides of Crowley's tarot cards and 400 feet of Anger's in-the-works *Lucifer Rising* film project. Behind the projection screen The Orkustra played, calling itself "Wizard" for the occasion.

Anger presided over the event, which turned into a fiasco, primarily on account of some acid he bum tripped on. While presenting his black magic invocation, Anger freaked – due to a malfunction with the videotape projection – and started doing all kinds of strange magickal mumbo-jumbo ad-libbing. Anger's antics – a combination of ritualistic dance movements, acid inspired invocations and manic gesticulations – turned into a bit of an embarrassment for all parties concerned, including Beausoleil.

With his eyes painted like the Egyptian Ra, and adorned in a flowing gold lame robe, Anger employed a wide range of magickal symbols during his satanic sideshow, including the Nazi swastika. Anger's Straight Theater spectacle is captured in his film *Invocation of my Demon Brother*. When all was said and done, the event failed to make back its guarantee in gate receipts, so Anger wrote a check to the Straight Theater for $666.66 to pay for the expenses. Afterwards, Anger and Bobby had a falling out over the nights' proceedings, as the filmmaker for some reason blamed Bobby for the whole disastrous affair.

The next day – sensing that his stay with Anger had run its course – Bobby returned to the Russian Embassy to gather his belongings, only to discover that Anger was gone and that sheets were draped across everything in the house. Bobby took this symbolism as some sort of purging ritual; a deliberate magickal act of expunging him from the premises.

According to Beausoleil, Anger purchased an odd-looking vehicle for him in payment for work on the ill-fated *Lucifer Rising* project, recorded with his new band The Magickal Powerhouse of Oz: a converted Studebaker that'd cost $400, and had subsequently been registered in Bobby's name. Beausoleil described this strange vessel as a cross between a spaceship and outhouse. The vehicle had been cut in half, with a small log cabin built in the back. When Bobby went to retrieve the Studebaker, it had been stripped, evidently by Anger, torn apart in some sort of twisted ritual, and locked up in the Russian Embassy ballroom. The car's disconnected battery was up on an altar, a ritualistic offering to the automotive gods, the cord of electronic life ceremoniously severed.

Seeing no other option, Bobby broke in and removed the battery from the altar and returned it to his vehicle, then took the car – with the remainder of the disassembled parts – to a nearby garage where they helped reassemble it. Once the vehicle was back in working order, Bobby hit the road.

Afterwards, Anger claimed that Bobby had stolen the vehicle, in addition to camera equipment and, more importantly, the *Lucifer Rising* film footage. And while it can't be denied that Beausoleil had a well-established background as a petty thief, Anger's assertion that he ripped off the film doesn't carry much weight, given the fact that footage from the aborted *Lucifer Rising* project appears in Anger's 1969 film, *Invocation of my Demon Brother*. In fact, the original version of *Lucifer Rising* eventually evolved into *Invocation of my Demon Brother*, and included in its cast The High Priest of The Church of Satan, Anton LaVey. The soundtrack that accompanies *Invocation of my Demon Brother* was supplied by none other than Mick Jagger on Moog synthesizer.

As for the Jagger connection, Anger claimed to be the main influence in The Rolling Stones decision to use the images from Aleister Crowley's Tarot deck on the cover of *Their Satanic Majesties Request*. Whatever the case, Jagger's infatuation with diabolism came to an abrupt end at 1969's Altamont Rock Festival when an eighteen-year-old black named Meredith Hunter was knifed to death by Hell's Angels' members during the Stones' rendition of "Sympathy for the Devil." A week after, Manson and his minions were arrested for the Tate/LaBianca murders.

In the early 70's, Led Zeppelin guitarist, Jimmy Page, entered into an agreement with Anger to supply the soundtrack for a new version of *Lucifer Rising*. Page even let Anger use the cellar of his Scottish estate at Boleskine – formerly owned by Aleister Crowley – for film editing. The end result of Page's participation in this project consisted of twenty-three minutes of material, which Anger considered totally useless, and subsequently went public with his displeasure in 1976, slamming Page as a junkie and a half-ass occult dabbler. It was later rumored that due to their falling out, Anger cast a curse upon Page that resulted in the rash of bad luck experienced by Led Zeppelin in the late 70s.

Ironically, the *Lucifer Rising* soundtrack was eventually produced by Anger's old adversary, Bobby Beausoleil, recorded in the Tracy Prison music room. The soundtrack evolved out of several jam sessions with prison players, including former Manson Family member, Steve "Clem Scramblehead" Grogan, then serving time for his involvement in the Shorty Shea murder.

After nearly a decade in production, *Lucifer Rising* was released in 1980, featuring Mick Jagger's one time girlfriend, Marianne Faithful, in the role of Lilith. As usual, weirdness followed Anger. During a screening of the film in Hawaii, Anger was approached by an agitated young man, who afterwards he recognized as John Lennon's assassin. Instead of moving on, Chapman kept asking him, "You know Mick Jagger? You know John and Yoko? How often do you see them for dinner?" After shaking Chapman's hand, he was given two 38-caliber bullets by the future assassin. "These are for John Lennon," said Chapman.

‡

Beausoleil formed a short-lived group The Devil's Band, which played some gigs in the Bay Area before he moved to Topanga Canyon in the fall of 1967. It was there Bobby formed a friendship with Gary Hinman, a piano teacher, small-time drug dealer and practicing Buddhist. Hinman was pals with Beach Boy Dennis Wilson, and it was through Hinman that Bobby became chummy with Wilson, independent of the later Manson/Wilson connection. Bobby – although a talented and improvisationally inclined musician – had no formal music training prior to meeting Hinman, and it was Hinman who taught Bobby how to read music and write down compositions.

At the time Beausoleil and Manson met, he and then girlfriend Laurie were living with Hinman. To his ultimate misfortune, Hinman adopted a habit of letting people in transit crash at his pad. On several occasions, Manson Family members took up temporary residence there, all part of the loose-knit communal Topanga Canyon scene.

At some point – after Hinman kicked Beausoleil out of his house – some of Charlie's girls informed him of Bobby's transient status, whereby Manson invited Bobby to come join their Magical Mystery Tour. The offer was tempting, what with all the cute girls Charlie attracted, not to mention the opportunity to play music with Manson, but Bobby declined the offer and decided to go his own way. Bobby's response impressed Charlie, even though it was clear Manson was big on having hangers-ons, he evidently respected Beausoleil's independent nature. Bobby described his relationship with Manson as "open-ended." His reason for keeping a healthy distance from the day-to-day operations of Charlie's Family was his intuition that "something (was) going to be coming down. If we merged the two personalities, I knew, and so did he with that way he knew things, that'd we'd indeed raise hell on earth."

Unfortunately for Bobby, he didn't listen closely enough to his own inner voice, eventually being carried away by whatever ill winds swirled through the Santa Susana Mountains in the summer of 1969.

CHAPTER 11
The God of Fuck

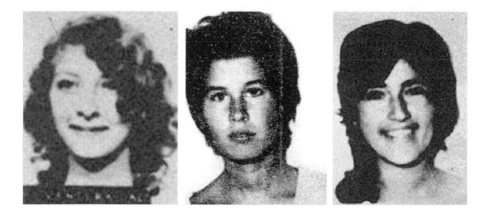

In early 1968, Charlie and the girls were hanging out at abandoned homes and camps in Topanga Canyon. At this time a heavy influence seeped into the Manson Family group-mind in the form of The Beatles' *Magical Mystery Tour*. In fact, the Fab Four made a movie by the same name about a magical bus trip where anything could happen, perhaps inspired by the psychedelic adventures of Ken Kesey and the Merry Pranksters. This all apparently rubbed off on Manson, providing the impetus for the Manson Family's Mystery Tour; a mystical transformation fueled by acid, role playing/name changing and brain re-arranging to arrive at the ultimate ego loss state of freedom, which Charlie's Family referred to as becoming "unprogrammed."

In February 1968, Beausoleil moved into a "burnt-out basement" on Horseshoe Lane in Topanga Canyon, and – knowing that Manson and his group were temporarily homeless – invited them to live on the property, where a Mansonoid tent scene soon unfolded, which included new converts Nancy "Brenda" Pitman, Linda Baldwin (aka Little Patty aka Madaline Joan Cottage), Ella Jo Bailey (aka Yeller) and fourteen-year-old Diane "Snake" Lake, who gained her reptilian appellation in "tribute to the transverse ophidian wiggles she made during intercourse." Another prized acquisition to Manson's pack of pubescent pretties was Deidre "Didi" Lansbury, daughter of Angela Lansbury. During their stay on Horseshoe Lane, Beausoleil and Manson formed a short-lived six-piece electric rock band dubbed The Milky Way that appeared for one weekend of public performances at a local nightclub, The Topanga Corral.

After leaving his "burnt-out basement", Beausoleil continued living the Topanga Canyon lifestyle, sharing a teepee with four young ladies, whom he referred to as his "wives." During this period, a film was being shot in the surrounding hills, and when the assistant director happened upon Beausoleil's well-constructed teepee, he hired Bobby to construct movie set tents. The film in production was *Ramrodder*, a softcore sexploitation Western. In addition to making tents, Bobby landed a role in the film as an Indian. During shooting, Beausoleil met Catherine Share, soon to be known in Manson Family lore as Gypsy, who also had a part in the movie, which included a sequence where she is chased through the woods wearing only a G-string. Evidently, Beausoleil had sexual relations with the leading lady of *Ramrodder*, who happened to be the producer's wife. Having worn out his welcome, Bobby split with Gypsy – and his wife Gail – and went to live with Gary Hinman for a while.

In March of 1968, Manson's was reunited with his former jail mate, Phil Kaufman. One time – when he and Manson were driving with to San Francisco – Kaufman realized that Charlie was trying to indoctrinate him. Charlie'd tell him something, then say, "You know that, don't you?" or "What do you think about that?" In this manner, Manson attempted to plant thoughts in Kaufman's head, which was the same method he used to manipulate his girls. Kaufman knew then that he had to get away, and said, "You got a good road game, Charlie. Don't blow it." In the vernacular of jail talk, "Road game" was a hustle or scam.

"I haven't got a road game," was Charlie's reply. But then, after awhile, he finally conceded: "You're too smart, Phil – You don't want to be around here." In other words, Kaufman was *thinking*, instead of blindly following "The Way of the Bus." Manson was a master at "planting seeds", as more than one former Family member has pointed out. Manson had a knack of getting others to believe they'd come up with an idea on their own, when in reality – through subtle persuasion – he'd coaxed them into a thought or action by planting a suggestion in their minds. This subtle persuasion was magnified under the influence of acid, which only heightens the power of suggestion. The girls – who all thought they were so in tune with Charlie's heavy guru vibes – in reality were being led around by their noses, according to Kaufman.

A friend Kaufman's, Harold True, rented a house at 3267 Waverly Drive, near the Silver Lake area of Los Angeles, where Charlie and his troupe visited in 1968 for "pot and LSD parties." True's house was located next door to the home of Leno and Rosemary LaBianca, future Manson Family murder victims.

One of the rarest Manson recordings – described by Nat Freedland in *The Occult Explosion* – is a tape made after an LSD orgy at True's house. Throughout this recording, Manson was unable to sing more than a couple lines of any tune before his attention span broke and he began spouting – as Freedland termed it – "the little acid guru epigrams he always punctuated with a high, self-conscious laugh," mouthing such meaningful maxims as: "Everything is the way it is because that's the way love says so." Or: "When you tune in with love, you tune in with yourself. That's not really a philosophy, that's a fact and everybody's who's got love in their hearts knows it," as in the background the girls chanted "Yeah" to every heavy word that issued forth in trippy trails from Charlie's pseudo-mystical mouth.

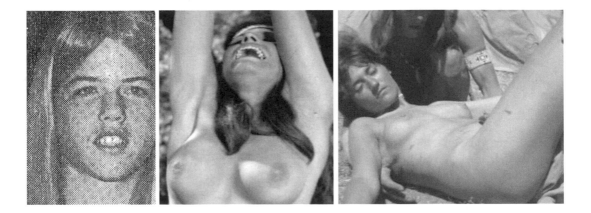

CHAPTER 12
Year of the Pig

For quite sometime, Charlie and his tribe had lived in transience aboard the black magic bus, never knowing where they might end up from one day to the next. At one point, Manson decided to cool his heels for a spell, setting up temporary residence in a cabin not far from The Spiral Staircase, on Summit Drive. During this period, Paul Watkins (soon to be known as "Little Paul") stumbled on to the scene, when he dropped by the Summit Drive shack looking for a previous tenant, and instead found Charlie and a roomful of naked girls. In short order, Little Paul was initiated by way of a Manson Family orgy as Brenda and Snake slithered across his body, "exploring orifices and contours with an amorphous precision like underwater jellyfish congealed in a single entity."

Although Charlie's Family had become accustomed to being hassled by the police, usually a few smiles and lash-batting by the girls would get the cops off their backs. But for some reason, the heat had been turned up, not only on Charlie's Family, but everywhere in early 1968. During this period, regulars in the Topanga and Malibu Canyons suddenly became aware of a new climate of police harassment, which coincided with the political unrest then spreading across the land. Arrests for archaic pot laws only helped escalate the level of resentment America's youth were starting to feel toward a new embodiment of the Inquisition.

Beatle George Harrison had recently penned a tune for the upcoming *White Album* entitled "Piggies", while simultaneously The Yippies launched the candidacy of an actual pig for president, a symbolic gesture signifying the direction the country was heading, as more and more people began referring to police as "Pigs." As was later evident, this symbolism sunk deeply into the sizzling heads of Manson's shock troops. Whether by orchestration – or artistic improvisation – this "piggie" symbol became the focal point of the Manson Family's retaliation against the Establishment.

On April 1st, 1968, Valentine Michael Manson – aka "Pooh Bear" – was born to Mary Brunner at the Summit Trail shack. To relax during birth, she inhaled deeply of a sacramental reefer. Papa Charlie played doctor, cutting and tying the umbilical cord, as the girls, now fifteen in all, performed as midwives.

After their Summit Drive sojourn, Charlie and his busload of babes hit the road, traveling up the California coast. They camped for awhile at Leo Carillo State Park, just south of Ventura, setting up tents in a gypsy-like fashion, singing around the campfire and smoking dope. It was here – Ed Sanders claimed – that Los Angeles Satanists would later perform blood sacrifices of animals.

Later in their journey, the black bus broke down in a wooded area south of Oxnard, so Charlie's Family decided to set up camp there. When Ventura County Sheriffs stopped to investigate, they were shocked to find a gaggle of naked hippies frolicking in the woods. But instead of the girls flashing smiles and batting eyelashes on this occasion, they got pissy, calling the cops "pigs" interspersed with other four letter imprecations. When one of the cops saw Mary Brunner's bare boob being suckled by Pooh Bear, she was booked for contributing to the delinquency of an infant, or some equally silly charge. Along with Mary, several others – including Charlie and Sadie – were arrested for possession of phony I.D.'s, and general overall nude, lewd and lascivious behavior, unbecoming of the Puritan ethic, as well as the statutes of the fair city of Oxnard. They were released the next day, fined ten dollars each. The Oxnard bust made the second page of the *Los Angeles Herald Examiner* with the provocative headline: "Nude Hippies Found in Woods."

After the Oxnard incident, Charlie's Family returned to Summit Trail. On May 2nd, police raided the cabin and arrested Manson, Sandra (Sandy) Good, Snake and Katie for possession of pot, and they were held in jail for a few days before being released. With all the hassles escalating around his Family, Charlie began to tune-in to the call of the desert. After his '67 release from Terminal Island, Manson had briefly visited the quiet solitude of the Mojave Desert, and it'd left an indelible impression. Not only were the insanities of the city taking their toll on Manson, but bus life, as well, had become a drag. What with the continued growth of his Family, it was becoming too overcrowded for comfort in the bus, inevitably creating stressful situations and sour dispositions. The desert was starting to look better from Charlie's perspective; it was somewhere that he and his throng could distance themselves from the long arm of the law, spread their wings and do their thing, free from the pigs breathing down their necks, day in and day out. This yearning for the desert hung in the back of Charlie's mind, growing larger each day.

CHAPTER 13
Dennis Wilson's "Wizard"

At 3AM, Beach Boy Dennis Wilson returned home from a recording session to his mansion at 14400 Sunset Boulevard. He parked his Ferrari at the rear, and as he got out, the back door swung open and out stepped a short fellow, with shaggy hair, dressed in a work shirt, jeans and moccasins.

"Who are you?" a bewildered Wilson asked.

"I'm a friend," Charlie Manson replied, inviting Dennis into his own house.

Inside, Wilson was taken aback by the scene unfolding, which featured about a dozen hippie chicks, smoking pot and dancing to a stereo blasting Beatle tunes. Most of the girls were topless, and not bad looking, either. In fact, Wilson recognized two of them, who he'd previously picked up hitchhiking. One went by the nickname of "Yeller" and the other called herself Marnie Reeves (aka Patricia "Katie" Krenwinkel). Earlier that day, Wilson had driven them to his house to show off his gold records, and ended up having sex with the girls, bragging about the incident later that evening in the recording studio. Afterwards, he would discover they'd given him the clap.

That night Dennis was introduced to the Way of the Bus, his initiation in the form of one of Charlie's well-orchestrated orgies. As usual, Manson himself oversaw the holy dispensation of drugs – LSD, STP, mushrooms, whatever was handy – always insuring that he gave himself a smaller dose than the rest of the group, so as to remain in control of the proceedings. Next Charlie would start to strip, and like clockwork, the girls would follow his lead. Then everyone would lie down on the floor and, under Charlie's direction, start rubbing up against one another, with their eyes closed, until they were all touching. Then Charlie would suggest various positions and sex acts.

Needless to say, Wilson was duly impressed with Charlie and the seductive scene surrounding him. Enough so, that he asked Charlie's Family to move in with him, beginning what the media later referred to as Manson's "Sunset Boulevard" period. During this time, Charlie was able to plug himself into the world of rock musicians and counted Terry Melcher – an up and coming rock music producer – among his many contacts established through Dennis Wilson. Melcher just happened to be the son of America's eternally virginal sweetheart, Doris Day, and produced the early Byrds records.

In 1966, Melcher rented a house at 10050 Cielo Drive, and was living there in the summer of 1968. Around this time, Manson became acquainted with Gregg Jakobson, a songwriter who worked for Melcher's music-publishing company. In time, Jakobson become intimate with Charlie's Family, recording Manson several times, and was privy to the benefits of rubbing elbows with a crazed little guru surrounded by sexually adventurous girls willing to impart favors to advance his career.

Manson was singing and playing guitar when Melcher encountered the would-be-rock-star at Wilson's house. Afterwards, Charlie visited Melcher's home on several occasions, once even borrowed his Jaguar.

According to Ed Sanders, the Manson/Melcher association was more extensive than has ever been admitted, and that an "area of silence" had been erected around the whole sordid affair. As one can imagine, such negative publicity revolving around a relationship between Manson, and the son of America's #1 sweetheart, was something that needed to be squelched at all costs. All it would take was one scandalous headline in the tabloids to shave precious Nielson rating points off of Doris Day's then highly rated CBS sit-com.

As Gregg Jakobson recounted: "One day Dennis called me up and said, 'Hey, Gregg, you should have been down here. Some guy pulled in with a big black bus... and he's got about thirty girls.'" The following night, Jakobson visited Dennis' house and was blown-away by the scene: a gaggle of subservient and half naked young women, waiting hand and foot on Charlie and Dennis. Jakobson perceived Manson as someone who "could discuss almost any subject, just like he said (later, in court) he had a 'thousand hats' and he could put on any hat at any time. In another situation he would have been capable of being a president of a university..."

One night, Wilson and Jakobson accompanied Charlie and the girls to the Whiskey A Go Go, and were treated to a magical spectacle on the dance floor. "Charlie started dancing, and I swear to God, within a matter of minutes the dance floor would be empty and Charlie would be dancing by himself. It was almost as if sparks were flying off the guy." Jakobson thought if he could only capture this psychedelic whirling dervish on film, the whole world would then see the wild energy of Manson. Charlie was "like fire, a raw explosion, a mechanical toy that suddenly went crazy."

Wilson was so in awe of Manson that he bragged about his friendship in an issue of the English rock magazine *Rave*. "Fear is nothing but awareness," said Wilson in the interview, mimicking Manson's guru-driven mumbo-jumbo. "I was only frightened as a child because I did not understand fear – the dark, being lost, what was under the bed! It came from within... Sometimes the Wizard frightens me – Charlie Manson, who says he is God and the devil! He sings, plays, and writes poetry and may be another artist for Brother Records."

While living in grand style at Wilson's house, much of Charlie's Family's habits stayed the same, such as their dumpster diving forays, this despite large deliveries to Wilson's house each day by the Alta Dena Dairy, as well as the generous cash supplements he shelled out to buy additional food. Nevertheless, Manson would pile his girls in Wilson's Rolls Royce in the middle of the night and seek out supermarket garbage bins for edible treasures cast off by a wasteful "piggie" society. Dennis thought these food runs were great fun, and even went on a few himself, driving the girls up and down Sunset Boulevard in his silver Ferrari.

Wilson underwrote everything during his time with the Mansonoids. In return, he was waited on hand and foot by the girls, and allowed to partake in Charlie's orgies. Before long, Dennis' entire wardrobe had been added to the communal Manson Family clothing pile. On one occasion, Manson ordered the girls to cut everything up into large swatches and sew them into robes for everyone to wear. "One day Dennis walked into our house in Benedict Canyon," his estranged wife Carol recalled. "I'll never forget him coming down the dark hallway. He was barefoot and wearing a robe they had made for him out of patches of clothing."

Manson drained Wilson of well over $100,000 that summer, including bills for wrecking his Mercedes-Benz, not to mention constant doctor's visits to cure Charlie's Family of the clap, in what Wilson referred to as "The largest gonorrhea bill in history."

Another benefit of taking refuge at Wilson's house was that it afforded Manson the privilege of using the address with his parole officer as a place of residence. For a free-wheeling vagabond with a busload of underage girls, this facade became a necessity. Even after Dennis let the lease run out – and had given Charlie and his girls the boot – Manson still used the address on his I.D.

‡

During this period, Deane Moorehouse returned in Los Angeles and began living with Charlie's Family in the guest house at Wilson's estate, working as a groundskeeper. Moorehouse – the former proselytizing minister, who had earlier sentenced Charlie to eternal damnation for defiling his daughter – underwent a sudden and illuminating transformation, apparently facilitated by a paradigm-shattering dose of acid, on top of an even bigger dose of Charlie-anity. Soon Moorehouse was rapping the word of Man's Son, as his grew long, gobbling acid on a daily basis.

Moorehouse – now officially another of Charlie's acid eating apostles – began recruiting others into the fold, including a young Texan named Brooks Poston. As was the custom for new recruits to bestow all of their worldly goods unto the Church of Charlie, Poston forked over a credit card belonging to his mother that was used extensively during Manson Family travels in 1968. As legend has it, Poston quickly grew to believe that Charlie was Jesus Christ.

Another Texan who wandered into the Manson Family sphere during this period was Charles Denton Watson aka "Tex." Born in Copeville, Texas in 1946, Watson was a high school athlete, starring on the football team, and at one time holding the Texas high hurdles record. Watson attended North Texas State College, dropping out in 1966 and moving to Los Angeles in early 1967. In L.A., he worked for awhile as a wig dealer, operating a popular hair store called Love Locs on La Cienega Boulevard. The young entrepreneur supplemented his income by dealing grass on the side. During this period, Watson lived in an upscale Malibu pad, affecting the lifestyle of a mod swinger.

Watson became acquainted with Dennis Wilson one day when he picked up The Beach Boy drummer hitch-hiking, and gave him a ride home. According to Watson, Dennis had "wrecked his Ferrari, and his Rolls Royce, so was having to use his thumb." At Wilson's invitation, Watson moved in with him at 14400 Sunset Boulevard and obligingly partook of the luxurious surroundings filled with drugs and chicks. Here Watson met resident guru, Deane Moorehouse, and in short order became a protégé of the former Protestant minister.

It was Moorehouse who first introduced Watson to such pseudo-mystical concepts as "ego loss", which Tex was to hear more of later from Charlie and his unwashed acolytes. Watson in his memoir, *Will You Die For Me*, remembered Moorehouse as a "kind of wandering guru, teaching a lot of people in the film and music industries that true 'awareness' and real 'religion' came through opening yourself up with acid. When people became aware, according to Deane, they could be free to die to themselves, to die to their egos. Then they would understand that Charles Manson was the reincarnation of the Son of God..."

At Wilson's, Tex soaked up all the feel-good vibes, especially when Charlie performed his songs of love, and his semi-nude girls gathered around, singing angelic harmonies, and initiating Tex into their group-gropes. Amidst all the harmonious vibes, a peculiar mix of humans came and went, including young drop-outs, drug dealers and people in the entertainment business. At this time, it was chic to "play the hippie game" as the children of big stars partied with resident gurus, Deane and Charlie.

Although Watson had smoked plenty of dope, he'd never dabbled with acid until Deane Moorehouse took him on his first trip. To the young Texan, LSD was a sudden revelation. All the baggage of his past – all the hang-ups, fears and conditioned societal attitudes – were laid bare in the searing light of truth, illuminated by the divine sacrament. There was no fear now, as Tex just let himself go with the cosmic flow, "letting things slip away like glass beads falling slowly through my fingers." He could be at peace for the first time in his life, because nothing had to be a hassle anymore; it was all so obvious, it was laughable. The answer was just to let it go, not to fight it at all, to submit. Sure, it might hurt some to let go of all that past conditioning, all that you had once been – but eventually it would heal in the wash of what one was be free to become.

When Tex first started using acid, he claimed that Charlie was not an important figure in his life. But Moorehouse babbled on incessantly about Manson, an evangelist for the "gospel according to Charlie." Charlie's girls also carried the message about overcoming one's ego, and that the only true way to freedom of mind was to let go, and experience "ego death." The truth was what the Beatles were singing: *I am you and you are me and we are all together.* The rap was that everyone was all part of the same thing, no separate *me* or *you*, everybody everywhere just cosmic ripples in the one great wave. True freedom meant giving fully of one's self, letting that musty old ego die a fitting death, so that one could be free of the ego-self that keeps us all from one another; that which creates walls and barriers and prevents us from living life as it was truly meant to be. It was like that song Charlie sang: "Cease to exist, come say you love me." The girls on cue repeated it over and over – *cease to exist, kill your ego, die* – so that once you cease to be, you can be totally free to love, and come together.

The girls kept urging Tex to join them. Charlie, they said, had died more completely than anyone on Earth, not only in his present incarnation, but long before, on a cross. So, according to Manson Family logic, in becoming one with him – in dying to themselves – they could really unite with Man's Son, and become one with love itself, with "God." With each subsequent acid trip that Deane and Tex took together, it started making more sense.

In August 1968 – while Dennis was on tour – Moorehouse began putting pressure on female guests at 14400 Sunset Boulevard to have sex with him. When Dennis learned of Moorehouse's unwanted advances, he promptly gave the lecherous old guru the boot, kicking both he and Watson out. Despite this, Moorehouse remained on good terms with Terry Melcher. Moorehouse, along with Watson, visited Melcher on several occasions at his residence at 10050 Cielo Drive. In fact, Moorehouse was a familiar presence at parties there, where he was well known as a dirty old man. Once Melcher even lent him his Jaguar and credit cards so that to Moorehouse could drive up north to face charges of giving acid to underage girls.

On Moorehouse's trip north, Tex accompanied his psychedelic guru, smoking joints and rapping about "ego loss." As the two were zooming through Atascadero they were stopped by a CHP and ticketed. As they drove on, Tex crumpled up the piggie citation, and tossed it out the window, since he never planned on being anywhere near Atascadero again. Little did he know that two years later he'd back, this time as an inmate of the state mental hospital.

‡

During the period Manson magically materialized into Dennis Wilson's life in the form of "The Wizard", his brother Brian Wilson was also going through his own strange changes, becoming increasingly alienated from the rest of the Beach Boys.

Throughout 1966, Brian spent a lot of time alone in his home studio composing and recording what was to be the follow-up to *Pet Sounds*. This project-to-be was the *Smile* LP. Unfortunately, when other band members heard this would-be psychedelic masterpiece, they were dumbfounded, thinking Brian was trying to ruin their careers with his LSD-inspired excesses. The only one who encouraged Brian was Dennis, himself recently illuminated by LSD. Ultimately, the collective decision was made to trash all the wonderful experimental psychedelic music Brian had produced, and record more traditional Beach Boys' music. Of course, this approach only further alienated Brian. The *Smile* sessions sat gathering dust in the Capitol vaults, although fragments of the sessions found their way on the later *Smiley Smile* album, but this effort paled in comparison to what Brian had originally envisioned. Over the next couple of years – as The Beach Boys continued producing fairly pedestrian albums – disturbed genius Brian remained busy at work behind the scenes in his laboratory/home studio, concocting revolutionary experimental music. But alas – as all this back scene creativity was taking place, Brian was slowly unraveling.

Another composition Brian recorded with a mini-orchestra was called "Fire", which he described as "weird and eerie." The song built slowly, like the beginning of a giant conflagration, "and grew so intense it was possible to picture the kindling catching, spreading, and being whipped by the wind into a raging, out-of-control inferno. It created a disturbing picture that mirrored the screams that filled my head and plagued my sleep for years."

The following day – after recording "Fire" – Brian learned that a building next door to his studio had burned down the same night as the recording session. Several days later, he was informed that after the session an unusual number of fires had broken out across Los Angeles. Now all that remains of this music is roughly two minutes of material, locked safely away in the Capitol vaults, per Brian's request. As he later explained, "I was dabbling into some kind of musical witchcraft. I can't let it happen again. It's too scary."

During the winter of 1968, the Beach Boys recorded *20/20* in Brian's basement studio. Perhaps the oddest cut on the album was a song Dennis supplied, entitled, "Never Learn Not To Love." Although Dennis was credited as composer, it was actually written by his strange new friend, Charlie Manson and was originally entitled "Cease To Exist." All told, Dennis swung a deal to acquire the rights of two Manson songs: "Cease To Exist" and another tune, "Be With Me", for an unspecified amount of cash and a BSA motorcycle.

During this period, Dennis brought Manson and the girls to Brian's home studio to produce a demo tape of some of Charlie's tunes. When Manson arrived for his first session, he was totally unprepared. "He brought nothing," studio engineer, Steve Despar remembered, "except a half dozen girls, and they stayed in the studio with him and smoked dope. I guess I got on Charlie's good side, because the first thing that happened was he pulled out a cigarette and didn't have a match, so I went to the kitchen and got a match for him. He was very impressed that someone would actually go to the trouble just for him. He made a big deal about that."

Eventually, though, Manson's true nature manifested, and Despar became uneasy. "What struck me odd was the stare he gave you. It was scary. We were in there two or three nights, and then he got pretty weird. (He) pulled a knife on me, just for no reason really, just pulled the knife out and would flash it around while he was talking. I called Grillo (the Beach Boy manager) and said, 'Look, this guy is psychotic… I don't know if I'm going to say something that's going to tick him off and he's going to pull a switchblade on me.'"

Grillo told Despar that the eight songs thus far recorded were enough, and called off any further sessions. In the meantime, Grillo hired detectives to look into Manson's background, and soon information came trickling in detailing Charlie's checkered past. These revelations, combined with the changes that Brian saw in his brother, Dennis, deeply disturbed the elder Wilson. Brian became convinced that Manson was experimenting with evil powers and sent word to Dennis that neither Manson nor any of his extended "Family" was to ever set foot on his property again. Later, when Vincent Bugliosi was investigating the Tate/LaBianca murders, he expressed interest in hearing the tapes that Manson had recorded. Dennis Wilson claimed that he had destroyed the tapes in question, because "the vibrations connected with them don't belong to this earth." Among the songs demo'd under Wilson's aegis during 1968 were: "Look at your Game Girl" (second version), "Ego", "Mechanical Man", "People Say I'm no Good", "Home is Where you're Happy", "Arkansas", "I'll Never Say Never to Always", "Garbage Dump", "Don't do Anything Illegal", "Sick City", "Cease to Exist", "Big Iron Door", and "I Once Knew a Man".

Another Hollywood player that Wilson tried to interest in Manson's music was Rudy

Altobelli, a show biz talent manager who owned numerous Los Angeles properties including the 10050 Cielo Drive house. When he first met Manson, Altobelli was living in the guest house at the property, then being rented by Terry Melcher. Altobelli previously met Manson at Wilson's house, and even though everybody was raving about Charlie like he was some sort of musical genius, Altobelli was unimpressed, and declined to promote Manson's career. According to Altobelli: "(Melcher and Wilson) talked to me on many occasions about Manson. They wanted Deane (Moorehouse) to come and talk to me... They were telling me about his philosophy and his way of living and how groovy it was."

So it was that in March of 1969, Sharon Tate – now living at 10050 Cielo Drive with husband Roman Polanski – had a brief face-to-face encounter with the man later charged with masterminding her murder. Altobelli was taking a shower in the guest cottage when he heard the front doorbell ring. He went to the door and found Manson, recognizing Charlie from their previous meeting at Dennis Wilson's house.

"When I saw him standing there," Altobelli later recalled, "I was surprised. He said he was looking for Melcher, and then skillfully turned the conversation around to his tapes. I told him Melcher had moved, and that I had no time to discuss it, because I was preparing to leave for Europe." Altobelli sent Manson away, although – as it turned out – Charlie did not immediately leave. Afterwards, Altobelli dropped by the main house where he met Sharon Tate's personal photographer, Shahrokh Hatami, who stated that: "(Manson) arrived at the door and asked for someone whose name I did not recognize. I don't think it was Melcher. I felt a little protective towards Sharon and I said loudly, 'This is the Polanski residence. There is no one here of that name.'"

Manson repeated the name, then turned to go. As he did, Sharon and the others – Jay Sebring, Woytek Frykowski and Abigail Folger – came towards the door. Sharon said, "Who was that guy?" At that instant, Manson turned and looked back, observing four future victims of the Cielo Drive murders.

CHAPTER 14
Spawn Ranch

In April 1968 – while standing on the corner of Topanga Canyon and Ventura Boulevard – Paul Watkins' path crossed once again with Charlie's Family, when he was picked by Snake and Brenda, returning from a garbage run. The girls informed Paul that they were now living at a placed called Spahn Ranch, and invited him to come with them and say hi to Charlie. The trio drove up Topanga Canyon to Santa Susana Pass, as the girls raved about how life at the ranch was so blissful and how deeply they all felt Charlie's love.

"Charlie," Brenda intoned, "is just a hole in the infinite through which love is funneled." It sounded pretty hokey, and Paul didn't pay much attention to this screwy rhapsody until Snake flashed a beatific smile and declared, "Charlie is Jesus Christ." Both girls giggled. Paul let the comment slide, thinking it was an inside joke.

They took a back road off Santa Susana pass, which led to a patchwork of weathered wooden buildings, sheds and lean-tos set against rocky, rolling foothills covered with brush and discarded automobiles. The ranch was an old western movie set, with buildings fronted by a boardwalk. As they slowly drove by, Brenda pointed out the old movie sets: The Longhorn Saloon, Rocky City Cafe, an undertaking parlor, a jail, a hotel, a carriage house filled with old vehicles, and a number of smaller stores. Out behind these structures lived the owner of the place, a half-blind old geezer, George Spahn. About a quarter mile farther down the road was the main ranch house, which at this time was occupied by a group of hippies unaffiliated with Manson's bunch. A little ways passed the main house were the "outlaw shacks" – two small dilapidated redwood structures – where Charlie's Family was then staying. Scenes from *Ramrodder*, and many other B-westerns, were shot at Spahn Ranch.

As Watkins and the girls pulled up before the outlaw shacks, the door opened and out stepped Charlie, Sandy, and Squeaky. Charlie gave Little Paul a warm, brotherly hippie-type embrace, and said he had to split, but would be back later. It was Little Paul's plan just to say hello, and hit the road for Big Sur that afternoon, but before Charlie left he gave Snake a knowing wink, which instructed her to show Little Paul a good time. It was in this manner – Watkins later suggested – that Manson's talons subtly dug in via sexual manipulations cleverly used to lure in young male recruits, such as he. Before long, Watkins would be performing the same service for Charlie, picking up high school chicks and bringing them back to the ranch in hopes of recruiting them into Charlie's Family.

‡

As the summer progressed, Dennis Wilson grew disillusioned with Manson. The turning point came one day when Charlie pulled a knife on him, and said, "What would you do if I killed you?" Dennis simply shrugged, and said, "Do it." With that, Manson lowered the knife, having not received a sufficient quotient of fear vibes from Wilson to continue on with his mind game. This wouldn't be the last time that Manson held a knife to someone's throat in order to test them, to feed off their fears.

Relief from this tense atmosphere came in the form of a Beach Boys' summer tour, as Dennis was in and out of L.A. with frequent regularity. Because he could never muster the courage to kick Charlie and the girls out of his house, Dennis opted instead – in early August, three weeks before the lease expired – to move to a small rented house in Palisades, leaving 14400 Sunset to Charlie and the girls. The rent went unpaid, and eventually Charlie's Family was thrown out by plainclothes detectives hired by Nick Grillo. Charlie was not particularly upset by Dennis' actions, as he now had a secondary residence at Spahn Ranch. However, Charlie continued to show up at Dennis' new Palisades pad whenever he needed anything.

On one occasion, Charlie paid a visit to Dennis' Palisades pad and found his fifteen-year-old girlfriend, Croxey Adams, there instead. When Manson encouraged Croxey to get naked, she refused and told him to get out. Manson pulled a knife and said: "You know, I could cut you up into little pieces..." Croxey ran out of the house, and down to the Pacific Coast Highway before she gathered up enough courage to return and confront Charlie. "I belittled him so much that he left, " Croxey remembered. "I told him, 'Go ahead! Go ahead, you wimp! Try and get it up, you motherfucker! You're a punk peon! You got me in a spot, so go for it, buddy! Get that knife out and kill me! Slice my throat!'" Faced with the challenge, Manson seemed cowed and backed down. His play on fear had backfired. Later, Croxey realized how lucky she had been when details of the Tate/LaBianca murders became known. Just the same, she had used the right tactic in dealing with Manson: when anyone turned Charlie's "Fear Game" back on him, he didn't know how to react, and usually backed down.

In Manson's psychological bag of tricks, the main trump card he continually played on was "Fear." Charlie's whole theology was hinged upon the precept of experiencing fear fully, submitting and becoming one with it. In this manner, he would enlighten and his children to the ultimate meaning of existence, as it meanwhile heightened their awareness and strengthened survival instincts.

Manson was constantly pushing the limits of paranoia within himself and his followers, playing mind games with sharp knifes, heavy vibes and piercing eyes; taking his "Family" to the heart of their innermost fears, that they in turn would overcome them, becoming stronger in body and mind. At least that's one way of interpreting these machinations, although it's probable that Charlie's tactics were consciously employed to break down egos and demolish morals, replacing them with his own twisted system of thought. This concept of overcoming fears and inner demons was undoubtedly related to the initial period of an LSD trip, where one must conquer the trepidation and anxiety that comes with the experience, or – failing that – become prey to a bummer trip, and an expense paid vacation in Hell.

The concept of embracing death became another power tool Manson used to instill his will. One of Charlie's favorite games was to hand a knife to someone, and suggest that they kill him. When they refused, Charlie would then say that he now had the right to kill them. Such tactics insured that his followers remained always on edge, and in the process became aware of everything around them, just like the coyotes of the desert that Charlie so profoundly admired. Charlie had a word for this heightened state of awareness: *Coyotenoia*. It all revolved around fear as the source of all awareness, as Charlie taught his children; wild animals live in a constant fear, super-aware of everything in their environment, totally lacking self-consciousness. That, said Charlie, is how they all should be. The purpose of fear was to get rid of all thought; if you were really afraid, then you were conscious of nothing but the moment, the present situation at hand. That was what Charlie dubbed "being in the *Now* ", which was true clarity, true awareness.

CHAPTER 15
The Witches of Mendocino

Not long after settling into Spahn Ranch, Charlie instructed Sadie and some of the girls to take a bus trip up the California coast. Why Manson chose this time to split up his Family, one can only guess. Some have suggested that Charlie was sending the girls – Sadie, Mary, Katie, Ella, and Susan Scott (aka Stephanie Rowe) – on a missionary trip to bring back new members to Spahn Ranch. An alternate explanation is that the girls were out scouting for a permanent place to settle Charlie's Family. Whatever the case, they loaded up in the black school bus one spring morning and headed north with Sexy Sadie at the helm. The girls ended up in the little Mendocino County town of Philo, and launched a satellite version of the Family there, with Sadie filling the role as head-Manson-mama.

One day – while Sadie was in San Francisco replenishing their LSD supply – a gang of high school boys from Philo raided the house where they were staying, and with threats and sheer brute-strength, forced the girls into having sex. When Sadie returned, the gang of the boys was still there, continuing to threaten the girls, so she thought by dispensing acid to the boys it might chill them out. However, this had the opposite effect, and soon the boys went berserk, and began take out their negative, spaced-out energy by destroying the house, as well as tearing apart the black bus and rendering it totally unusable. Eventually, the majority of boys split, but that was only the beginning of the girls' troubles. A little after midnight, one of the boy's mothers phoned the Mendocino County Deputy Sheriff's office requesting an officer be sent to her home because someone had given her son dope. When the police arrived, they found the disoriented seventeen-year-old speaking of his legs as if they were snakes. The boy informed police that "The Witches" at the Philo "hippie" house had given him acid.

That night the Sheriff's deputies raided the so-called "hippie lair" occupied by five females (later referred to as the "Witches of Mendocino"), three males and an infant, Pooh Bear. The police searched the house and surrounding area. In an outside woodshed they discovered a film canister containing marijuana in addition to a plastic bag filled with groovy blue tabs. The girls were subsequently arrested on charges of drug possession and contributing to the delinquency of minors and sentenced to three months in the Mendocino County Jail. Their sentences were later reduced to time served while awaiting trial, plus probation. Altogether, the "Witches of Mendocino", spent about a month in locked up.

During this time, Pooh Bear was taken away from Mary and placed in a foster home. In the interim, Roger Smith – Manson's former federal parole officer – and his wife were appointed foster parents for the child. In January 1968, Smith had left his job as a parole officer and established a drug treatment program at the Haight Ashbury Free Clinic. During the Summer of Love, Charlie's girls often visited the clinic to clear up venereal diseases. Al Rose, the clinic's administrative head, was so intrigued by Charlie's Family that he later visited them at Spahn Ranch and – in collaboration with a Dr. David Smith – wrote a formal paper in 1968 entitled "The Group Marriage Commune: A Case Study", later published in the November 1970 issue of the *Journal of Psychedelic Drugs*. The authors wrote that the group was distinguished by its:

> ...spiritual leader... a "father-figure" (known as) Charlie, a 35-year-old white male with a past history of criminal activity...He was never arrested or convicted of a crime of violence... He was an extroverted, persuasive individual who served as absolute ruler of this group marriage commune... Tales of Charlie's sexual prowess were related to all new members... Charlie would get up in the morning, make love, eat breakfast, make love and go back to sleep. He would wake up later and make love, have lunch, make love and go back to sleep. Waking up later, he would make love, eat dinner, make love, and go back to sleep – only to wake up in the middle of the night to have intercourse again.
>
> Such stories, although not validated, helped him maintain his leader-ship role. Charlie had a persuasive mystical philosophy placing great emphasis on the belief that people did not die and that infant consciousness was the ultimate state... Charlie used the words of Jesus, "He who is like the small child shall reap the rewards of heaven," as a guide for the group's child-rearing philosophy...However, Charlie's mysticism often became delusional and he, on occasion, referred to himself as "God" or "God and the Devil." Charlie could probably be diagnosed as an ambulatory schizophrenic...
>
> Charlie set himself up as "initiator of new females" into the commune. He would spend most of their first day making love to them, as he wanted to see if they were just on a "sex trip" (a term used by the group to label someone there only for sexual gratification), or whether they were seriously interested in joining the group... An unwillingness, for example to engage in mutual oral-genital contact was cause for immediate expulsion, for Charlie felt that this was one of the most important indications as to whether the girl would be willing to give up her sexual inhibitions... Charlie felt that getting rid of sexual inhibitions would free people of most of their problems...

In conclusion, the authors asked why this type of communal lifestyle held such appeal for "adolescents and young adults. Why, for example, were these young girls so attracted and captivated by a disturbed mystic such as Charlie?"

Another connection linking Charlie's Family and the Haight Ashbury Free Clinic comes in the form of Inez Folger, mother of Abigail Folger, who worked as a volunteer at Roger Smith's drug treatment program. Mrs. Folger helped the clinic receive a $25,000 grant, as well as holding several fund raising events. Abigail – as well as Sharon Tate's parents – attended one of these benefits. It also appears that one or more Manson Family members attended this same fund raising cocktail party.

†

The Spahn Ranch cast of characters during the summer of '68 was steadily growing. The female population had swelled to ten, consisting of Snake, Brenda, Squeaky, Sandy, Sadie, Katie, Mary, Bo, Stephanie and Yeller. The male contingent included Charlie, Little Paul, T.J. Walleman, Brooks Poston, Tex Watson, a kid named Kim, and Steve (Clem Scramblehead) Grogan.

Grogan – a sixteen-year-old from Simi Valley – was living with a group of hippies at the rear of Spahn Ranch, prior to joining Charlie's Family. His criminal record included drug use and possession, shoplifting, grand theft, prowling, child molestation, indecent exposure, not to mention having recently escaped from Camarillo State Mental Hospital. Clem eventually became a sort of creepy carbon copy of Manson, parroting Charlie's rap in almost word for word perfection, while following around the girls with an insipid grin on his face. Charlie told the group that Clem should be an example for everyone because he needed very little "deprogramming." Clem was innocent, like a child before his mama got hold of him, killed his soul and laid society's whole fucked up trip on him. Clem took Charlie's mantra "no sense makes sense" to heart, because Clem hardly ever made any sense. Nevertheless, he was a talented musician, able to copy Manson's guitar style and singing voice almost exactly. Another male that drifted in and out of the Manson Family scene that summer was Juan Flynn, an Irish Panamanian who worked as a wrangler at the ranch.

During this period, Charlie's Family spread out like a day-glo fungus through the woods and streams surrounding Spahn Ranch, building lean-tos and setting up tents. Like a psychedelic field commander, Charlie oversaw the operation, roaming about in hippie regalia and supervising the various construction projects. "All my women are witches and I'm the Devil," he told other people living at Spahn's. And witches they were, fashioning occult items about the ranch, such as a steer skull atop a stake, painted with arcane emblems. Manson's tent was decorated with occult symbols, including eyeballs and pentagrams. Another example of the girl's "witchiness" consisted of a ritual ceremony performed before each garbage run when they would form a mental picture in their minds as to what store would provide the best gourmet garbage, then drive to a supermarket garbage bin, and – lo and behold! – the food envisioned would magically appear. Much of this purported witchiness came to the fore during the Tate/LaBianca trial testimony of star prosecution witness, Linda Kasabian, who joined Charlie's Family in the summer of 1969.

Kasabian became known as "Yana the Witch." When later asked if she actually considered herself one, Kasabian answered, "No, they told me I was. They said they all were. I was made to feel I was." But she added that as far as the murders were concerned, she regarded herself as a "good witch."

To illustrate the overall level of Manson influenced witchiness, Kasabian testified that – before she and the rest of Charlie's killing crew drove off from Spahn Ranch on the evening of the murders – Manson came to the car window and said: "Leave a sign. The girls know what I mean – something witchy." At the trial, Manson's attorney, Ronald Hughes, asked Kasabian: "Your state of mind before you went to the Tate residence was that you were a witch?" In response, Kasabian answered, "I thought I was a witch, yeah."

Hughes then displayed gory photographs of the Tate/LaBianca murder scene, and asked: "You considered that witches had supernatural powers?" Kasabian answered, "Yes, but I didn't... have any powers. I was made to believe I was a witch, right from the beginning." The young women at the ranch kept saying to each other, she recalled, "I'm a witch; you're a witch."

In her testimony, however, Kasabian stated that she could communicate with animals – not with words – but through "vibrations." Kasabian added that Manson had influenced her through power of suggestion, or "vibes."

Later, Paul Watkins explained Charlie's unusual hold over his followers. "How did he do it? Well, by the time Charlie was 35 he had done just about everything there was to be done. We were all terribly impressed by his experiences. He had been in jail a lot, bummed around the country, and always had harems of young chicks... He was big on Scientology and Black Magic. It was pretty powerful stuff. He was continually hypnotizing us, not the way they do in night clubs but more like mental thought transference."

CHAPTER 16
Getting The Fear

In June 1968, Leslie Van Houten (later known in Charlie's Family as LuLu) met Bobby Beausoleil, who at the time was living with two other women, his wife Gail and Gypsy Share. Leslie joined the trio, roaming the California coast in Bobby's Studebaker. As she later recalled: "Nothing was planned, everything happened for the moment, at the moment. Just freedom. When someone would ask us to come over, we would go over. There was no idea for tomorrow, because we never, you know, we didn't know tomorrow would even ever be there. Everything was pleasurable."

Eventually, this three-women-to-one-man arrangement fostered jealousy and Gypsy decided to split for Los Angeles. Later – while hanging out with Bobby in San Jose – Leslie heard about some hippies that were in the area, stranded in a prune orchard where their bus had broken down. In the past, Gypsy had spoken highly of this group, and so Leslie went in search of the broken bus and its occupants. She eventually found the group – including Gypsy – camped communally in the orchard. Immediately Leslie was accepted into the tribe. "It was like I had known them forever. It was like walking into a group of old friends."

The group abandoned the bus, and hitched back to Spahn Ranch. Once there, Leslie was introduced to the group's leader, Charlie. "He just walked up and smiled real nice, you know, and I just smiled back. And he wasn't any different than all the others. But I could feel much strength in meeting him. I felt a very good feeling toward him."

That summer, another new initiate joined the group, Joan "Juanita" Wildebush. Wildebush – described by Ed Sanders as an "eager young lady with a Rubenesque Frame" – was a schoolteacher on summer vacation, who just happened to pick up four hitchhikers – T.J., Tex, Ella and Clem – near Palo Alto, California. They persuaded her to drive them down to Spahn Ranch, so that Juanita could meet Charlie. Apparently, it didn't take long for Manson to cast his love-spell. After an all-day grope-session, Wildebush withdrew $11,000 from her trust fund and handed it over to Manson.

Around this time, Manson acquired a 1956 white GMC school bus, which his Family painted light green. This same bus was seen at 10050 Cielo Drive that summer, driven by Tex and Mary, who were apparently looking for Terry Melcher, although Melcher wasn't home at the time. However, this wasn't the only occasion that Tex visited 10050 Cielo Drive, prior to the murders. In the summer of 1968 – in the company of Deane Moorehouse – Watson attended several parties there hosted by Melcher and his girlfriend, Candice Bergen.

Later that summer, Charlie's Family moved from the Spahn Ranch outlaw shacks to better digs in the jail, which adjoined the saloon. Manson still had designs on the main ranch house, but would have to wait until the group of hippies living there gave it up. In the interim, Charlie converted the new quarters in such a fashion as to accommodate his entire Family.

The saloon was authentic Old West, complete with mahogany bar, mirrors and low hanging overhead fans. The girls cleaned up the place, and knocked out a wall to connect the jail to the saloon, where they set up a kitchen, using the common area for meals, parties and other happenings. The floor was covered with mattresses and tapestries hung over the walls. Their food supply was stored in George Spahn's house, and the girls cooked on his stove, preparing meals for old George at the same time. Charlie – looking to stay in old man Spahn's good graces – assigned one or two of the girls to take care of his needs, which included a little nookie now and then. In due time, Squeaky became the old man's favorite Manson girl. When, on occasion, he would slide his hand up Squeaky's leg and pinch the inside of her thigh, she'd invariably flinch and make a little "eek" sound. That is how she came to be known as "Squeaky."

Once a week they'd set aside an evening to drop acid. However – as Paul Watkins pointed out in *My Life with Charles Manson* – drug use was never indiscriminate or casual. Rarely did they smoke dope during the day, and Charlie forbade anyone to take acid on their own. "Drugs were used to a specific purpose: to bring us into a higher state of consciousness as a Family; to unify us."

Many of Charlie's after dinner sermons dealt with the meaninglessness of time. Manson never allowed calendars or clocks at the ranch; time meant nothing when you lived in the eternal *Now*. "We are ageless, " he would say. "We will never die. But nothing else is secure because time is running out for the world. The end of the world is coming. Society is killing the planet... Time is running out and we've got to get out into the country, into the desert, to live off the land...

"But despite this," Charlie went on, "we have to continue to live one day at a time. You should have thrown away all your clocks and watches. That's a must. There *is* no time. We're ageless. There *is* no time. Everything is now.... Love is free. Love just loves...We are all one... God is everywhere and everyone is God... No sense makes sense...There is no such thing as no such thing."

Charlie explained that the burden placed upon his shoulders was not one he necessarily wanted, but was a mission he had been chosen for. The vision came to him one day in prison, "...when the Infinite just came into my cell and opened up my head. He showed me the truth. But I didn't want it. I cried and yelled at him, 'No. No. Not Me.' But he showed me the truth."

Manson was a mental magician; a natural born charmer – of people, as well as snakes. One Manson Family legend tells of Charlie walking through a gully of sidewinders, gliding gracefully, caressing them gently on their tails in passing. None of the rattlers struck out, as the vibes Charlie sent out put his reptilian friends at ease. Similar were the charming effects Manson had upon humans. Twisting himself into their minds, he had the uncanny ability to meet a person and immediately psyche them out; to instantly understand their deepest fears and hang-ups, and how to manipulate their vulnerabilities.

Charlie's eyes were hypnotic. They could bathe you in everlasting love, or at a moment's notice scare you shitless. Charlie knew tricks he could play with his face, and used these manipulations to reflect and project his thoughts on others. It was all about altering perceptions, and erasing institutional blackboards in his follower's minds: replacing all authority with one authority, *The Soul*.

Economically, Charlie's Family managed quite well, as Manson assigned the girls various jobs. In the early Haight-Ashbury days it was survival by panhandling, or using parent's credit cards or shoplifting. Later, the girls became noted for their junkets to shopping centers were they raided garbage dumpsters for discarded food. Mary Brunner had a contact at a local bakery in Santa Monica that supplied the group with bread, cakes, cookies, and assorted pastries. Charlie contributed by running various scams that netted his Family old cars or donations. Plus people were always giving Manson things – such as Dennis Wilson – who contributed not only money, but automobiles, clothing and food. Added to that, all bank accounts became community property, so that a general cash reserve was always on hand when someone needed it. Just like all well-managed cults, Charlie made it known to new members that the only way they'd be able to join his Family was by giving up all their worldly possessions – that meant giving everything to Charlie.

One special project that Mary and Squeaky began during the Summer of Love was Charlie's ceremonial vest – embroidered by hand with every color imaginable – with flowers that flowed across the shoulders on vines. Soon, little scenes were added to the vest depicting the Family's black bus travels, and finally, their arrival at Spahn Ranch. There were scenes of love making, smoking dope, riding horses, dancing, making music, and eventually their trek into the desert. In time, the vest became a living, breathing entity, beautiful in design and execution; a vibrant chronicle of events all the way from the Haight-Ashbury beginnings through the Helter-Skelter period. Over time – one by one – all the girls made a contribution, in some way or another, and it was understood that each contribution represented their personal love for Charlie, chronicling the days and nights of Man's Son. It was likened unto a medieval tapestry depicting a legend or myth. During the Tate/LaBianca trial, after the girls shaved their heads, they took their cut locks and wove tassels into the vest.

Over a two-year span the girls worked on the vest continuously, sometimes twenty-four hours at a stretch. The only other person that Charlie let wear the ceremonial vest was Little Paul Watkins, who Charlie had positioned as his second in command. On occasion, Charlie would tell Watkins that "someday this will all be yours" referring not only to the vest, but also to the leadership of his Family. Later, when Watkins fell out of grace, Bruce Davis would accept the role of heir apparent, while Manson was in jail on charges for Tate/LaBianca. During the trial, Davis was filmed in the documentary *Manson*, wearing the ceremonial vest, in his role as the voice and conscience of Man's Son. Later the girls sewed their own vests, similar to those worn by biker gangs, with stitching that read: "Devil's Witches – Devil's Hole, Death Valley," complete with skull and crossbones.

Another fancy piece of haberdashery fashioned for Manson during the Tate/LaBianca trial was a velvet gold cape that the girls were preparing for the day when Charlie would be released from jail and reunited with his Family in Death Valley. Lined with a parachute to insulate against the hot or cold, the cape was topped with a braided hair collar, taken from the girl's locks.

In the early 1970's – while Manson was housed at San Quentin – Squeaky sent Charlie his much-prized ceremonial vest, which he immediately cut up into several swaths and handed out to fellow inmates. To an "outsider", this act might have appeared totally irrational. But to a wizened con like Manson, it was simply a means of survival, as he realized that the other prisoners – once they got a load of his beautiful vest – would become jealous, attack him and take it away. So, to avoid a beating – as well as the prospect of anyone else wearing his Family coat of arms – Charlie took a pair of scissors to his precious vest, then distributed it among the prison population.

According to Paul Watkins, the Manson Family's main goal during the Spahn Ranch period was to form a bond of love that would reach such a pure and high plateau that they could set an example for the rest of the fucked-up world of just how good things could be. Charlie espoused the doctrines of the old Zen Masters: "Turn off your internal dialogue and come to *Now*." (Or to quote John Lennon, Tim Leary and the Tibetan Book of the Dead: *Turn off your mind, relax and float downstream – it is not dying... it is not dying...*) This method of supposed spiritual purification was practiced through psychosexual therapy, with Charlie at the helm of the Magical Mystery Tour, stripping down his follower's psyches to their bare essence, then ripping to shreds all the societal conventions and values that had formerly existed; all the hang-ups about sex and sharing love uninhibitedly. As Paul Watkins noted: "Basically, Charlie's trip was to program us all to submit: to give up our egos, which, in a spiritual sense, is a lofty aspiration."

Following Manson's after dinner lectures, the group would sing Charlie's songs, such as "Cease To Exist", "Your Home Is Where You're Happy," or "Old Ego Is a Too Much Thing." Then the girls would pass around some grass, and they'd play a game called The Circle, which centered around the transmission of energy by joining hands and passing it around the group. The focus would be to turn off the internal dialogue and just go with the flow, getting into the rhythm and vibrations. Gradually, Charlie would program in sexual energy by touching the person next to him, and this energy would be passed along until they'd progress to positions on the floor, touching each other in various places, trying to get into a harmonious space. Charlie would often direct these maneuvers by sign language – winks or nods – or by physically guiding people in the various motions.

Manson's ultimate goal in these sexual experiments was to have all the participants come into the "Now" at the same time, in one big group orgasm. Charlie's believed that if they reached this ultimate plateau as a group, then they would be bound together as one person/one soul in an eternal state of love. Charlie often said that if the group was to ever share this peak experience, they'd make it through "the last door." But invariably, this Big Bang Theory of Sex never quite panned out, because someone would invariably start freaking out – or go through some heavy ego death scene – and the rest of the group would have to turn their focus to guide that person out of their bum trip.

From Watkins' perspective, life with Charlie's Family was a "game of awareness" which, in essence, meant being aware of what Manson was trying project at any given moment. Watkins attributed his success within the Family hierarchy – as Charlie's right hand man – due to his ability to play the various roles and games laid down by Manson.

Watkins learned to pick up quickly on Charlie's signals, and knew when Manson moved in a certain way – or assumed a certain expression – just what he wanted. Charlie and Little Paul often picked up girls together, and took them back to the ranch, Manson using his younger protégé as a recruiter. As Charlie was so much older, Watkins helped him to bridge the generation gap, luring foxy prey into tne fold, to eventually be molded into Manson girls. Watkins felt that because he and Charlie were about the same height – and spoke the same hep cat psychedelic rap – that it was easier to relate to each other, and this was one of the reasons why Charlie took the young disciple under his wing.

In time, Charlie gave more responsibility on Little Paul. Watkins' became the ceremonial holder/dispenser of drugs, administering the doses that Dr. Manson prescribed for his patients. In *My Life With Charles Manson*, Watkins corroborated the oft repeated claim that Charlie normally self-prescribed a smaller dose of drugs to himself than the rest of the tribe, to allow him to better control the proceedings, and imprint his program; to *plant seeds*.

‡

From the very beginning, Charlie's sights were set on the Spahn ranch house, and it was only a matter of time before he was able to convince George Spahn to turn it over to his Family. On their first night in the ranch house, they built a roaring fire and enjoyed a communal feast. To celebrate the event, they played music, then dropped acid. As usual, they were all naked, and – as Little Paul was tripping to the colorful trails pulsating from the fire – Charlie suddenly rose to his feet and crouched before him like a predatory beast. Without warning, he lunged at Little Paul, fastened his hands around his neck, sending him reeling backwards against a beanbag chair. When Little Paul looked up, he was expecting to see a playful twinkle in Charlie's eyes. Instead, he found a leering, demonic expression; a face he'd never seen before, contorted with madness. As the *Fear* grew large in Little Paul's blazing brain, his escalating emotions seemed to feed the fury of Charlie's sudden madness all the more.

As Watkins' fear grew, so likewise did Manson's power. Little Paul could see the waves and pulsations of his own stark fear-juice being absorbed directly into Charlie's hands, animating them with some ungodly force. Little Paul could see Charlie strangling him with *his own fear.*

"Okay, Paul," said Charlie. "I'm going to finish you off, now... I'm going to kill you."

At precisely that second, the *Fear* began to leave Paul. He relaxed, looked up at Charlie, and – as he consciously withdrew his fear – Little Paul immediately felt Manson's savage power begin to wane, losing strength. Charlie's hands began to shake, and then his whole body. Soon Charlie's hands popped off of Little Paul's throat, and he was literally ejected from his body. He sat up, his body dripping with sweat, and seemed as shocked by the whole incident as Watkins, yet there was a twinkle in his eye.

"You saw it, huh," Charlie asked, almost reverently.

Little Paul nodded, rubbing his neck. "Yeah, Charlie... I saw it."

What Watkins had seen was the fear-manipulation game Charlie played as a way of controlling his Family. Becoming intimately aware of this "fear factor" on a first-hand basis, this eventually put Little Paul on a sort of par with Manson, as he later realized that Charlie had staged the whole bizarre incident to test him; the classic confrontation of master and pupil.

Charlie's standard procedure in programming "Fear" was to locate deep-seated hang-ups in a person's psyche. Access to these psychological realms was particularly effective when under the influence of acid, where various personal blocks, inhibitions and frustrations became all too apparent to an astute student of human nature, such as Charlie. Manson would ask his followers to submit to him – as well as to their innermost fears – and instead of reprogramming or dismantling the targeted "fear" or "hang-up", Charlie would leave it operational on a subconscious level, instructing them: "Don't let anyone in your head but me." In this manner, Manson took up residence in people's minds. "I am you and you are me" was one popular Manson mantra mouthed somewhat meaninglessly by his mixed-up minions; a programming matrix used to subtly instill his philosophy. Thus – with a subconscious handle on people's heads – Manson could trigger or dissolve these targeted "fears" at will. For most people then, he became both saviour and Satan. On the one hand, he had programmed people to give up their past lives, so that eventually they had no frame of reference, and nothing to relate it back to – no right or wrong – no roots. Now Charlie was their only frame of reference.

Charlie preached that once an individual had achieved this level of perfect detachment – as had he – then all things would become the "same" in that "sameness" which is God. Then, with the death of the ego – to quote the *Bhagavad-Gita* – "a man who has reached a state where there is no sense of 'I', whose soul is undefiled – were he to slaughter all those worlds, slays nothing. He is not bound." While it's unknown if Manson ever read the *Bhagavad-Gita*, it seems evident that he borrowed many of his ideas from eastern mysticism, then twisted the words to meet his own ends.

Charlie played both sides of the coin: Love was hate and hate was love. Not only were the lines blurred, but the map itself was a "Magical Mystery Tour" where his Family could create its own version of reality, irregardless of the eventual consequences. At first it was all a communal lovey-dovey do your own thing philosophy. But as the boundaries expanded, more taboos fell by the wayside, in the gradual heap of litter which steadily grew around Charlie's Family, eventually transforming flowers to gore.

Simply stated, Charlie's philosophy was: "Don't think." Or, in other terms, don't become inwardly divided in thought, another eastern mysticism precept. At least that's the line Charlie was selling. But, as with everything, there was a catch. In the Manson canon, "Don't think" was the only defense against the Establishment's programming. Overcoming fear was the key to Charlie's "Don't think" mantra. This, he felt, gave him the liberty to dispense "fear" as a tool to de-program his disciples from what he interpreted as their previously fucked-up thought patterns. But to "deprogram" was – in reality – just another program.

CHAPTER 17
A Chameleon and His Influences

As ringleader of the "Magical Mystery Tour" game of role-playing and name-changing, Charlie became a chameleon-like character with a different mask or mirror for his many reflections and moods. With the many faces that Charlie tried on for size, came a myriad of names to accommodate the games: Count von Bruno Giordano, Riff Raff Rockess, the Gardener, the Black Pirate, and Chuck Summers. (Not to mention Jesus Christ, and his alter-ego, The Devil.) As Diane Lake later recalled:

> Charlie used to pride himself on how many faces, how many people he could become... I can remember looking in a mirror with him and watching him change his looks – he would have been a great actor by changing his appearance. A hat, a mustache, it was just phenomenal... He was a man of many, many faces.

Charlie was a changeling. Not only in appearance, but in movements. One moment they'd be slow, almost trance-like; the next moment a whirling dervish, bouncing off walls with unbelievable energy. Charlie changed his hair and beard constantly, and with each change he would be born anew as Hollywood slickster, a hardened ex-con, a rock star, child, guru, hobo, angel, devil, or the only begotten son of God. Charlie's Family was famous for the huge pile of clothing from which they all borrowed, changing dress to fit moods, and assuming new roles each day at the ranch – just like their leader.

Manson's alter-ego, Chuck Summers, became a familiar figure on the Sunset Strip. This was a return, in fact, to Charlie's late 50's stomping grounds, in his previous incarnation of second-rate pimp and hustler, running two-bit scams on Hollywood and Vine. Manson – in the Chuck Summers persona – maintained many of his former criminal contacts within this murky milieu, rubbing elbows with bikers, prostitutes, petty criminals and porn models in the sleaze clubs and greasy-spoons down around the Strip bearing such names as The Galaxy Club, The Omnibus or The Melody Room.

Chuck Summers' favorite hangout was the Galaxy Club, which he visited in the mornings, according to the club manager. The manager also happened to be a stage hypnotist, who later opened the Hollywood Hypnotism Center, and he and Manson often discussed the finer points of the craft.

Around this time, Manson made the acquaintance of biker clubs such as The Satan's Slaves, The Straight Satans, and The Coffin Makers. Charlie eventually developed a closer association with The Straight Satans, in his attempt to build a his own army à la Rommel's Desert Corps.

During this period, Ed Sanders suggested that Charlie's Family became associated with three satanically inclined cults:

    1) The Process Church of the Final Judgment;
    2) The Solar Lodge of the Ordo Templi Orientis;
    3) The Kirke Order of Dog Blood.

Sanders' maintained that these three groups were familiar with one another, and that their similarities and connections with the Manson Family could not be discounted. It was The Process – according to Ed Sanders in *The Family: The Story of Charles Manson's Dune Buggy Attack Battalion* – that Manson encountered first. In fact, one Manson Family member placed Robert DeGrimston – the head of The Process – hanging out at The Spiral Staircase during the same time frame as Charlie's Family. The Process Church subsequently brought a $1.5 million libel suit against Sanders and his publisher, Dutton, and all material referencing the "English occult organization" was excised from later editions of the book. The following statement was released on March 8, 1972, from the publisher's attorney:

> E.P. Dutton, publisher of "The Family: The Story of Charles Manson's Dune Buggy Attack Battalion" said today that the book will be revised to remove all reference to The Process-Church of the Final Judgment. A close examination has revealed that statements in the book about The Process Church, including those attributing any connection between The Process and the activities of Charles Manson, accused and convicted murderer, have not been substantiated. Dutton announced further that no additional copies of the book in its present form would be printed. This release will be inserted in all existing and unsold copies of "The Family" still in Dutton's possession.

It should be noted that The Process Church lost their case against the British publisher of *The Family*. Similarly, in 1980, a former Solar Lodge member brought a lawsuit against Dutton, and also lost their case. For a period of time after the publication of *The Family*, Sanders went into hiding after receiving death threats.

There are largely two schools of thought concerning the legend of The Process Church. The first asserts that The Process was a cult "that never quite made it." In regards to the size of its membership, The Process never officially counted more than a few hundred members. The other school – promulgated by authors Ed Sanders and Maury Terry – fingers The Process as behind the reigns of a vast Satanic underground dealing in pornography, drugs and murder.

The Process began in London circa 1963. Its founders – Robert Moore and Mary Anne MacLean – met at the Hubbard Institute of Scientology, where both were auditors and instructors. During his Scientology stint, Moore graduated to the level of "clear", just as Charles Manson claimed to have reached the same lofty level while studying Scientology in prison. Shortly after leaving the Church of Scientology, Moore and MacLean married, changed their names to DeGrimston and took along with them some of Scientology's principles and methods, incorporating them into a new venture first called Compulsions Analysis, then renamed later The Process.

In March of 1966, The Process moved into a mansion on Balfour Place in London's Mayfair district, followed by twenty-five young acolytes, who turned over all their money and worldly possessions to DeGrimston. The garb worn by The Processians was neo-Gothic, consisting of tailor made magician's capes with the Mendes goat of Satan stitched in red on the back with matching black uniforms. After moving into Balfour Place, Robert and Mary Ann each got themselves a large, vicious Alsatian dog, a variety of German shepherd. Other members soon acquired their own Alsatians and a dog pack was assembled.

The Process made forays into pop music, attempting to attract into their ranks the likes of the Beatles and Mick Jagger. They published a magazine to further the cause called *Process*. Around this time, they attracted Mick Jagger's girlfriend, Marianne Faithful, into the fold. In *Process* issue #3, Faithful appeared on the cover, lying down as if dead, holding a rose.

"The Death" issue of *Process* published in 1971 featured a brief article by none other than

Charlie Manson appeared entitled "Pseudo-profundity in Death", which Charlie penned during the course of the Tate/LaBianca trial. In this article, Manson described death as "total awareness... Coming to Now... and Peace from this world's madness and paradise in my own self." While, on the one hand, The Process took measures to distance themselves from Manson , the inclusion of Charlie's essay only furthers to muddy an alliance that, at the very least, shared many of the same philosophical tenets.

Process members arrived in Los Angeles in early 1968, and stayed in public view until a few days after Robert Kennedy's assassination in June of 1968, after which they dropped from sight. By this time, The Process had become subdivided into three groups: the Luciferians, the Satanists and the Jehovans. The Luciferian branch were fun-loving hedonists, celebrating sensuality. The Jehovah branch were uptight, narrow-minded zealots, both anti-sex and austere. The Jehovans beat each other as punishment, and were into self-flagellation. The Satanists were both cold and calculating, on the violent end of The Process spectrum. According to an individual's personal desires they could become an advocate of any three of the above branches; it didn't really matter anyway, because in the long run they were all going to unite in the End Times.

The best illustration of The Process philosophy was summed up in this paragraph from Robert DeGrimston's 1967 book called *As It Is*:

> Christ said: Love thine enemy. Christ's enemy was Satan and Satan's Enemy was Christ. Through love, enmity is destroyed. Through love, saint and sinner destroy the enmity between them. Through love, Christ and Satan have destroyed their enmity and come together for the End. Christ to judge, Satan to execute judgment.

It was this marriage of Heaven and Hell that Manson himself grooved with – the unity of Christ and Satan. In his *Rolling Stone* interview from June 25, 1970, a reporter asked Charlie: "What did you mean when you once said that God and Satan are the same person?" Manson replied: "If God is One, what is bad? Satan is just God's imagination. Everything I've done for nineteen hundred and seventy years is now in the open. I went into the desert to confess to God about the crime I, you, Man has committed for 2,000 years. And that is why I'm here. As a witness." Manson's philosophical spin – although similar to The Process – projected a more simplistic dualism, as he was known to his followers as both Satan and Christ. Like the Process, Manson preached the Second Coming, and that when Christ returned, it would be the Romans (i.e. The Establishment) who went up on the cross.

Here is a list of other similarities shared by Charlie's Family and The Process:

*Manson spoke frequently of the bottomless pit; The Process, of the bottomless void.

*Within its organization, The Process called itself "the family," and referred to its members as brothers, sisters, mothers and fathers.

*Fear was another Process/Manson focal point. A special issue of *Process* magazine dealt exclusively with the topic. "Fear is beneficial," wrote the author of one article. "Fear is the catalyst of action. It is the energizer, the weapon built into the game in the beginning, enabling a being to create an effect upon himself, to spur himself on to new heights and to brush aside the bitterness of failure."

*The Process Church symbol was an inverted swastika, the same symbol Manson later carved into his forehead.

*The Process and Manson both attempted to recruit biker groups to be used as a military wing, on a par with Hitler's SS troops. The two biker gangs closest to Charlie's Family shared the initials of S.S.: The Satan Slaves and The Straight Satans.

*The Process – like Manson – sought out "The Beautiful People." Besides John Phillips, The Process managed to rub elbows with Warren Beatty and Cass Elliot, and they approached Terry Melcher right around the same time that Melcher first met Manson. John Phillips recalled that: "Terry Melcher and Dennis Wilson and the people who were living with Manson at Dennis's house used to call me all the time, you know, and say come on over... I'd say no, I think I'll pass."

Sources suggest that Manson and his minions actually did cross paths with Phillips. One witness claimed to have seen Manson's bus parked for awhile in the fall of 1968 outside Phillip's Bel Air house. Allegedly, Manson also attended a New Year Eve's party thrown for the cast of *Hair* by John and Michelle Phillips.

Robert DeGrimston wrote: "If a man asks: What is the Process? Say to him: It is the End, the final ending of the world of men. It is the agent of The End, the instrument of The End, the inexorable power of The End." In order to bring about their End Times paradigm, the Process Church reversed the commandment of Moses to "Thou shall kill." DeGrimston went on to exhort his followers to "release the Fiend that lies dormant in you, for the world can be yours, and the blood of men can be yours to spill as you please." Perhaps these highly charged words were simple posturing on the part of DeGrimston, but nonetheless the power of words can never be underestimated, for once released into the cosmos, the law of cause and effect will somehow manifest itself. Working from this presumption, many believe that Charlie's Family was a lesson in the laws of bad karma; a magical working unleashed by Process members that took the form of Manson and his knife-wielding nymphs – whether consciously intended, or not. Perhaps it was all just street theater on the part of the Process, designed to shake up the status quo and blow the minds of the Establishment. But – following the karmic laws – those who play with fire, eventually get burned.

Some observers have described the Process as a society dedicated to aiding and abetting the end of the world by stirring up violence and chaos. In the Process "End Time" scenario, they would survive the wrath of the apocalypse as the chosen people, which is where Manson was coming from, if one believes the gospel according to Bugliosi.

Robert DeGrimston and other Process members descended on Haight-Ashbury during the Summer of Love, taking lease of a property at 407 Cole Street. Meanwhile, Manson and his girls lived at 636 Cole Street, only two blocks away. One of the more outrageous claims I've heard suggesting contact between Manson and the Process comes courtesy of John Parker's *Polanski* wherein Parker claims that Manson was a regular visitor to the Process headquarters, "reaching the fourth of the six levels of initiation, that of 'prophet'."

In December 1968, Bruce Davis traveled to England where he spent roughly five months. While there, he was employed for a short period by the Church of Scientology, working in the mailroom and studying Scientology courses in his spare time. The Church eventually fired Davis after a couple of weeks because of drug use. According to a homicide investigator close to the Tate/LaBianca case, Davis then began to hang out at the Mayfair headquarters of the Process. Davis later returned to England in May 1969 in the company of five women alleged to be witches, who were seen roaming around the Manchester area, a purported witch-haven and the stamping-ground of Alex Sanders, "King of the Witches".

Bugliosi's *Helter Skelter* recounts how Charlie – during the Tate/LaBianca trial – was bragging about his relationship with the Process, until one day when he was paid a visit in jail by two Process Church brethren named "Father John" and "Brother Matthew." After their departure, Manson seems to have clammed up about the Process, and since then has made no further comments. Prior to the visit by these two mysterious Processians, Manson was asked by Vincent Bugliosi if he knew Robert DeGrimston, and his reply was, "He and I are one and the same." When the two Process members met with Bugliosi, they assured him that Manson and DeGrimston had never met, and that DeGrimston was thoroughly opposed to any form of violence.

Ed Sanders claimed that Manson was in New York City during July 1969, using his Chuck Summers alias. At the same time, Robert and Mary Anne DeGrimston are believed to have been there, and ominous rumors abound that Manson and the Process founders met at this time.

After Manson was arrested for the Tate/LaBianca murders, an article appeared in a Berkeley newspaper alleging that Charlie had been a member of a homosexual "death-cult" operating in 1968 out of a house on Waller Street in Haight-Ashbury. Known as "The Devil House", the article described a trial conducted by the cult, which was called the Final Church of Judgment, a name closely resembling the Process Church of the Final Judgment. Other former Waller Street house residents were allegedly associated with the Process.

The source for this article – an individual named Blaine – first heard about Manson in 1964 when he was a prisoner at the U.S. Medical Center. There Blaine met a man named Richard, who had recently been transferred from McNeil Island prison, where he claimed he had been Manson's bitch. Blaine and Richard met at the Medical Center Prison Library, and Richard had made this pronouncement: "Charles will be a great man some day because he knows all about magic."

After prison, Blaine moved to the Haight to indulge in the legendary Summer of Drugs and there, by chance, met Manson. Later – in the Summer/Fall of '68 – the two met again, when Blaine became involved with the Final Church of Judgment. "The Final Church is the name Manson chose for the church he eventually founded," Blaine wrote. The cult was evidently led by one Father P., and operated out of the aforementioned Waller Street "Devil House."

According to Blaine's account, Manson supposedly showed up at a "medieval trial" in the summer of '68, where it was to be decided whether to put a former cult member to death. There a strange scene unfolded, and though the former cult member who "went wrong" was not ultimately put to death, he did get the crap beat out of him with a wooden crucifix, as Father P. shouted: "I'm God! I'm Satan! I'm Jesus." Blaine alleged that Manson – in the company of Sadie – left the next day to drive back to Spahn Ranch, and that Father P. visited Manson soon after in Los Angeles.

Another of Ed Sanders' claims was that the Process had three closed chapters that conducted secret rituals in Marin County, Santa Barbara, the Santa Cruz Mountains and the Santa Ana Mountains of California. Of particular interest are the activities that transpired in the Santa Cruz Mountains, where occult sacrifices were said to have taken place.

In the fall of 1968, police discovered exsanguinated and decapitated animals in the remote Santa Cruz wilderness, and one witness recounted ritual executions observed in a grove on Route 17 south of Santa Cruz. Informants told police that there were approximately forty people present at this ritual sacrifice, where a human heart was said to have been eaten. One man told about fire-dances and blood-drinking rituals at Boulder Creek, near Santa Cruz, and stated that glue-sniffing was part of the ceremony. Another informant reported to police that he had seen a group of hippies dancing wildly around a parked car, on the hood of which were the carcasses of five skinned dogs. Corroboration of this story came from the Santa Cruz Animal Shelter, which reported during that time span to have turned up a number of skinned dogs in the area, all drained of blood.

One alleged witness to these sacrifices was Stanley Dean Baker, who had been arrested for an out of state murder. Baker told police that he was a member of the Santa Cruz cult, and showed them a finger bone he carried around in a leather pouch. Also in Baker's possession was a satanic bible and a recipe for LSD. Noted Baker: "I have a problem. I am a cannibal." In one of Baker's killings, the left ear of the victim had been severed (à la Gary Hinman in the first Manson Family murder) and there was blood writing on the wall saying "Zodiac" and "Satan Slaves." According to Baker, the cult worked its rituals on a stellar timetable, and possessed a portable crematorium to do away with victim's remains.

The group supposedly responsible for these ritual sacrifices was the Four P Movement, an alleged Process splinter group. Supposedly the name of the group derived from a Process symbol which consisted of four P's coming together to form an iron cross/swastika-like image. The leader of the group held the title of Grand Chingon, however this individual was not Charles Manson. With that said, let it be noted that several times in the presence of Ed Sanders, Manson Family members referred to Charlie as The Grand Chingon. The leader of the Four P was alleged to be a prosperous Los Angeles businessman.

As for the two other groups that allegedly inspired Manson's murderous minions, little is known of The Kirke Order of Dog Blood, whose membership was said to worship a reincarnation of the goddess Circe (or Kirke). The cult carved the Star of Circe – a four-pointed star with a rectangle – into their chest, a symbol of adoration for Circe. Apparently, Circe was rumored to have red-hair and to be of British descent. The cult held outdoor ceremonies twice a month – during the new and full moons – on secluded Los Angeles and Ventura County beaches where they sacrificed dogs, cats, roosters and goats. Animal vampirism was also rumored to have been involved in these gory rituals.

Sanders hinted that these blood sacrifices were filmed and that Manson Family members were involved.

A former Manson Family hanger-on, Larry Melton (aka White Rabbitt), claimed to have seen several of the so-called Manson Family films, and admitted having stolen a short film showing Family members sacrificing a dog. An editor of a national magazine later viewed this film, and said: "There's very little question in my mind that the film's authentic. Nobody's trying to manufacture a rip-off would produce a loop of such incredibly poor quality. I've been assured that if I knew the Manson group's faces well, I'd be able to identify them in the film; but, thanks to my ignorance, I can only tell you that, while the camera does some gratuitously pyrotechnic pan-in/pan outs, a group of people, sitting around a fire, *apparently* slaughter a dog (or a cat, or a goat – or maybe a teddy bear), then *apparently* anoint themselves with blood, then *apparently* take some of their clothes off, then do a weird – but not *too* weird – little dance."

Retired Captain Dale Griffis of the Tiffin, Ohio Police Department believes that Mary Ann DeGrimston was the mysterious "Circe" who went underground in the early 1970's. According to Griffis, Circe surfaced in Toledo, Ohio in the mid 1970's where she opened an occult shop and acquired property adjacent to a location reputed as a site where human sacrifice rituals were performed. In 1985, law enforcement officials dug up the site, discovering ritualistic paraphernalia, although no evidence of murder was discovered. Shortly before the police raid, the Toledo occult shop closed and "Circe" disappeared.

Although Robert DeGrimston was the figure head of the cult, former members claim that Mary Ann was the real power. In 1974, the two were divorced, as Robert was ousted from The Process; an ouster that has been attributed to a number of reasons, from the philosophical to the adulterous. Afterwards, Robert made efforts to revive the Process with a faction of members still loyal to him, but was ultimately unsuccessful in these attempts. In 1979, Mary Ann's faction evolved into the Foundation Church of the Millennium, now called the Foundation Faith of God, a fundamentalist Christian sect. In 1984, Mary Ann's "Foundation" formed a non-profit organization called The Best Friends Animal Sanctuary, and acquired a 33,000 acre compound near Kanab, Utah where she lived until her death on November 14, 2005.

It wasn't until early 2004 that these Process/Best Friends connections were revealed in an edition of The Rocky Mountain News, and it was at that time that Best Friends' President Michael Mountain (aka Father Aaron in The Process) came forward to dispute some of the more sinister allegations regarding his group. Mountain – attempting to put a positive spin on the story – trumpeted Best Friends' efforts toward promoting humane treatment of animals, while at the same time distancing his organization from their shadowy past. According to Mountain: "Charles Manson had been in prison for about a year, and somebody had the bright idea that we would go and interview (him). We thought it would help sell (our) magazine... It was a mistake."

As for Robert DeGrimston, last reports place him in Staten Island, New York, employed as a business consultant for AT&T and occasionally teaching classes at a New York college.

‡

Another alleged Manson influence was the Solar Lodge of the O.T.O., an offshoot of the Ordo Templi Orientis, a magical order founded in Germany in 1902 and later revived in England in 1911 by Aleister Crowley. The Solar Lodge was founded in late 1966 by Georgina "Jean" Brayton. Like Manson, the Solar Lodge believed that an apocalyptic race war was imminent and made plans to escape the forthcoming Helter Skelter high weirdness by retreating to the desert. Brayton shared Charlie's philosophy in regards to cutting ties with old acquaintances, and issued forth – from her lofty perch – the grand pronouncement that "the family was public enemy number one" because it inhibited the individual from truly severing themselves from the bonds of conformity. Manson spoke to this same theme in his song "Your Home is Where You Are Happy."

So burn all your bridges
Leave the old world behind
You can do what you want to do
'Cause you're strong in your mind

According to Ed Sanders, Brayton took her cue from Aleister Crowley, using drugs and sadism as her calling cards in the arena of ritual magick. Just as 60 years before Crowley ingested peyote to demolish his ego and open himself up to powers and devils, likewise did Brayton's group open up similar dark currents. Brayton's methods were similar to those of Charles Manson: tearing down the mind through pain, perversion and drugs – and rebuilding it in the image of their leader, be it Brayton or Manson.

According to former Solar Lodge members, the group used a potpourri of recreational drugs, including marijuana, LSD, Demerol, scopolamine, jimson weed, belladonna, datura root and ether. Apparently the source of many of these drugs was Brayton's second in command, Robert Duerrstein of the USC's Dentistry Department, who also managed the two "Eye of Horus" bookstores owned by the Jean Brayton and her husband, Richard.

To attract new initiates, Brayton put on what were known as "profane parties" where indiscriminate drug use was encouraged. It's has been speculated that Brayton owned the notorious Spiral Staircase House. Manson and others have referred to the Spiral Staircase owner as a lady named Jean or Gina. A perhaps more concrete connection linking Brayton to Manson was a house at 1251 West Thirtieth Street in Los Angeles, where occult chicken sacrifices were said to have taken place in homage to whatever evil deity digs dead foul. This was one of several properties owned by the Braytons and reportedly frequented by Manson.

In early 1969 – when certain Manson Family members were staying with The Satan Slaves at the Hollowberry Hill Ranch in Malibu – this association with Brayton's Solar Lodge allegedly began. Apparently, some of Manson's biker contacts were part of the outlaw fringe of Brayton's Lodge, and it was they who introduced Manson to the cult.

As part of their own perceived Helter-Skelter-coming-down-fast worldview, the Solar Lodge established an End Times outpost on a ranch located between the desert towns of Blythe and Vidal in the southern California desert. The most prominent structure there was known as the Ark, the construction of which began in the summer of 1967. Built from the remains of an old army Quonset hut, the Ark – a pyramidal structure – served as the group's temple of worship, wherein many rare books and grimoires were housed, including magical robes once owned by Aleister Crowley.

Brayton's apocalyptic vision corresponded closely with Manson's Helter Skelter scenario: sometime around May 20th 1969, she announced to her flock that Armageddon was nigh at hand. As Brayton was marshaling her forces to split Los Angeles before the eschatological shit-hit-the-fan, a scandal took place at the cult's ranch. It seems that a young boy – one Anthony Gibbons, age six – started a fire that resulted in the Ark, and all of its magical contents, being burnt to the ground. As punishment, Brayton first held lit matches to the boy's fingers. After he still seemed unrepentant, another punishment was devised, this time consisting of solitary confinement in a locked wooden packing crate with the boy chained to a metal plate in the ground. Reports vary as to the actual amount of time the boy spent in the crate. Ed Sanders claimed that for fifty-six straight days, young Anthony withered away under the desert sun with temperatures averaging 110 degrees. However, according to the account of former Solar Lodge member Frater Shiva in *Inside Solar Lodge/Outside The Law*, the child was in the crate for no more than 10 hours over the course of a two-day period. Frater Shiva goes on to assert that many of allegations made regarding the beating and burning of the child were outright fabrications produced by Solar Lodge detractors.

On July 26th – the day of Gary Hinman's murder – a couple local ranchers stopped by to look at some horses for sell at Brayton's ranch, and at that time noticed the boy in the crate. The men immediately drove to a store in nearby Blythe and notified authorities, who subsequently raided the compound and arrested eleven cult members for felony child abuse, among them the parents, James and Beverly Gibbons.

The boy-in-the-box trial was held in October/November of 1969, resulting in charges filed against several Solar Lodge members. However, most of these charges were dismissed, or only short jail sentences served. During the period that the Solar Lodge was under scrutiny from the authorities, Jean Brayton and many of her inner circle – who were not arrested during the boy in the box fiasco – fled the country, sensing they were under siege. Brayton and her exiled compatriots spent a considerable time in South America and Canada before eventually returning to the states a couple years later.

Brayton died in Los Angeles in 1984.

CHAPTER 18
The Beautiful People

The eldest of three daughters, Sharon Tate was born on January 24th, 1943, in Dallas, Texas to Colonel Paul Tate and his wife, Doris. Tate was a career military intelligence officer, and because of this he and his family had lived in various parts of the United States and Europe. In her early twenties, the family moved to San Pedro, California, a few miles from Hollywood's bright lights. Sharon – her sights set upon those bright lights – began auditioning for movie studios, pursuing fame and fortune. Her first break came in 1963, when Sharon's agent sent her to New York to audition for Petticoat Junction, a CBS sitcom produced by Martin Ransohoff. Legend has it that the first time Ransohoff laid eyes on the comely Miss Tate, he proclaimed: "Sweetie, I'm going to make you a star!" and signed the young beauty to a seven year contract.

In 1963, Sharon met Jay Sebring, exclusive hair stylist to the stars. Soon after they began a relationship, and at one time considered marriage. Sebring's famous clients included Paul Newman, Warren Beatty, Frank Sinatra, Peter Lawford, Sammy Davis, Jr. and Steve McQueen. The character of George in 1975's *Shampoo*, starring Warren Beatty, was based largely on Sebring.

In 1965, Ransohoff gave Sharon a featured role in *13* (*Eye of the Devil*), being filmed in London. *Eye of the Devil* – co-starring David Niven and Deborah Kerr – featured Niven as the victim of a cult practicing human ritual sacrifice. Sharon's role was that of a country girl with witchy powers The production company hired an English magician Alex Sanders – the so-called "King of the Witches" – to serve as technical advisor. Sanders became fast friends with Sharon and before filming finished, he allegedly initiated the young starlet into witchcraft.

In early 1966, Ransohoff hired Roman Polanski to direct *The Fearless Vampire Killers*. Due to Ransohoff's influence, Sharon landed a leading role, and as the making of this horror-spoof progressed, Sharon and Roman became romantically involved. The film was released in 1967, featuring Sharon as the beautiful victim of a vampire who ends up biting her lover (Polanski) in the neck, creating yet another monster. Later in the year, nude photos of Sharon appeared in *Playboy* in a series called "The Tate Gallery" shot by Polanski.

When Process Church members arrived in Los Angeles in early 1968, it was John Phillips who put them in touch with real estate agent Artie Aarons. Once a week, these Process members went around cleaning and repairing properties owned by Aarons. In return for their services, Aarons let them stay rent free at a large, two-story house in south central L.A. In the following weeks, the Process group – while working for Aarons – visited the old John Barrymore mansion at 1301 Summit Ridge Drive in Beverly Hills, which was located several blocks down the hill from where Roman

Polanski was then renting a house from actress Patty Duke at 1600 Summit Ridge.

Shortly after moving into the Summit Ridge house, Sharon and Roman threw a housewarming party where a strange event occurred involving Roman and some vicious dogs from down the hill. Apparently, the Polanskis had agreed to take care of Patty Duke's sheep dog while renting the house, and the dog had a habit of getting loose and running away.

On the night of the party – according to Ed Sanders – the sheep dog once again ran away and Polanski went after it. Somewhere down the hill, Polanski encountered a vicious Alsatian dog pack belonging to – as Sander's phrased it – "a group of English occultists who were in America to promote the end of the world." Somehow – during his attempt to retrieve Patty Duke's pooch – Polanski got locked in a garage while trying to escape the cult's dog pack, and managed to break out a rear window and flee to safety.

In early 1969, Sharon and Roman moved to an upscale house in Benedict Canyon at 10050 Cielo Drive, which was set at the end of a long, steep driveway, providing a spectacular view of L.A. The estate – protected by electronic gates – was a spacious ranch style affair with lawns, gardens, swimming pool and a large two-story living room with a loft.

When the Polanski's moved in, there was a string of Christmas lights strung along a split rail fence on the property's edge that could be seen at night from Sunset Boulevard, a mile below. Sharon and Roman decided to leave the lights up as a beacon to all their rich and famous friends, the ranks of which were growing legion: Kirk Douglas, Warren Beatty, Steve McQueen, James Coburn, Yul Brynner, Mia Farrow, Peter Sellers, Lee Marvin, and Jane and Peter Fonda were among the celebrities who frequented the Cielo Drive party house, along with rock stars Jim Morrison, Janis Joplin and the Mamas and the Papas.

Another up and coming member of the "Beautiful People " scene was Woytek Frykowski, an old Polanski friend from Poland. While in New York, Frykowski met the wealthy American coffee heiress, Abigail "Gibby" Folger, and the two began living together. When Polanski decided to move to Hollywood after *Rosemary's Baby*, Woytek and Gibby tagged along, soon becoming regular fixtures of the Polanski's social scene. According to Ed Sanders, Woytek and Gibby acquired some dubious friends during this period, including mutual friends of the Manson Family.

Frykowski's ambition was to become a major movie mogul, but in the interim – in order to make ends meet – took to dealing drugs. According to investigators, it was Folger's money that set Frykowski up in the drug trade. Frykowski bought marijuana, LSD, speed and other drugs from underworld distributors, then sold the stuff to affluent La-La Land denizens. Along with Sharon's former fiancé – Jay Sebring – Woytek became the major drug source for those in the Polanski/Tate social circle.

In mid-February, when Sharon and Roman moved into 10050 Cielo Drive, they threw a huge housewarming party. One noteworthy incident that occurred at this party was a minor brawl involving uninvited friends of Woytek and Gibby. Evidently, twenty-year-old Harrison "Pic" Dawson – the son of a prominent State Department Official – stepped on the foot of Sharon's agent, William Tennant, which precipitated a shoving match. Others soon joined the skirmish, including two men in their twenties, both siding with Dawson. Polanski got pissed-off and threw Dawson and his friends out of the party. Their names would later resurface during the Tate/LaBianca murder investigation.

During this period, Roman and Sharon commuted frequently between Los Angeles and London, until later that year when Sharon traveled to Rome to start work on a new film. Shortly after Sharon left for Rome, Polanski returned to London where he was preparing several film projects. In their absence, 10050 Cielo Drive became a free-wheeling drug and sex pad.

"Half the weirdos, kooks and creeps in Hollywood were hanging out there," a detective later said. "Stars and starlets mingled with convicted dope pushers, addicts, prostitutes, homosexuals, sadists, hippies and motorcycle bums."

According to David Hanna in *Cults In America* – after Sharon came back from Rome – many of these shadowy characters remained, as her house became the center for a cult practicing black magic and witchcraft.

In J.D. Russell's *The Beautiful People*, an unidentified friend of Sharon Tate's was quoted:

Sharon was a student of black magic, voodoo and occult arts, including spiritualism. She has spent hours with me theorizing about ghosts and the world beyond. While she was in London she visited many of the stores that sold black magic books and herbs that are supposed to induce a variety of spells. She told me she had once tried scopolamine, the active ingredient in henbane, which is called 'The Herb of the Devil'.

While they were making 'Rosemary Baby's an initiation ceremony into the world of black magic was held at the home of a friend. One of the guests told me that he was met at the door by Sharon, was blindfolded and led into a dark room filled with white-robed people wearing animal masks. They lit black candles on a crudely made wooden alter; then Jay offered me two antique goblets I had seen earlier at his home. One contained wine, he said, and the other, rat poison. He said for me to take my pick.

I realized he was serious, so I left in a hurry!

Prior to moving to 10050 Cielo Drive, Woytek and Gibby rented a house on Woodstock Road – near Cass Elliot's home – and at that time became intimate with the corpulent singer. Concurrently, Gibby was involved in various forms of social work, including a stint as a volunteer helping children in the Watts ghetto, and working on a variety of community projects.

Gibby took an active role in the mayoral campaign of Tom Bradley – Los Angeles' first black mayor – and subsequently became interested in a black group called the Street Racers, who served, at rallies, as Bradley's security force. Along with her philanthropic and humanitarian activities, Gibby also developed a heavy drug habit, and just prior to the Tate murders was attempting to "kick", visiting a psychiatrist once a day for help with her problem. As well, she had began to tire of Frykowski and his drug induced excesses, as arguments between the two were becoming louder and more frequent.

Early in July 1969, Canadian associates of Frykowski promised him samples of a new drug called MDA, an euphoric stimulant with purported aphrodisiac effects, also called the Love Drug. According to police sources, Frykowski was being groomed as a wholesaler of the drug. Allegedly, Frykowski and Folger were enjoying MDA's euphoric effects the night all hell broke loose at 10050 Cielo Drive.

CHAPTER 19
I Am Charlie

In October 1968, Charlie decided to move his Family to Death Valley, but before doing so, Manson wanted to center the energies of the group by taking one final Spahn Ranch acid trip. The girls made special garments for the occasion; velvet embroidered shirts and pants with peacocks, sunsets and flower designs. They called them the "no-sense-makes-sense-clothes" with buttonholes with no buttons, or pockets not completely sewn on. In the past, Charlie had always taken less of the drug than the rest of the group – in order to maintain control – but on this occasion he took the same amount as everyone else.

Little Paul was strumming a sitar when the acid kicked in, as the notes from the instrument began to sound like semi-trucks rumbling through the room. He glanced at Charlie – as did the others – and they all saw uncertainty in his eyes, which was totally out of character. Squeaky – sensing the unsteady vibes – clung tightly to Charlie's arm, trying to rest her head against him. When Charlie asked Squeaky what she was doing, she replied, "I'm hanging on to you." After a long silence, Charlie shook his head, and said, "No, I'm hanging on to *you*." As he said these words – pregnant with import – the group as a whole realized its unsettling implications. Charlie was being totally sincere. And even though Manson always preached against clinging to anyone or anything, that's exactly what he was doing in this instance, and Squeaky didn't dig it one bit. She started freaking out, screaming, "No, no, I'm hanging on to you, Charlie!" Squeaky began flailing about wildly. As Charlie attempted to restrain her, she rolled over on to the woodpile by the fireplace, screaming and kicking. "Charlie... Charlie! It's not so!"

Manson – feeling the walls closing in – told his right hand man, Little Paul, to look after Squeaky, because he was splitting. Charlie changed his "no-sense-makes-sense" clothes and left the house. All those remaining – who had been abandoned by their hippie messiah – sat in a state of psychedelic shock. After awhile, Little Paul was able to calm down Squeaky, but before doing so, she accidentally kicked a male Family member, Kim. Whatever negative psychic energy Squeaky released sent Kim racing into the bathroom where he went berserk and pulled a sink out of the wall and smashed the bathroom mirror to pieces. Kim bounded back into the living room, screaming at the top of his lungs, "I'm the devil... I'm the devil," then crashed through the front window.

Everyone began screaming: "Charlie... Charlie... where's Charlie!?" which sent Squeaky off on a return journey to bummer land, as once again she resumed thrashing about in the woodpile. In response, Kim came sailing through the broken window and started ripping tapestries from the walls and smashing glass out of the remaining windows.. "Charlie... I'm the devil... I'm the devil," he continued jabbering. For his next act, Kim dove into the fire, a feat of which only a true devil could perform without getting burnt. Although Little Paul tried to restrain him, Kim broke away and plunged into the flames again. As Little Paul explained this surreal scene in *My Life With Charles Manson*:

> Everything seemed to slow down: time became elastic and incalculable. I looked at Kim in the fire and saw all around his body – conforming to every contour – a glowing force field – an aura. It had occurred to me in flashes while struggling with him earlier that he was *not* getting cut or burned! Not even his hair was singed. His body was totally protected by this force field. For what seemed like an eternity I watched him lying in the fire, the flames spitting and flickering up around him. His legs were drawn up to his stomach, his body immersed in smoke. When I finally reached in and pulled him out, I saw that the force field had protected my hands. They were unmarked. As Kim lay on the floor, his frenzy subsiding, I obeyed an impulse and reached into the fire and withdrew a small handful of glowing coals. I gazed at them lying in my hands. They felt almost weightless, like a handful of dry cotton. I experienced sensation but no pain. Then a thought jolted me: "You idiot, you just burned the shit out of your hands!" As this notion claimed my mind, I could see the force field starting to change shape, I could see blisters forming, not on my hand, but on the aura itself as though the blisters were working their way to the skin. As soon as I dismissed the thought, the aura returned to its original, mirage-like shape. I tossed the coals back onto the fire as Charlie appeared in the doorway…

Manson tried to restore order, yelling, "Cool it… cool it… the cops are coming!" Then – as quickly as he'd materialized – he was gone again. Right on cue, everybody went bonkers: "Charlie… Charlie… Where did Charlie go?" Some of the group pummeled one another, while others flopped and flailed about the floor like epileptics. "Charlie… Charlie!" The insane refrain rang out, and the words reverberated in Little Paul's brain: "Charlie… Charlie!" Soon the name sounded foreign to his ears, like a word from an alien language. "Charlie?" Little Paul muttered. "Charlie? Who the hell is Charlie?" Then he flashed on the words: "All is one; I am you and you are me." It then struck Little Paul that no one else was standing, only he; no one else even seemed real. "I'm Charlie," he blurted. "I am Charlie…"

‡

At first, Manson's teachings seemed complex to the group; a hodge-podge of Eastern religion, Scientology and pop-psychology. But at the core stood a simple, yet powerful message: *All is one.* Charlie's believed that the programming, which had been instilled in individuals by parents and society, built barriers around them, keeping them in broken fragments; torn from their connection with the infinite Whole, and that the only way to break down these barriers – between themselves and true oneness – was with love. There was no "you" and "me." In Charlie's mystical view, there was only "it."

Manson's definition of love was that of totally giving one's self to each other – and to Charlie without reservation – without clinging to anything of themselves. According to Manson, the only way to find that kind of love was to completely "kill the ego", and that no one was truly independent of the infinite Whole, and to realize that any idea they'd had of a separate identity was mere illusion. To become one, a person first had to become individually "nothing" and undergo "ego death." This was the message of Man's Son. And the more acid they gobbled, and the more they listened, the more sense it all made. It was not just a matter of belief; Charlie's Family lived this reality everyday, experiencing exactly what he was talking about. As Tex Watson noted, "The time came when we could look into each other's faces and see our own features, when we could be sitting together and suddenly all think the same thought. It was as if we shared one common brain, when we could project something – a visit, people bringing up some grass – and it would happen; the friend would appear, someone would knock on the door with a lid. You couldn't argue with evidence like that."

There was no talk of killing... yet. But, as Tex Watson stated in *Will You Die For Me*, Charlie's theology of death – death *as* life – laid a future foundation for murder. After the killings, the world was horrified that Charlie's Family expressed no remorse or sympathy for their victims. But why should they, if the death of any particular individual had no more meaning "than breaking off a minute piece of some cosmic cookie?" There could be no wrong – according to Charlie – when killing the mortal body simply opened up the inner soul to a new experience of the *one*, the infinite Whole.

Charlie's interpretation of Death incorporated the ancient mystical belief that we are all of one body, an integral part of Hinduism, Buddhism and Christianity. According to Corinthians 1: "For as the body is one and hath many members, and all the members of that one body, being many, are one body; so also is Christ." Of course, Charlie went one step further in his interpretation of the holy writ, in his belief that he – and his fellow human beings – are God and The Devil at the same time, and that we are all part of each other. Thus there is no death; if one kills another, you are only killing a part of yourself. And as you live on, the dead person you have killed will live on in you. So in essence, Death has no real meaning.

Ego death was another precept that echoed the thoughts of world religions, such as the Arabic proverb, spoken by the Prophet Muhammad, which says, "Die before you die", and a similar Buddhist saying: "Die while alive, and be completely dead." The end goal of Hinduism and Buddhism is to pass into a state of awareness – through "ego death" – in which time and space are totally transcended, and one is literally "dead" to the world, but alive in timeless eternity.

Everyday brought a different role, Leslie Van Houten later recalled, taking them more out of themselves: "Everyday was Halloween... One of (Manson's) things was to stop you during the day and have you put your palms up to his and then he'd move them in any direction or he would make a series of faces and then you were supposed to try to keep up with them and the whole thing was always geared toward the complete mirroring of him." According to former executive Scientologist, Jim Keith, what Charlie was doing with this mirroring process was identical to a Scientology process called "Opening Procedure by Duplication" aka "Op Pro by Dup" taught on the Hubbard Qualified Scientologist Course.

These games Charlie's Family played on a daily basis were attempts to rid themselves of their former identities and achieve ego death, thus making them totally free: first, by cleaning their mental slates with ego loss and fear games. Then, secondly, in stretching the limits of their sanity through the use of mind-bending drugs and breaking down sexual taboos via group sex with Manson as puppetmaster, pulling the strings of his naked marionettes, under the guise of helping them discover their "true selves."

Dissolution of identity was another key element of Charlie's deprogramming, accomplished through various steps; first with the nicknames and aliases used by the group, along with various role playing games – not to mention the acid trips and orgies – all eventually leading to a total submersion of each Family member's individuality, as they became one with the group mind, which – in essence – was the magnified mind of Man's Son. They were part of Charlie and Charlie was part of them. *I am you and you are me and we are all together*. "I became Charlie," Paul Watkins later noted, after breaking free of the group. "Everything I once was, was Charlie. There was nothing left of me anymore. And of all the people in the Family, there's nothing left of them anymore, they're all Charlie too."

‡

In late '68, Sadie's baby was delivered by Manson, with Mary, Yeller, Squeaky, Stephanie, Gypsy, Little Paul and Ruth Ann Moorehouse (aka Ouisch) in attendance. After the birth, Manson danced around the room with a guitar, composing songs in honor of the "new leader" of the Manson Family, soon to be christened Zezos Zeze Zadfrak. It was Manson's contention that the children were the real leaders of the group, unencumbered by psychological armor and over-developed egos; their responses were more instinctive and natural; they were always "at Now."

During testimony at Leslie Van Houten's 1978 retrial, prosecution witness Paul Crockett was asked: "Did Charlie ever tell you he was the leader of the Family?" Crockett replied, "Charlie never told me he was the leader of the Family. He told me that the youngest one in the group, which was Pooh Bear (the Manson/Brunner child)... that the baby was the leader."

Crockett's testimony suggests that Charlie believed youth and innocence ought to be the leader of their group. This also suggests a fear of growing up and accepting responsibility; forever living in a fantasy world, like the one Charlie's Family created at Spahn Ranch.

CHAPTER 20

Death Valley Daze

Charlie learned about a potential hideaway in Death Valley from former Buffalo Springfield groupie, Cathy Myers (aka Cappy Gillies.) Cappy, seventeen at the time, had been raised at a mining claim – in the high desert mountains bordering Death Valley – known as Myers Ranch. Into this setting, it has been conjectured, Manson withdrew with his Family to escape the paranoia he felt rising in the cities in the form of the black menace, a looming shadow growing long across the land like a huge Superfly afro. Many claim that this scenario helped hasten Charlie's transformation from acid gobbling peace and love guru to a drug crazed mass murdering cult leader.

Unlike their Spahn Ranch sojourn, the Family's Death Valley transmigration was of a more nomadic nature. At Spahn Ranch, Charlie's Family was situated within close proximity to one another, as opposed to Death Valley where they spread over a vast area, encompassing Goler Wash and the Panamint Mountains, holing up in mining claims throughout the area. Barker Ranch and Myers Ranch were two of the sites occupied by the Manson tribe, with Barker Ranch eventually becoming the central hub and unofficial Manson Family headquarters. Their previous Spahn Ranch stomping grounds fit more into the traditional role of what one normally considers a ranch, although it was a bit of a misnomer in reference to Barker and the other so-called "ranches" in the desert. These sites were actually comprised of forty acre mining claims usually staked out in an area near a spring, or other water source.

In the beginning, life at Barker Ranch helped strengthen the bond of the group, bringing them closer together. Each night they played their music and got tighter, refining old songs and writing new ones, as Charlie taught the girls to sing harmony. Although Manson was always the lead vocalist, everyone got involved in one way or another. Brooks and Clem played guitar, and when Bobby Beausoleil was around, he also played guitar and sang background vocals. Little Paul alternated between the French horn and flute, Gypsy played violin, and Mary also played flute.

One supposed myth that Charlie has tried time and again to dispel was that his rag-tag bunch was ever officially known as "The Family." According to Manson: "It wasn't the Manson Family trial because there was no Manson Family 'till we got busted. There was a music group known as The Family Jams, but, y'know, all that Manson Family thing – the D.A. put that together..."

As a singer, Manson had a magnetic pull, as all his violence and vitality were expressed through the music. As Paul Watkins attested, Charlie's Family was programmed most effectively through music, and had the general public been exposed to Manson through this medium, they might have well understood the intensity of Charlie's mercurial presence.

It was the tonal quality of Manson's voice that first charmed and beguiled so many a new comer, and – as it has been expressed by those who fell under the "Manson spell" – there was a magical quality to his singing and speaking voice that entranced the listener, perhaps even more than the actual spoken words.

When they weren't singing or working around the ranch, Charlie's Family took expeditions into the mountains. At night they'd often hiked up to Myers Ranch, build a fire and listen to Charlie rap. More and more Manson preached that there were no leaders, no rules, and that the only thing that mattered was opening up one's self to the cosmic vibrations and "coming to Now."

One of the things that most appealed to Charlie about the desert was that it was a ready made acid trip, from its enchanting rock formations to its wondrous sunsets, filled with myriad colors, where the Indian shamans and holy men had experienced transcendent visions for many a moon. There was a certain magic to be found, particularly in places like Joshua Tree or Death Valley.

Death Valley is perceived of as a place where nary a trickle of water runs; a place devoid of life. But contrary to popular opinion, life does indeed abound there, but it is only the heartiest and wiliest of animals that survive in these harsh environs. Case in point, the coyote, which, if there was ever to be a true Manson Family mascot, would surely be it; a creature alert and industrious, totally aware of itself and its surroundings, more scavenger than hunter, making use of the garbage and dead remains others have left behind – in the same manner as Charlie and his pack.

It was in this harsh environment that Charlie's Family came looking for some special sort of magic; to commune with nature, and attain a level of *Coyotenoia*. Manson's philosophy of Coyotenoia went as follows: "Christ on the cross, the coyote in the desert – it's the same thing, man. The coyote is beautiful. He moves through the desert delicately, aware of everything, looking around. He hears every sound, smells every smell, sees everything that moves. He's always in a state of total paranoia and total paranoia is total awareness. You can learn from the coyote just like you learn from a child. A baby is born into the world in a state of fear. Total paranoia and awareness..."

The Manson Family's sojourn into the desert was a societal withdrawal from the continual harassment they'd begun to experience from The Man. It was also a spiritual quest where – it was felt – they could finally become one as a family. Another aspect of the desert which fascinated Manson was that it was "a land where rivers ran upside down", a fact that appealed to Charlie's "no sense makes sense" worldview.

Death Valley is part of the Great Basin, where literally thousands of streams run, although not one of them ever reaches the sea. Death Valley is the sink of the Amargosa River, most of which is below sea level. Here the stream beds are on top, and the water beneath the sand and gravel, a phenomenon that always perplexed Charlie, who – from the time he arrived in Death Valley – began speaking of "a hole" in the desert that would lead his group to water, and perhaps even a lake and a place to live.

Many days, Charlie would walk the desert floor in search of this mystical "hole." The idea of a "hole" was by no means a crazy one, since all water flowing into the Death Valley eventually emerges elsewhere in the form of springs. This entire mythology of subterranean worlds fell into place with Manson's "magical mystery tour" concept of *I am you and you are me* and *no sense makes sense*, which was more readily acceptable to the minds of his minions in the magical atmosphere of the desert. As Little Paul later noted: "The cosmic vacuum of the desert was a perfect place to program young minds."

A parallel to Charlie's vision of a magic hole was the Hopi Indian legend of "Emergence from the Third World" which spoke of a large underground world from which the Hopi Nation would emerge – back to the Earth's surface – after Armageddon. Manson believed in the geological possibility of just such a hole. Evidently there have been claims in the past, as well, about a huge city-sized cave beneath Death Valley, with a river running through it, fed by the mighty Amargosa.

While exploring the many hot springs of Saline Valley in September of 1969, Manson discovered a spring that was so deep his feet couldn't touch bottom. So Charlie – thinking he might have discovered the secret entrance to the "bottomless pit" – commanded Clem and Ouisch to jump in and see if they could swim to the bottom. Swimming, though, didn't work out, as the water was way too hot, so instead they tied the end of a string to a rock and sunk it down, but the spring crevice went off at an angle. Charlie mentioned something about getting skin-diving equipment to further explore the springs to see if they led to "The Hole."

Even after Manson was incarcerated for the Tate/LaBianca murders, his fickle flock was still going out on "Hole Patrol" in the attempt to find the hidden opening into this underground world. Remaining Manson Family members came to believe that there was some sort of occult conspiracy in effect to conceal this secret entrance, and only Charlie held the keys of access to this subterranean paradise.

‡

According to Vincent Bugliosi, Manson's main motive behind the murders was to provoke a race war that would later be blamed on black militants, due to a false "bloody panther paw" trail of clues left by Charlie's shock troops. This, in turn, would lead to the aforementioned race war (Helter Skelter!) when the whites would retaliate against the seeming black menace. While this war was raging overhead, Manson and clan would be safe underground, in their haven of paradise, The Bottomless Pit, staying high and making love.

This fascination with the bottomless pit first began to exhibit itself at Dennis Wilson's house, when Manson took to sporting a Bible, cracked open and folded down to Revelations 9. Of this, Charlie read knowingly: "From the shaft of the bottomless pit... came locusts on the earth, and they were given the power of scorpions. They were told not to harm any green growth or any tree, but only those who have not the seal of God on their foreheads...Their faces were like human faces, their hair like women's hair... They have a king over them, the angel of the bottomless pit."

Tex Watson described The Bottomless Pit as "an underground paradise beneath Death Valley where water from a lake would give everlasting life and you could eat fruit from twelve magical trees – a different one for each month of the year. That would be Charlie's gift to us, his children, his Family. If anyone back in the Sunday schools I'd attended in Texas had ever mentioned that The Bottomless Pit was one of the names for hell itself, I'd forgotten it."

In *Will You Die For Me*, Watson took the politically correct stance of labeling Manson as an anti-Christ manifestation; a beguiling silver tongued snake using the masquerade of Jesus' thorny crown to conceal his jutting red horns.

Tex, like St. John before him, had simply been a messenger – albeit a dark one – bringing forth The Word of Charlie for those with ears to hear. But instead of uttering *The Kingdom of Heaven is at hand*, the message Tex delivered for his false messiah was *Helter Skelter!*, with an exclamation point of stab wounds ritualistically delivered on Cielo and Waverly Drives. *I'm the Devil, and I'm here to do the Devil's business!* Later, Tex would become one of many Judas Goats who would betray their former leader, along with Sexy Sadie – and Manson's former right hand man – Little Paul Watkins.

One possible entrance to "The Hole" was thought to be the so-called Devil's Hole in the northwest corner of Death Valley. The Devil's Hole, which is fenced off, is a forbidding pit of water, murky and ominous, inhabited by blind fish, where a couple of skin divers drowned in the early 60's trying to reach the bottom. For three straight days, Charlie sat crossed-legged before Devil's Hole, meditating with all his metaphysical might, contemplating the ultimate meaning of this bottomless well. After the third day, it dawned on Charlie that the water in the Devil's Hole was the door – or blocking mechanism – preventing entrance into the Underworld. All Charlie had to do was find a way to *suck* the water out, and – lo and behold! – the secret passageway would be revealed.

Isolation – such as that found in the desert – was another tool Manson used to program his followers. It was just this sort of atmosphere that has enabled many a cult leader to separate their followers from outside influences – such as parents – until the subject becomes totally dependent and, in time, entirely adopts the cult's belief system. Often this new set of values evolves into an "us against them" mind-set; for once someone has been placed in a vacuum, there is no longer anything to contrast or compare one's perceptions against. Cut off from mainstream society, Charlie created a timeless land for his followers, with their own value systems and beliefs. Such a scenario leads eventually to a group-mindset that is further intensified through programmed drug use.

Even the name Death Valley took on great significance with Charlie's Family, because – as it has been noted by the likes of Tex Watson – "Death was Charlie's trip." This statement can be construed in a number of ways – from Charlie's constant preaching about how it was paramount for each individual to "die to their ego" – to the eventual carnage that went down on those hot August nights of 1969.

Charlie was always rapping about "making love" and "death", and after a time the two became interchangeable, as "making love" and "death" melded together through all of Charlie's songs and raps. "It's through death (ego death) that we come to love" was the much repeated Manson mantra. Only later would it become painfully clear where such guidance can lead a wayward soul; for instance Sadie, and her much bragged about orgasm when delivering the fatal stab wounds to Sharon Tate and her unborn baby.

‡

In late November 1968, Gregg Jakobson and Dennis Wilson drove to Death Valley to retrieve Jakobson's jeep, broken down in Goler Wash, where Charlie had left it. From there they towed it to the nearby town of Trona to be repaired, Manson riding along with them. On the way, Jakobson ran over a scorpion, which set Charlie off, as he informed them that the life of a scorpion was more important than that of a human. At this time, Manson accompanied Jakobson and Wilson on their return trip to L.A to celebrate the impending release of The Beach Boys' "Never Learn Not To Love" the tune Manson had written, formerly titled "Cease To Exist."

In December, Capitol Records released the Beach Boys' single, "Bluebirds Over The Mountain," the b-side of which was "Never Learn Not To Love." Concurrent to this historic event, a recording of even greater magnitude was released, the Beatles' *White Album*. In time, this recording was to take on great significance within Charlie's Family.

After Manson's trip to L.A. with Wilson and Jakobson, he returned to Barker Ranch in an agitated, although enthusiastic state. Charlie spoke of escalating violence in the city, and that the blacks were on the verge of a revolution. "It's just a matter of time, " Charlie declared, "The shit's gonna come down... it's gonna come down hard." Charlie had alluded to this black/white race war before, but this time his attitude had changed: instead of advocating passive resistance – and remaining aloof from the imminent conflict – Manson began outlining his Family's role in the forthcoming revolution.

"What we need to do is program the young love to split... when the scene comes down, they're gonna need some place to go. Well, we got that place. We're here, and we can show the young love to come. And we can show them with music." The "young love" was Charlie's term for jailbait hippie honeys, and music was the proposed method of mass indoctrination. But where once peace and flowers had prevailed in the minds of Manson's minions, now things had changed. Suddenly they were no longer "coming from nowhere and going nowhere" with "nothing to do but love." Charlie's Family now had a purpose.

It was time to prepare.

CHAPTER 21
We All Live In A Yellow Submarine

It was another ceremony around the Barker Ranch campfire, like so many before in the high desert, or at Spahn Ranch. But all the peace and love vibes that had once been so prevalent in Charlie's rap had gradually begun to dissolve, more and more each day, and in their place paranoia was oozing in at steadily increasing doses. A large part of Charlie's sudden mood swing could be attributed to The Beatles' *White Album,* of which he spoke of solemn tones around the campfire.

"Are you hep to what the Beatles are saying?...They're telling it like it is. They know what's happening in the city; blackie is getting ready. They put the revolution to music… it's 'Helter-Skelter.' Helter-Skelter is coming down. Hey, their album is getting the young love ready, man, building up steam. Our album is going to pop the cork right out of the bottle."

Although growing steadily more paranoid about the general state of the modern world, Charlie's optimism about his recording career had been renewed by his recent trip into L.A., and the release of "Never Learn Not To Love."

Paul Watkins – in his Tate/LaBianca testimony – gave his own spin on the Manson Family mindset during this period:

> Our music was going to lure Whitey's daughters to the desert, away from Haight Ashbury. Blackie would have no other means of releasing his tensions, so would turn to the white establishment. The murders were going to start in rich places like Bel Air and Beverly Hills in the summer of 1969. The super-atrocious crimes would disturb the rich piggies; the spades would scare Whitey. They'd go to the ghetto and shoot the garbage man and the Uncle Toms. The Black Muslims would be in hiding. The whites would split up the middle, some saying, 'Look at the things you are doing to the blacks!' The whites would kill each other off. Then the Black Muslims would come in and kill the rest of them. Helter Skelter is the end of the cycle. What was on top had to go on the bottom. The karma of the whites is over and the black's karma begins. But then Revolution 9 takes over. This is described in Revelation 9. The black man would have to clean up the mess the white had made of the world, rebuild the cities and all that. But Blackie can't do it all alone. He will have completed *his* karma, and he'll have to come to the 'family.' Charlie will pat his fuzzy head and kick him. Charlie will have to show him how. Meanwhile, the 'family' will have grown to 144,000 like the twelve tribes of Israel in Revelation. Charlie encourages the girls to get pregnant. And we'll have buses to collect all the children when Helter Skelter comes down, so we can save them

and raise them in our hole in the desert. The bottomless Pit. That's in Revelation 9, too... Charlie's mission is to complete the karma of the world.

Throughout late 1968 and early 1969, Charlie's Family was spread throughout Death Valley, Topanga and Laurel Canyons, and one or more in England, allegedly with The Process. One former Manson Family associate claims that four to six members of the group lived on Laurel Canyon Boulevard in late 1968 in a log cabin once owned by actor Tom Mix. In Manson's famous letter to the *Hollywood Star*, he reminisced about the Tom Mix house: "...We had a pool full of naked beauties and strobe lights in the living room & sex in 5 bedrooms & all the closets had secret doors that go from bedroom to bedroom plus guest house, big beds, pool shacks, and mattresses in the living room, a tree house, sex all over the grounds, in the rose gardens, under the trees. NEIL DIAMOND used to come over. MIKE LOVE, of the Beach Boys, DORIS DAY's son, ANGELA LANSBURY's daughter Dee Dee, NANCY, SINATRA's daughter, used to be at the beach pad..."

Around this time, Charlie and gang moved into a house at 21019 Gresham Street in Canoga Park, about twenty minutes from Spahn Ranch. The house was painted a bright canary yellow, and became known as "The Yellow Submarine." From there, Charlie said, the Family would remain "submerged beneath the awareness of the outside world" while working on their music.

According to Charlie – in *Manson In His Own Words* – within four weeks of moving into the Yellow Submarine, it had become a "concert hall for musicians, a porno studio for kinky producers, a dope pad, a thieves' lair, a place to dismantle stolen cars and just about everything but a whorehouse..."

Shortly after moving into The Yellow Submarine, Charlie sent a squad back to Barker Ranch to retrieve his remaining Family members who had been left behind to look after things: Brooks, Juanita and Gypsy. It was Charlie's practice to leave a few members behind at their various hangouts in order to keep a foothold, such as Spahn Ranch, where Charlie always left a pretty young thing or two to see after George Spahn, and keep the horny old man happy. Among the new girls who joined around this time was seventeen-year-old Barbara Hoyt.

The legendary "Death Mock-up Party" was a prime example of the mounting weirdness that began to take hold during the Gresham Street period. Charlie and his tribe were sitting around stoned in the middle of the living room one night, apparently postulating their own deaths, when Charlie – strategically positioned in the middle of the throng – said, "Die," so they all laid down and pretended to die. Bo started screaming, "Charlie", and then "Oh-h-h-h-h!" In response, Manson started moving his fingers about in strange reptilian patterns, talking about the confusion in the air, and how groovy it was.

Meanwhile, Brooks Poston had gone into a deep trance, and Charlie commanded him to die. Thus Brooks Poston died in his own mind, and stayed in this "Death Trance" for five days. As he lay wasting away on the living room couch, the girls would periodically clean up after his bodily functions. On the fifth day of Brook's death, Charlie commanded that his very own ceremonial vest be placed beneath the ego-dead disciple as a sort of symbolic diaper, and – lo and behold! – with this one humble messianic act, Charlie was able to resurrect Brooks back to the world of the living, just like Jesus in the Bible awoke Lazarus. Charlie looked down upon Brooks and said, "I command you to live again!" With Charlie's commandment, Brooks' eyes opened, and slowly and painfully he rose to his feet. Then saith Charlie: "Now I accept you."

Another apocryphal tale from this period told of a Manson Family acid orgy where Bo Rosenberg went batty while giving Charlie a blowjob and bit off his cock in one mad chomp. Manson, it is said, immediately healed his severed penis with a magical wave of the hand, then continued on with the wild drug fueled orgy as if nothing had happened. Hallelujah!

Shortly after moving into the Gresham Street pad, Charlie was visited by Dennis Wilson and Gregg Jakobson, who – after hearing Manson and his gang play a few tunes – were enthused about the new "desert music." Because of this, Dennis, Jakobson and Melcher scheduled a couple of recording sessions at a Westwood Village studio.

At this session, Charlie brought the whole mob with him – fifteen all told – invading the place like some sort of hippie free-for-all. Immediately, the studio manager instructed Charlie and his gang on what they could and couldn't do; where to sit, where to stand, which way to face, even how to hold the microphone. At first, they complied with his requests, but when it came time for Manson to lay down his vocal tracks, the girls wanted to be looking at him as they sang background. As the girls moved away from the place where they'd been positioned, the studio manager came unglued. In the end, the whole scene was a repeat performance of what went down at previous recording sessions, as Charlie felt the studio wouldn't let him perform his music the way he wanted to, free from the restraints and deadlines of studio managers and record producers pushing their trip on him. Nevertheless, Manson managed to record a dozen songs, two of which were spontaneously composed. It was at this session that Manson freaked-out Terry Melcher with a little spontaneous guitar vamp ditty and scat-singing of apparently non-sense syllables "digh-tu-dai, deigh-du-doi, di-tew-deigh" which gradually became clearer until "di-tew-deigh, die-tew-dai," became "die today, die today, die today."

Much ado has been made about Charlie's failed music career. Some suggest his failure to "hit the bigtime" was the main motive behind the Tate murders; that Charlie felt spurned by Terry Melcher, and in retaliation sent his shock troops to 10050 Cielo Drive to settle the score. Manson dismisses such accusations, insisting that his musical career was never of great importance to him.

Manson – never shy about name-dropping – claims to have met and influenced many of the movers and shakers of the 60's music industry. Among those who Manson says "stole his chops" were The Beach Boys, Neil Diamond, and The Buffalo Springfield. According to Sandy Good, former Buffalo Springfield member Neil Young was amazed at Charlie's rhythmic style of playing, and supposedly gave Manson a motorcycle as a gift. Young's song "Mansion on The Hill" from *Ragged Glory* has long been rumored to be about his meeting with Charlie in the 60's. (Manson on the Hill.) The lyric of this song goes: "His words were kind but his eyes were wild, he said 'I got a load to lug but I want one more trial.'" Another Manson influenced tune by Young is "Revolution Blues."

Young – who met Manson through Dennis Wilson – was quoted as saying: "He wanted to make records. He wanted me to introduce him to Mo Ostin at Reprise. He had this kind of music that nobody else was doing. He would sit down with a guitar and start playing and making up stuff, different every time, it just kept on comin' out, comin' out, comin' out. Then he would stop and you would never hear that one again... Musically, I thought he was very unique. I thought he really had something crazy, something great. He was like a living poet."

During the Yellow Submarine period, Manson began recruiting former prison buddies, in addition to outlaw bikers and mechanics, to help him score and repair dune buggies and Harleys. From his experiences in the rugged terrain of Death Valley, Manson decided that dune buggies best fit the bill for his Family's envisioned mass exodus into the desert, as they were great for outrunning the cops, and were light enough so that two or three people could lift them over impassable boulders and gullies if they became high-centered. Manson would later outfit his sacred dune buggies with huge gas tanks, giving them a 1000 mile distance capability, and even put on machine gun mounts in preparation for Helter Skelter. Charlie's own personal dune buggy was adorned with hanks of human hair, affixed to the roll-bar, donated by female Family members.

One of Charlie's ex-con recruits was Bill Vance (aka William Rex Cole.) Vance – a hulking six-footer in his late forties – had been heavyweight champion of Tennessee's Brushy Mountain Prison, one of the roughest prisons in the U.S., for nine years. Vance hit it off immediately with Yeller, and Charlie used this liaison to his advantage.

On March 23rd, 1969, Bobby Beausoleil signed a songwriting contract with the Gerard Theatrical Agency on Sunset Strip. Beausoleil was given a key to the front door of the agency, and allowed to use the tape recording equipment there to produce a demo. During this period, Beausoleil was cultivating a relationship with Dennis Wilson, Terry Melcher and Gregg Jakobson, with designs of furthering his musical career. In fact, Jakobson went twice to the Gerard Agency to listen to Bobby's tapes, and in April, Bobby stayed for about a week at Jakobson's house on North Beverly

Glen. There he met seventeen-year-old Kitty Lutesinger. In late May 1969, Kitty became pregnant courtesy of Bobby, and moved to Spahn Ranch. Beausoleil also approached Frank Zappa, asking him to come out to the ranch to hear the Manson Family's music, but Zappa declined. Apparently, Zappa and Beausoleil had formed a loose relationship during the early Haight-Ashbury days, and Bobby had even performed a cameo on Zappa's first album, *Freak-Out*.

The Gerard Agency specialized in supplying actors and actresses for porno flicks, and topless dancers for nightclubs. After hearing Bobby talk about the agency, Bill Vance – acting as an "agent" for Sadie, Yeller, Stephanie, Katie, and Mary – was able to land jobs for the girls as dancers at strip joints in the valley. Charlie encouraged them to take these jobs in order to buy vehicles and other supplies for his Family's forthcoming desert exodus. During this same period, Charlie and some of his girls allegedly made a porno movie at the Malibu property of a "Mrs. Gibson", who – after receiving numerous complaints from neighbors – inspected her house in the company of a lawyer and discovered a bloody machete, which police said Manson used to slash somebody's arm during the course of the filmmaking.

Karate Dave – a twenty-six-year-old Vietnam vet – hooked up with Charlie's Family during the Yellow Submarine period, and lived in a tree house in the backyard with Bo Rosenberg. It was through Dave and Bill Vance that other outlaw types were enlisted to help prepare for "Operation Helter Skelter." These were guys who could score motor parts, camping gear and building supplies, and who would later work on various Spahn Ranch projects.

As the months passed, preparations for Helter Skelter accelerated, and though Manson rarely allowed this fringe biker and ex-con element into the inner circle of his Family, he was able to keep them around through enticements of dope and sex. One favorite trick of Charlie's was the strip and suck command. Executed with a wave of the hand, Manson would have his girls undress and go down on his biker associates.

By mid-March, Manson had acquired three dune buggies and three Harleys. In addition, Charlie bought three hundred dollars worth of topographic maps to chart an escape into the desert. The escape route began behind Spahn Ranch, up into the Santa Susana Mountains by way of Devil's Canyon, then through Simi Valley, bypassing highways, going over and under culverts, across the Mojave Desert and eventually leading them to Death Valley. This clandestine route was to be used at the time of Helter Skelter, when everything was going crazy in the cities – and the highways leading out of L.A. would be in violent gridlock – an escape route that would be a quick exit away from the chaos.

According to Paul Watkins, it was at the Gresham Street pad that Charlie started getting heavy into the Beatles' *White Album*, which he interpreted as modern day prophecy, and the Fab Four as messengers of the Apocalypse retitled "Helter Skelter." Charlie spent endless hours quoting Revelation, specifically the verse from chapter 9:

> And the four angels were loosed
> Which were prepared for an hour
> And a day, and a month, and a year,
> For to slay the third part of man
> And the fifth angel sounded,
> And I saw a star fall from heaven
> Unto the earth: and to him was
> Given the key to the bottomless pit.

For those with ears to hear, the implications were clear: the four angels were the Beatles, and the fifth angel Charlie! The "third part of man" was the white race; those who would die in the resultant Helter Skelter carnage, wiped out for "worship of idols of gold, silver, bronze, stone and wood," (Verse 20) which Charlie related to cars, houses, and money; those modern idols worshipped by the piggies.

The passage, "And he opened the bottomless pit... and there came out of the smoke locusts upon the earth; and unto them was given power as the scorpions of the earth have power" was not only a reference to the Beatles (i.e. locusts) but also implied that the power of the scorpion would prevail. (Charlie was a Scorpio.) Manson found references to dune buggies, as well as the motorcycle gangs he was trying to recruit, in such passages as "horses prepared to battle" and horseman that would roam the earth, spreading destruction.

In describing the locusts (The Beatles), Revelation said that "their faces were as the faces of men," yet "they had the hair of women," and wore "breastplates of fire," which Charlie interpreted as electric guitars. Another Revelation verse spoke of "fire and brimstone" coming from the four angels' mouths, which Charlie interpreted as the Beatles' music and lyrics. Some have suggested that it really wasn't Charlie who invented "Helter Skelter", but that he just became hip to the concept through channeled Beatles messages.

In the same manner that Manson became a self-styled Bible student, likewise he threw himself into *White Album* interpretation, which he listened to with headphones as a means to decipher the messages hidden in the vinyl grooves. Soon, it has been suggested, Manson began to hear the Beatles whispering to him: "Charlie, Charlie, send us a telegram", on the song "Revolution #9." At one point, Manson actually tried to call The Beatles in London, but was unsuccessful. *The White Album* became such an influence upon Charlie's Family that Beatles lyrics punctuated their speech. It was all there, Charlie would tell them; just listen to the music. Didn't they have a song called "Sexy Sadie" that described Susan Atkins to a tee, not long after Charlie himself had christened her Sadie? Didn't the Beatles tell blackie it was time for him to rise up in their song "Blackbird": "Blackbird singing in the dead of night... All your life/You were waiting for this moment to arise..."? Not only that, but The Beatles actually knew about Charlie out in Los Angeles – and were urging him to speak out, to sing the truth to the world, in their song "Honey Pie":

Oh honey pie, my position is tragic
Come and show me the magic
of your Hollywood song

In this song, the Beatles even went so far as to beg Charlie to come to England:

Oh honey pie, you are driving me frantic
Sail across the Atlantic
To be where you belong

Charlie felt that the Beatles were beaming subliminal messages that on a conscious level were unknown even to them. During the Tate/LaBianca trial, Manson was quoted: "I think it's a subconscious thing. I don't know whether they did it or not. But it's there. It's an association in the subconscious. This music is bringing on the revolution, the unorganized overthrow of the Establishment. The Beatles know in the sense that the subconscious knows."

According to Tex Watson and Paul Watkins, Manson's interpretation of *The White Album* was more significant than Charlie was willing to later admit. It was their contention that *The White Album* was both a message to this "returned Jesus" (Charlie) to speak out, to call the chosen, and as a preparation for Helter Skelter. According to the Manson mythos, The Beatles were setting the stage for Charlie's coming, and that Charlie was to give the world an album that would light the fuse the Beatles had prepared. In this album would be message songs, like the Beatles', with lots of subtle symbols aimed at different parts of society involved in the coming changes. Charlie's album would contain the "plan" which the Beatles were asking him to reveal in the song "Revolution #1." In the song "I Will", The Beatles urged Manson to speak the word:

And when at last I find you
Your song will fill the air

Sing it loud so I can hear you
Make it easy to be near you...

Other *White Album* songs that Manson allegedly interpreted as direct messages from the four angels:

    * "Happiness is a Warm Gun" which instructed Charlie's Family to arm themselves for the coming race war.

        * "Piggies" about fat rich capitalist pigs and how they deserved a "damn good whacking", which is exactly what the blacks were going to give them. "Pig" was written at the Tate residence, and "Death to Pigs" was written at the LaBianca's home.

    * "Helter Skelter" was a prophecy about Manson emerging from the bottomless pit. "Healter Skelter" [sic] was written in blood at the LaBianca's.

The most experimental piece on *The White Album*, "Revolution #9", took on great significance to Manson, who equated it with Revelation 9. "Revolution #9" was the result of John Lennon ingesting several tabs of LSD-25 then feeding tape splices into reel-to-reel machines of archived BBC recordings. Because of this unorthodox recording process, many were led to believe, including Charlie, that hidden messages had been deliberately inserted, ala backward masked subliminals, amid the strange collage of taped sounds – warfare, church hymns, crying babies, football games, BBC announcers – thrown together in overlapping anarchic patterns, and highlighted by the chilling "Number Nine-Turn Me On, Dead Man" phonetic reversal.

Like Manson, the number nine held great significance in Lennon's life. In numerology, nine is the final number, the last single digit and highest counting number before starting over again; the beginning and the end.

Lennon's numerological odyssey began with his birth on October 9th, 1940; his son Sean was also born on October 9th, 1975. As a Liverpudlian lad, Lennon grew up at 9 Newcastle Road. Brian Epstein discovered the Beatles on November 9th, 1961. The Beatles played their first gig at the Cavern Club in 1961. Nine years later – in 1970 – they split up. The group rocketed to stardom after appearing on the Ed Sullivan Show on February 9th, 1964. Several of Lennon's tunes featured the number nine theme, such as "Revolution #9" and "Number 9 Dream" from *Walls and Bridges*.

John met Yoko on November 9th, 1966 and the two were married in 1969. The couple moved from England to New York in 1971, and lived there for nine years, until Lennon was shot to death outside the Dakota Building on December 8th, 1980.

After receiving the fatal gunshots, Lennon was transported to Roosevelt Hospital on 9th Street, and was pronounced dead at 11:07 pm (1+1+7=9). In England, John's birthplace, it was already December 9th.

The Dakota Building is located on West 72nd Street. (7+2=9) The Lennon's apartment number at The Dakota was 72. (Once again, 7+2=9.) Above Lennon's bed at the Dakota hung the number 9. Eerily enough, one of the apartment buildings Lennon purchased at The Dakota was used in the making of Polanski's *Rosemary's Baby*.

The Beatles' last album – *Abbey Road* – was recorded in 1969. That same year, Lennon changed his name from John Winston Lennon to John Ono Lennon, bragging that between John Ono Lennon and Yoko Ono Lennon there were nine O's. Lennon claimed to have seen a UFO while standing on the roof of The Dakota at 9am. John and Yoko's Tarot card reader performed a pagan nuptial ceremony in 1975 to celebrate their 6th wedding anniversary; the ceremony commenced at 9pm.

Number nine, number nine, number nine...

August 8th and 9th – when the Tate killings occurred – coincide with other significant historical dates:

    * On August 9th, 1945, the atomic bomb was dropped on Nagasaki.
    * August 8th, 1907, was the birthdate of the infamous cannibalistic serial killer Ed Gein.
    * On August 8th, 1985, the LAPD first announced that the Night Stalker – a Satanic serial killer – was haunting the city.

* On August 8th, 1974, Richard Milhous Nixon became the first President in history to resign from office.

* On August 8th, 1969, Disneyland opened the doors to a new attraction, *The Haunted Mansion* . Later that night macabre history was made again on 10050 Cielo Drive when Sharon Tate and her house guests were murdered. The next evening, August 9th, the Mansonoids paid a visit to the LaBianca's house, formerly owned by Walt Disney.

In a 1970 *Rolling Stone* interview, John Lennon acknowledged that he, George Harrison and Ringo Starr took their second LSD trip at a location loosely referred to as "Doris Day's house." However, Lennon may have been referring to the house that Day's son, Terry Melcher, was subleasing at 10050 Cielo Drive. According to Lennon:

> …We were on tour, in one of those houses, like Doris Day's house or wherever it was we used to stay. And the three of us took it [LSD]. Ringo, George and I. I think maybe Neil [Aspinall, a roadie]. And a couple of the Byrds…[David] Crosby and the other guy, who used to be the leader…[Roger] McGuinn. I think they came round, I'm not sure, on a few trips.

The reference to Byrds members Crosby and McGuinn lends credence to the hypothesis that John, George and Ringo actually dropped acid at the house where Sharon Tate later met her fate, as Melcher produced the first two Byrds albums.

CHAPTER 22
Let's All Do The Creepy-Crawl!

For nearly two years, Charlie's Family had been almost totally removed from television, radio and newspapers, living in relative seclusion at Spahn Ranch or in Death Valley, out of touch with mainstream society. Now, suddenly – at the Yellow Submarine house – they found themselves in the midst of civilization again, subjected to TV newscasts filled with violence and bloodshed; the body counts from Vietnam and student demonstrations in the streets. Everything seemed to validate what Charlie had been rapping about of late; a revolution on the horizon.

In March, Charlie began sending his followers out on "creepy-crawls" to houses in and around Canoga Park. As Charlie explained the ultimate meaning of creepy-crawly in his midnight sermons: "When it comes down, we got to be prepared to save the babies. It might mean sneakin' and peakin' around... takin' some chances." The Manson Family "creepy-crawl" M.O. was to dress entirely in black, and move about like Ninjas, through the shadows in total silence, blending into the night, as they snuck into houses and moved from room to room. The girls got into the act by fashioning special creepy-crawl costumes with capes. To some, the Manson Family's sudden fondness for black attire during this period has drawn comparisons to The Process Church of the Final Judgment, and their similar dark and dramatic duds.

The Process, at this time, were preparing the "Fear" issue of their magazine, later published in the fall of 1969, which included such articles as "Satan Is Fear", a page with quotes from Hell's Angels members, and a grim photo of The Process's collection of Alsatian dogs all lined up in a row with fangs bared. The centerfold of the magazine was a picture featuring the Lamb of Christ and the Goat of Satan, which read "The Lamb and the Goat must come together – pure Love descended from the pinnacle of Heaven, united with pure hatred raised from the depths of Hell."

During this period, Bill Vance took Tex and some of the girls out on their very first creepy-crawl, teaching them to remove screens, slip locks, avoid watchdogs, and implement the tools of the trade, such as penknives, razor blades and bobby pins. In retrospect, these early creepy-crawls appear to have been dress rehearsals for "Helter Skelter." Although it may have seemed that this kind of game was designed to blow people's minds – when they woke up the next morning and discovered their furniture rearranged in the night – the real purpose was to make those Manson Family members involved in creepy-crawls face their "fear" and go beyond it. When going out on these nocturnal excursions, Charlie shared the following advice: "Do the unexpected. No sense makes sense. You won't get caught if you don't got thought in your head."

In early April, Charlie's Family began gradually moving out of the Gresham Street house, as it had become over-crowded, what with all the people, vehicles and motor parts scattered about, not to mention an overabundance of paranoid vibes bouncing off the walls. By this time, the Charlie and his troops had acquired the aforementioned dune buggies and Harleys, as well as a milk truck and two diesel semi-trucks for hauling around their vast arsenal of vehicles, camping supplies, tools, equipment and motor parts. Another motivation for leaving the Yellow Submarine house was an unpaid stack of electric, water and telephone bills that had been piling up, as collectors were beginning to hound them.

Since Charlie's Family couldn't move back into Spahn Ranch *en masse* without causing a scene, they had to do so incrementally, by first establishing a campsite in a ravine just below the ranch. Charlie purchased several parachutes from an army surplus store in Los Angeles and, after dying them green, used them as tents beneath a grove of oak trees. Meanwhile, they began remodeling the saloon into a nightclub, knocking out the back partition behind the stage, painting the walls and ceilings black, bringing in strobe lights and hanging white Styrofoam balls from the ceiling. On the left side was a long bar where free popcorn, chips, soda and coffee were served, and on the floor were rugs and mattresses to encourage patrons to "do their thing." This new venture was called "Helter Skelter Club" and Charlie's Family painted a huge mural along the back wall, depicting – in Day-glo and black-light colors – a mountain, the desert and Goler Wash. In the mural, the Angel of Helter Skelter was seen coming out of heaven, to save the planet from destruction. The bottom of the mural read: "Helter Skelter, Goler Wash and Death Valley." Helter Skelter was also painted on doors, and on a jug that was passed around for donations. At the far right end of the saloon was a stage with guitar amps, a sound system and drums. "The Family Jams" was the house band, and soon word spread throughout the valley of the good music, nude dancers and other carnal pleasures to be found at Club Helter Skelter.

But alas, Charlie's psychedelic go-go club was short-lived, as underage kids started showing up, and their parents notified the police. The pigs came storming in one night, rousting everyone and bringing the Helter-Skelter Club up on several charges: contributing to the delinquency of a minor, possession of illegal substances and operating a nightclub without a license. In any event, Charlie was able to skate, as old George Spahn bore the brunt of the charges leveled during the raid.

Not long after returning to Spahn Ranch, a seventeen-year-old girl was picked up by a couple of male Manson Family members and taken back to Spahn Ranch. When they arrived, the police report recounted the following:

> Victim states that this was the strangest place she had ever seen in her life; 20-25 people sitting, standing, lounging around in a living room; men, women, girls, boys and even little children; strobe lights were going off and on; things hanging from the walls, everything psychedelic; some were on the floor plunking on some types of musical instruments; and that they were all drinking out of a dirty looking jug and smoking something.

When the girl asked somebody where she was, one of Charlie's Family replied, "This is where it is." The girl became hungry, and one of the Mansonoids offered her some cornflakes, but – as was custom – the flakes were first offered to a dog named Tom, because – within the Family hierarchy – dogs always ate first, before the women.

When the girl was introduced to Manson, he took her outside to get some privacy and explain the meaning of life. After that, Charlie allegedly raped her. Later, the girl had someone drive her to a liquor store in Chatsworth on the pretext of buying cigarettes, and there she was able to make her break, running home to her parents, who were reluctant to press charges due to the bad publicity that might result from the incident.

In mid April, Charlie's Family made their final exit from the Yellow Submarine. One day Charlie and T.J. pulled a semi-truck into the driveway and loaded everything inside of it, including Harleys, VW engines, a big diesel motor, and countless dune buggy and jeep parts. They then drove to a Mulholland mansion, which belonged to the rock band, Iron Butterfly, whom Charlie learned were out of town for a few weeks. Bill Vance broke the lock on the gate, and Charlie and his tribe spent about two weeks there, making music and planning Helter Skelter strategy. Around May, they left the mansion and moved back to Spahn Ranch, staying in a campsite on the property.

Charlie and his tribe were drifting more and more into a survivalist mode during this period. He told the girls to hang "witchy things" on the trees around their campsite – usually made of beads or feathers – so that by touch they would be able to return to the campsite at night, without the aid of moonlight. The girls set up a camp kitchen, and staple sustenance was provided by a hundred pound sack of brown rice. The girls were instructed to secure additional foodstuffs from the local vegetation, which at times proved difficult in the rough and unfertile woodlands surrounding Spahn Ranch.

Around this time, Danny DeCarlo – a tough, hard-drinking biker and treasurer for the Straight Satans motorcycle gang – started hanging out with Charlie's Family. DeCarlo later told authorities that his rapport with Manson was enhanced by the fact that he could sexually satisfy his girls, thus taking the pressure off Charlie to keep them all happy. Because of this, Danny acquired the nickname "Donkey Dan", a tribute to the size of his male member.

According to DeCarlo, it was Squeaky who persuaded George Spahn to allow the Manson Family to return en masse to Spahn Ranch. Charlie's plan was to get George to sign the ranch over to Squeaky when he died, since she was his favorite girl. It's not out of the realm of possibility that Charlie might have indeed ended up owning the ranch. Even after the Tate/LaBianca murders, Old Man Spahn was still eager to have Charlie's gals around.

By this time, Charlie's Family had begun to accumulate a small arsenal in preparation for Helter Skelter, which several small caliber handguns, two thirty gauge shotguns, a Schmizer machine gun, and a thirty-thirty. Charlie was particularly fond of a Buntline Special, Hi Standard .22 caliber Longhorn revolver he'd been given by Randy Starr, an old rodeo performer who hung around Spahn ranch.

Buck knifes also became a Manson Family staple, as both the men and women carried them around the campsite. Charlie – an expert with knifes – gave the girls lessons in knife throwing, later followed by detailed throat slitting lessons. Later that summer, he acquired a sword from "86 George", the President of the Straight Satans, when Manson paid one of George's traffic tickets in exchange for the homemade two-foot razor sharp weapon replete with knuckle-guard. Not long afterwards, Manson would use this same blade to sever Gary Hinman's ear.

One of Charlie's favorite games during this period was to gather his Family together, and have them imagine a rich piggie sitting in a chair in the middle of a circle. "Imagine we just yanked the pig out of his big car and stuck him here," Charlie'd instruct the group. They would then project their own fear on the piggie. Charlie directed the mental traffic of his group until they'd actually see themselves scaring the imaginary pig to death with their creepy vibes. During this game, they'd usually drop acid, and after awhile Charlie got into the habit of talking about things that could be done to the imaginary piggie, such as tying him up, stabbing him, then going to his house and murdering his family and stealing all their money. Family members would follow Charlie's lead and imagine the butchery and gore, and – according to Tex Watson – even though it was all just a game, the images would stay locked in their brains long after the game was over.

A couple miles from the ranch was a new suburban development with ostentatious homes, just the type of affluence that Charlie and his minions held in contempt. Gradually "the pig" in their fantasies became one of the people in this development, as Charlie began to talk about going in and taking over one of the piggie's houses. Manson had it all sketched out: they'd just barge in one night blazing on acid and scare the owners shitless by projecting fear onto them. Charlie's Family would then take control of the house and live there, with the girls pretending to be maids to keep up appearances, while they ripped off everything they could find to fund Charlie's Helter-Skelter campaign.

When this plan didn't pan out, Charlie set his sights on a gambling casino on the hill above Spahn Ranch. Charlie's first brainstorm was to rob the casino itself, but after a week of casing the joint, he gave up on that idea and decided they'd just kidnap one of the rich customers, then take over the pig's house and use his money for buying dune buggies and supplies.

All of the sudden, Charlie was brimming with ideas. Another light-bulb went off in his buzzing brain, and Charlie decided that instead of scaring his victims to death, he would build a jail in the L.A. sewers for them; a jail where he would be warden and dole out appropriate punishment to the pigs, to right all the wrongs and turn the tables of karma back upon all the judges, cops and prison guards that had abused him throughout his life. Fortunately, nothing came of this idea, either.

According to Tex Watson, in early 1969 Manson began ranting in his death trip lectures about The Process Church of the Final Judgment. Soon after, Charlie and other Manson Family members were wearing black capes and black-dyed clothing – just like their spiritual brethren. Of course – from the beginning of his three year odyssey with his Family – Charlie had always talked about death, but it was usually spiritual death he was rapping about: death of the ego. But now, it appeared, there was nothing spiritual or psychological about the dying which Charlie seemed ever more obsessed with. It was physical, violent death that Manson meant when he told his doped-up flock that "death was beautiful", because it was the one thing people feared most. On the other hand, saith Man's Son, death was nothing than a mere illusion of the mind, so killing fellow human beings was like destroying a fantasy. Manson kept repeating that the spirit, *The Soul*, could never be killed; it was one and eternal, and that the illusion of physical death opened up the spirit to the realization of its essential oneness with all that is.

In late May, Katie Krenwinkel bought about a dozen deer hides, and it was from these skins that the girls attempted to fashion buckskin outfits for the Family men-folk. These would be all-purpose buckskins; combat-ready clothing that would last indefinitely and be conducive to desert life, like a second skin that could be washed right on their bodies, with soap and water. When the girls' efforts proved less than satisfactory, Charlie took the hides to a guy named Brother Ely, who sewed the buckskin outfits at his Santa Barbara leather factory. Manson was wearing his buckskins when later arrested in Death Valley. Brother Ely was also the high priest of a clandestine Santa Barbara occult group, which the local police believed to be a "chapter" of The Process Church. Evidently, the police had a list of names of those associated with the group, one of them being Danny DeCarlo.

On May 27th, 64-year-old Darwin Scott – the brother of Manson's father, Colonel Scott – was hacked to death in his apartment in Ashland, Kentucky, and pinned to the floor with a long butcher knife. From May 22nd through June 18th, Manson was out of touch with his parole officer. During this same period, a motorcycle riding guru calling himself "The Preacher" appeared in Ashland, accompanied by several foxy females. On May 25th, it has been alleged that Manson and Sadie were seen together in Kentucky, zipping around on a motorcycle. The "Preacher", it appears, was generous with his drugs, doling out acid to local teens and attempting to set up a commune in a ramshackle farmhouse. Later, irate citizens burned down the farmhouse and drove off the remaining "hippies."

‡

With Helter Skelter looming just around the bend, Charlie had Tex construct a shelter across the road from Spahn Ranch where they could store supplies and hideout in case of an emergency. Using two-by-fours and plywood, Tex built a small lean-to, which was stocked with such provisions as camping gear, dried foods, and weapons. Family Members called it "Helter-Shelter", while Charlie referred to it as "The Just-in-Case Place."

Charlie's Family set up base camps and explored the mountains around Spahn Ranch, so that they knew every hill and gully, using their dune buggies and Harleys to roar through the canyons like a band of revolutionary guerrillas. Meanwhile, Charlie's mechanics worked on his fleet of vehicles, while the girls continued dancing topless, bringing home paychecks to cover the mounting expenses of Manson's planned paramilitary operation. Charlie's mechanics concentrated mainly on converting Volkswagens into dune buggies. For power to operate the assembly line, one of Manson's more talented thieves had stolen a truck with a gas generator and arc welder. The generator provided light for work at night for their assembly plant, called the Devil's Dune Buggy Shop. There the men would strip off the body and fenders of stolen Porches and Volkswagens, cut everything up, and load the cuts onto a truck and haul them away. Then they'd make dune buggies out of the skeleton Porsche and Volkswagen frames.

CHAPTER 23
Ego-Death Valley

In the spring of 1969, Paul Crockett was prospecting in Goler Wash and living out of Barker Ranch. Returning one day in April, Crockett and his partner, Bob Berry, found some hippies living at the ranch house, namely Manson Family members Juanita Wildebush and Brooks Poston. Poston, they noted, appeared zombie-like.

The miners decided to move into an adjacent bunkhouse, occasionally visiting their hippie neighbors in the larger house next door. In conversations, Wildebush and Poston spoke of a guy named Charlie who possessed Christ-like powers and oversaw a flock of wayward hippie kids.

At first – according to Wildebush and Poston – this Charlie character had preached the requisite *peace, love and drugs* so popular with the 1960's flower children. But only recently had Charlie's worldview turned apocalyptic, as he began prophesying the imminent doom of mankind, to be triggered by a forthcoming black/white race war.

From these discussions, Crockett arrived at the conclusion that these two wayward kids had been badly brainwashed. Gradually, Crockett and Berry welcomed the two lost youths into their world, helping them foster a respect for the desert environment, and recruiting them into their mining work. The end result was an overall improvement in the physical and mental conditions of both.

Later that spring, Paul Watkins and Bo Rosenberg showed up at Barker Ranch, bringing with them supplies for their two friends. Upon encountering Poston, Watkins was amazed at the transformation that had overtaken his once zombie-like countenance: he was now cheerful and alert, excited about the new life with the miners.

Watkins was disturbed by Crockett and his "deprogramming" of Wildebush and Poston, so he took upon himself the task of spreading the gospel according to Charlie, intent on combating the "negative" influence that Crockett had been asserting upon the minds of his friends. Watkins attempted to indoctrinate Crockett into Manson's philosophical system, but at every turn Crockett was able to counter Little Paul's interpretation of The Word.

Initially, Watkins thought he could overwhelm the miner with the canon of Charlie's teachings, revealing the imminent reality of Helter Skelter. However, Watkins greatly underestimated Crockett, whom he erroneously perceived as a middle-aged, straight-laced square. Little did Watkins know, but Crockett had steeped himself, over the years, in philosophy, theology, religion and history. Crockett, as well, had delved into Scientology, Theosophy, Rosicrucianism and other esoteric schools. This knowledge provided him with an arsenal of selected precepts to draw upon in his debates with

Watkins.

Crockett – mainly out of curiosity – listened intently whenever Watkins delivered "The Word of Charlie" detailing Manson's plan to avert the coming race war by leading his flock into a "bottomless pit." There – according to Manson's Revelation 7 interpretation – his flock would multiply to 144,000.

Through his deprogramming of Wildebush and Poston, Crockett was eventually able to break Manson's chain of influence. Watkins, though, was a harder sell, so Crockett's approach was more systematic. Piece by piece he had to dismantle Manson's philosophy right before Watkins' eyes, displaying the frail logic supporting Charlie's Helter Skelter vision. When Watkins returned to Spahn Ranch to convey the news that Crockett had overtaken Barker Ranch, it triggered an intensely negative reaction within Charlie's Family. Nevertheless, Watkins persuaded Charlie to let him return to Barker Ranch "to keep an eye on" Crockett.

On several occasions, the Mansonoids attempted to drive up Goler Wash, but something always seemed to go wrong. Soon it came to be believed that Crockett was sending out negative vibes preventing Charlie's Family from making it up to Barker Ranch. Crockett himself did little to dispel this myth and, in fact, promoted the idea that he had constructed a magical force-field around Goler Wash, which no one could pass through unless they carried true love in their hearts.

CHAPTER 24
The Manson Family Crime Syndicate

During the summer of 1969, Juan Flynn claimed that, on several occasions, he and Manson drove around Chatsworth, and that Charlie tried to get him to enter houses, tie up the residents, force feed them acid, kill children in front of parents, then kill the parents as they were freaking out.

There was another incident where Manson encouraged Flynn to kill a black man who lived in an apartment building near the Yellow Submarine house. Manson's motivation for the murder was because this individual had supposedly given dope to his girls and had sex with them. Later, when questioned about this incident, Manson denied it. Some investigators now believe that the true motivation behind this incident – and the murders to follow – stemmed from Manson's relationship with the California underworld and his rumored status as a hit man who contracted out for murder.

On August 12th, a few days after the Tate/LaBianca murders, Manson grabbed Juan Flynn by the hair, held a knife to his throat and said, "You son of a bitch, I am going to kill you... Don't you know I am the one that is doing all the killings?" At this time, Manson offered Juan the opportunity to wear a ring in his nose, and be Charlie's personal slave. Flynn wisely declined the invitation.

Prior to 1969, the majority of Manson Family drug transactions were small scale, but as Charlie began constructing his Helter Skelter plans, these activities increased to a larger scale in order to buy the dune buggies and other equipment required to fund their Death Valley exodus.

In the early summer of 1969, Charlie's Family stole an NBC station wagon loaded with film and recording equipment. Most of this equipment was eventually given away, but not before Manson and his mob made video porn with it in Death Valley in September. When Spahn Ranch was raided on October 10th, police seized the last of the stolen film equipment, consisting of a camera containing unexposed film. Supposedly, at this time, Bill Vance made off with some of this rare Death Valley footage.

Much has been made about the so-called "hemic films" that allegedly document Manson Family activities at such locations as Topanga Canyon, Malibu, Death Valley, Hollywood and Spahn Ranch. These films were improvisational, capturing "slice-of-life" Manson Family fun such as group acid freak-outs and orgies. According to Vern Plumlee, three super-8 cameras were used to film these events which included Charlie's Family dancing naked with knives and pretending to cut each other up. Family orgy footage is rumored by some to appear in the mondo-sleaze movie *Witchcraft 70*, which also features the Church of Satan.

On one occasion – when Ed Sanders was in Los Angeles posing as a pornography dealer – the opportunity arose to purchase seven hours of assorted erotic footage including Manson Family porn for the hefty tag of $250,000. There were also rumors circulating that a friend of Gary Hinman's had in his possession films of "Malibu and San Francisco axe murders." Sanders alleged that a Los Angeles dope dealer had sold "a film depicting the ritual murder of a woman to a famous New York artist whose name will not be mentioned here."

Another of Sanders' unnamed sources alleged that Charlie's Family held several Spahn Ranch happenings where home-made movies were shown on eight-millimeter projectors, with the soundtrack provided from tapes of Manson recordings. The films featured reels of Manson Family happenings, music jams, the previously mentioned knife dance caper and drug orgies.

Another unnamed Sanders' source alleged that Process Church members were involved with an obscure biker club located near Spahn Ranch, and that Charlie's Family was also involved with this same shadowy group and participated in outdoor ceremonies involving human and animal sacrifices filmed secretly at a beach located along the Pacific Coast Highway.

Afterwards, these films were screened at Spahn Ranch, featuring participants dressed in black and wearing crosses, some with black hoods. The informant identified two Manson female followers as taking part in the blood drinking rituals. One of the girls participated in sexual intercourse, while fresh blood was poured over her body.

During the same period, residents of 10050 Cielo Drive were allegedly making their own home movies. One day in July of 1969, caretaker William Garretson witnessed Woytek Frykowski taking pictures of a nude lady in the swimming pool. Later, a cable TV repairman came to the residence and stumbled upon a nude love scene going on there. Recently, former Manson Family member Catherine "Gypsy" Share disclosed that she and Susan Atkins visited the Polanski residence prior to the murders, both of them taking a dip in the spool. More recently, Terry Melcher confirmed this swimming pool incident. When Melcher moved out of the house, it was occupied for a period by another former Manson disciple, Deane Moorehouse. While there, Moorehouse was visited on several occasions by Tex Watson. All of these revelations appear to cast a shadow of doubt over the random killings theory.

In early July, Bobby Beausoleil and his pregnant girlfriend, Kitty Lutesinger, moved into the "outlaw shacks" at Spahn Ranch. Later – at his murder trial – Beausoleil testified that he returned to Spahn's because Gregg Jakobson had called him and said that the Manson movie deal was "on", and that Melcher was still interested in participating in the project. According to Beausoleil's testimony, Jakobson wanted him at the ranch to help with music for the film's soundtrack.

Throughout the summer, Manson stepped up his efforts to attract young males into his Family – preferably those with klepto tendencies – in his ongoing efforts to create a well-supplied dune buggy army assembled from stolen vehicles. John Philip Haught (aka Christopher Zero), Scotty Davis, and Lawrence Bailey (aka Little Larry) were three such youths. Zero, Scotty, Vern Plumlee and Bill Vance became Charlie's crack squad of car thieves, terrorizing San Fernando Valley, stealing cars and robbing gas stations.

On July 17th, 1969, sixteen-year-old Mark Walts disappeared while hitchhiking from Chatsworth to a fishing pier in Santa Monica. The next morning, Walts' battered body was discovered in Topanga Canyon, near Mulholland, in the same vicinity where two other bodies were found earlier that year. Walts – who had been shot three times and repeatedly ran over by a car – was a frequent Spahn Ranch visitor. His brother, Allen Walts, publicly accused Manson of the murder. Although charges were never filed, several police officers visited Spahn Ranch to investigate the death. Around the time of Walts' death, another corpse – identified as "Jane Doe #44" – was discovered near Lake Castaic, northeast of Spahn Ranch. Some have speculated that the corpse in question belonged to Manson Family member, Susan Scott, who was living at Spahn Ranch at the time of her disappearance. While the Castaic corpse technically remains unidentified, Susan was never seen again. An article of clothing "Jane Doe #44" had been wearing was identified as part of the Manson Family communal clothing pile.

‡

In late June 1969, Tex Watson was dating a girl named Rosina Kroner, who had an apartment in Hollywood. It was there that a dope burn went down involving a black drug dealer, Bernard "Lotsa Poppa" Crowe, who Watson ripped off for 2,500 dollars intended for a kilo of grass, then high-tailed it to Spahn Ranch. At around 2 A.M. the next morning, a call came in through the Spahn Ranch pay phone, placed by an hysterical Rosina Kroner, who stated that Crowe was at her apartment threatening to slice her up if she didn't come up with the money Tex had ripped off. Kroner had called Spahn Ranch asking for "Charles", as in Charles "Tex" Watson. Family member T.J. answered, and – thinking she meant Manson – summoned Charlie to the phone, who first talked to Rosina, then Crowe. Crowe threatened to bring his boys over and shoot up Spahn Ranch if Charlie didn't return his money. Manson informed Crowe that he would be right over to resolve the problem.

On his trip over to Rosina's, Charlie brought T.J. with him, as well as his Buntline Special .22 revolver. When a disheveled Rosina answered the door, Charlie and T.J. were met by two men, Dale Fimple and Bryan Lukas, a friend of Dennis Wilson's. The pair informed Manson that Crowe wanted his money back pronto, or else he was going to take his vengeance out on the girl, then raid Spahn Ranch.

A few minutes later, Crowe showed up and Charlie told him that "you can't take my friend's life – you must take my life." With that, Charlie took the Buntline Special from behind his back and – kneeling down before a seated Crowe – held the revolver out, butt-first. When Crowe reached for the gun, Charlie spun it around so that the handle rested in the palm of his hands, and sprang to his feet. Crowe rose up and made a move toward Charlie and in response, Manson pulled the trigger, but nothing happened. Charlie – in a spontaneous act – laughed and said, "How could I kill you with an empty gun?" The trigger clicked again, and this time a shot was fired, hitting Crowe, who fell down to the floor, clutching his stomach.

Charlie turned to one of Crowe's associates and, admiring his buckskin jacket, instructed the guy that he wanted it; Crowe's associate wisely handed it over. With jacket in hand, Charlie walked over to the fallen Crowe, knelt over, kissed his feet and said, "I love you brother." Charlie and T.J. split, under the impression that Crowe was dead.

Charlie was woke up the next morning by T.J., who came to tell him about a story on the morning news regarding a high-ranking Black Panther who had been shot dead, and his body dumped on the lawn of a Beverly Hills hospital. According to Charlie – in *Manson In His Own Words* – this is when paranoia set in at Spahn Ranch, as he suspected that Crowe was the "high-ranking Black Panther" mentioned in the news story, and that the Panthers would come seeking retribution.

Charlie went directly to the saloon and told every one present that they were going to have to make an immediate change in the way they 'd been living at the ranch; that they would all have to be more observant, more so than ever. It wasn't only the police now, it was the blacks rising up, as well. With the police, Charlie informed his flock, they didn't have to fear sniper shots, but with the blacks, it was a different story.

On Charlie's instructions, they set up lookouts, as Spahn's came to resemble more a military encampment than a dude ranch. No longer was it just a bunch of kids playing at fun and games. Now was a time for constant vigilance, as Charlie believed he had inadvertently ignited a race war.

The next day, three carloads of blacks pulled into Spahn's. From all appearances, the group was just innocently touring the ranch, but in the Manson Family's mounting paranoia they suspected them of being a Black Panther scouting party. Those among Charlie's Family who might have beforehand doubted Manson's proclamation that he had started a race war, now became firm believers that the blacks would soon be back in full force to exact their revenge. Little did Charlie know that – as all these paranoid vibes were reaching a fevered pitch – Lotsa Poppa Crowe was alive and well at the UCLA Medical Center. Crowe evidently stayed there until June 17th, after which he returned to home to recuperate.

In retrospect, one must wonder if Manson actually believed he'd ignited a race war. Some sources suggest that Charlie was much more familiar with Bernard Crowe than he has ever admitted. One former Manson Family member stated that in late 1968 Charlie's Family used to visit a "Bernie's house" in Laurel Canyon, and Diane Lake once referred to Crowe as "the Negro member of the Family." Given the fact that a friend of Dennis Wilson's was at the scene of the Crowe shooting further supports the likelihood that everyone involved in this incident were much more familiar with one another than has been officially disclosed.

Bryan Lukas – a first hand witness to the Crowe shooting – called his friend Dennis Wilson several days later and told him about the incident. Gregg Jakobson was there at the time and overheard the conversation, then immediately called Terry Melcher to inform him of the situation. As can be expected, Melcher was quite upset about the whole mess, and that may have been the final straw that caused him to sever ties with Manson.

Rumors later surfaced that Manson had been involved in a Hollywood "black dope syndicate", the facts of which were only partially uncovered by investigators. Whatever the case, there was definitely a group of black dope dealers operating in Hollywood during this period, a number of whom were arrested during the Tate/LaBianca murder investigation.

Bernard Crowe, it so happens, lived at 7008 Woodrow Wilson Drive above Sunset. According to reports, Manson and several associates were often seen hanging out around Woodrow Wilson and the Loyal Trail road that ran behind Crowe's place, and it is probable that Charlie and his pals were either visiting Crowe's during this period, or – according to other sources – Mama Cass Elliot's place, located in the same area. It may have been at Cass's pad that Manson became acquainted with Abigail Folger and Woytek Frykowski, not to mention various players involved in the Hollywood drug scene.

"I've heard that Charlie went down to Mama Cass' place and like they were all sitting around jamming for hours... Squeaky and Gypsy were down there. Everyone would jam and have fun and eat," related former Family associate Charles Melton (aka Crazy Charlie) in Sanders' *The Family*.

CHAPTER 25
The Tale of the Butchered Buddhist

Bobby Beausoleil's main drug connection was Gary Hinman, who made mescaline in a bathtub lab at his Topanga Canyon pad. Throughout the summer of 1969, Beausoleil had been dealing Hinman's mescaline to the Satan's Slaves biker gang, and one morning some of the bikers rode into Spahn Ranch claiming that the last batch Bobby sold them was bad stuff, and had made some of their member's deathly ill. When the Slaves demanded their money back, Bobby assured them he would take care of the situation. After they left, Manson placed a call to Hinman, informing him about what'd just gone down, but Hinman replied that there was nothing wrong with the mescaline batch sold to the Slaves, and refused to return their money.

That evening, Bobby, Sadie and Mary showed up at Hinman's place to get the biker's money back, but Hinman told them to buzz off. To show he meant business, Beausoleil brought along a nine-millimeter pistol and since Hinman wasn't budging, Bobby decided to check out the rest of the house for money or drugs. He handed the gun to Sadie, and went into the other rooms to look around. Soon after, a scuffle broke out between Hinman and Sadie and the gun discharged. Bobby grabbed the pistol and smashed Hinman several times with the butt, leaving his head a bloody mess. Following this altercation, Beausoleil placed a phone call to Spahn Ranch, and a short time later, around midnight, Bruce Davis and Manson arrived, equipped with Charlie's ceremonial sword.

At first, Hinman was relieved to see Manson, but when it became clear that Charlie was there to back up Bobby, Hinman became unglued, calling Manson a "phony little bastard" and telling him to get out of his house. In response, Manson hacked Hinman's ear with his sword, creating an ugly five-inch wound, cutting into the jawbone and deep into the ear canal. Charlie then turned to Bobby and said, "Talk to him, maybe he'll remember where his money is. Then bring him out to the ranch until he gets well."

According to Beausoleil's account, after Charlie left, Hinman started screaming bloody murder, and that is exactly what he got when Bobby repeatedly stabbed him in the chest to shut him up. As Hinman succumbed to the fatal wounds, the three Manson Family members laid him on the floor and fashioned a makeshift Buddhist shrine, giving Gary his prayer beads as he chanted his last rites of "Nam Myo Ho Renge Kyo – Nam Myo Renge Kyo", until he lapsed into his final sleep. They covered Hinman with a bedspread, then Bobby stuck his hand in Hinman's blood and on the wall in the room scrawled: "POLITICAL PIGGIE." To the left of the slogan was finger-painted the paw of a cat: a half-cocked attempt to implicate the Black Panthers in Hinman's murder. Afterwards, the Mansonoids wiped down the walls for fingerprints, hot-wired Hinman's VW bus and drove it, and his Fiat, back to Spahn Ranch.

That night, Charlie's Family got together for a songfest and tape-recorded a recreation of Hinman's murder in musical form, with each Family member playing a role in this gory rock opera. Supposedly, this tape was among several that Bill Vance had in his possession following the Tate/LaBianca murders. That night – when Sadie crawled into bed between Sandy and Yeller – she whispered, as she lay her head down upon the pillow: "Gary is dead." The next morning, Yeller split, fleeing Charlie's Family.

There are several theories explaining why the Hinman murder went down. Some suggest that the "dope burn" angle was just a cover story Charlie cooked up, and that he actually sicked his acid-munching minions on Hinman to encourage the aspiring Buddhist monk to come across with a certain five-figure sum he'd recently inherited.

Early on, Beausoleil stated that Manson had no role in the murder, and that the story about him showing up with his ceremonial sword was a myth woven by Vincent Bugliosi and Ed Sanders. Film director Kenneth Anger – an insider into the Manson Family scene – confirmed this in a late 1990's interview, adding that narcotic agents might have been involved in a Manson Family frame-up:

> ...(Bobby) left me in '67 and the Manson killings began in the summer of '69, beginning with Bobby and (Sadie)... He had sold some bad dope to the Manson Family that the Manson Family had resold to the (Satan's Slaves), and the drug agents had sprayed it with cyanide. And so all the (Satan's Slaves), about fifty of them, got extremely ill. They almost died, and then when they recovered they blamed the Manson Family. They said 'if you don't kill whoever you got that bad dope from, we will kill all of you'. That was California in the sixties (laughs), the so-called generation of love, or summer of love or whatever (laughs). That was a farce! And so that's how Bobby got mixed up in murder and why he agreed to murder and, you know, they were all dropping acid like it was breath mints, and generally cutting loose from their family connections. They were all middle to upper-class kids, you know, rebelling against their backgrounds...

Another critical event occurred on July 27th, the day Hinman was murdered: Jean Brayton's Solar Lodge ranch was raided. For all intents and purposes, Helter Skelter appeared to be coming down fast. That same day, Father Ryan of the Order of St. Augustine claimed that Manson, or a Charles Manson look-alike, approached the back door of his parish – located a half mile from the LaBianca residence – and informed the priest that he (Charlie) was Jesus Christ, then looked at Father Ryan with a cold, steely stare. Charlie asked Father Ryan why he had become a priest, and apparently displayed an intense dislike for the priesthood. Father Ryan slammed the door on Manson's face.

Later, on July 27th, Manson encountered a task force of California Highway Patrol and Malibu Sheriffs outside of Spahn Ranch. The cops – who were planning a raid – had gathered together near a turnoff to Spahn's, when they came across Manson's hidden dune buggy in the brush. According to Officer Olmstead of the Sheriff's Department, Manson said that he was out watching for Black Panthers, who he was expecting to attack the ranch at any time, and that the rest of his friends at the Spahn Ranch were heavily armed. Charlie also warned the officers that if they were suddenly to pull a raid, his friends might think that the attacking hordes were Black Panthers and open fire. Charlie got permission from the officers to proceed in first and alert his gun-wielding compatriots that The Man was on his way. He then raced back to the ranch, ordering everybody to disperse up into the hills to hide-away spots.

When the officers arrived, Charlie attempted to intimidate them by drawing their attention to the hills north of the ranch, where he said he had his people scattered with their guns trained and – at his command – would open fire. Charlie informed the officers that only specially equipped dune buggies could reach his hidden troops, and that patrol cars would be useless. At this point, Manson approached the officers with an offer to join up with his bunch, so that together they could get rid of the Black Panthers once and for all. The cops ran makes on the Manson Family vehicles, which included a red VW bus registered to recently deceased Gary Hinman, whose corpse had yet to be discovered at his Topanga Canyon house.

On August 4th, Bobby Beausoleil was arrested in San Luis Obispo, sleeping on the side of Highway 1 in Hinman's Fiat. During Beausoleil's arrest, the police found the murder weapon – a knife, stained with blood – in the vehicle's wheel well. Beausoleil was taken into custody and charged with murder.

About the same time, Charlie took a solo trip up the north coast. Some sources suggest that Manson was off on a recruiting trip, but as Charlie related the story – in *Manson In His Own Words*– his reason for the trip was two-fold: to score some drugs, then turn them over for a profit to pay off Bobby's debt to the Satan's Slaves; and to take a break from the Manson Family scene, which of late had become oppressive, what with all the Black Panther negative vibes swirling around his Family, as well as recent harassment they'd received from the cops. Some accounts say Charlie had even talked about an extended trip – for perhaps three months – but given the timing it seems more than coincidence that both he and Bobby took off immediately following the Hinman murder.

At the Tate/LaBianca trial, Susan Atkins testified that soon after Bobby was picked up on the Hinman murder, the girls started entertaining the idea of staging a copy-cat murder to help Bobby beat his murder rap. Apparently, one of the girls had recently seen a movie where copy cat murders were committed over a period of time, allowing the killer to get out of jail.

Manson left Spahn Ranch on August 3rd, driving a '52 Hostess Twinkies Bakery Truck equipped with a love bed in the rear. From there, he headed north to Big Sur, and early the next morning picked up an attractive seventeen-year-old hitchhiker named Stephanie Schram. That evening, Schram and Manson spent the night on the beach, as Charlie gave Stephanie her first hit of acid, initiating her in a session of LSD sex-therapy.

"He sure did send me on a trip that one day," Schram later noted.

When they woke up the next morning, Schram had fallen head over heels for Manson, promising never to leave Charlie. Manson was likewise smitten with the shapely Miss Schram, vowing not to leave her side for two weeks; a vow that would later cause much consternation among Charlie's girls, who would have never imagined such a thing possible. Usually he'd have sex with a new female recruit, then move on to a next "young love" – as Charlie called them – but Stephanie Schram was different. Charlie later told Paul Watkins that Stephanie – who was of Germanic extraction – was the result of two thousand years of perfect breeding, which evidently turned him on, forming some sort of Aryan love goddess image in Manson's mind.

On August 5th, Manson and his Aryan maiden drove north to a place which he described to Stephanie as a "sensitivity camp." This, of course, was Esalen Institute, which become popular during the late 1960's for its mineral baths and human potential seminars, featuring the likes of such tuned-in counterculture icons as Tim Leary, John Lilly, Allen Ginsberg and Carlos Castaneda. Also of note, Process Church leader Robert DeGrimston reportedly participated in an Esalen seminar during this period, although it is unknown if it coincided with Charlie's visit.

Into the Esalen milieu one could come, drop some acid and spout their way-out philosophy to a rapt audience of illumination seekers looking for a guru of the week. While at Esalen, Manson had "played his guitar for a bunch of people who were supposed to be the top people there, and they rejected his music. Some people pretended that they were asleep, and other people were saying, 'This is too heavy for me,' and 'I'm not ready for that,' and others were saying, 'Well, I don't understand it,' and some just got up and walked out..." This, to Vincent Bugliosi, was one further instance of what Manson considered a rejection from the establishment, occurring only three days before the Tate murders.

According to Ed Sanders, someone at the Polanski residence placed a call to Esalen six days before Charlie's appearance there, on July 30th at 3:07 PM. Sander's also hinted that during the weekend of August 1st and 2nd, either Abigail Folger or Sharon Tate may have stopped in at Esalen for – as he termed it – "one of those famous Esalen weekends where people pay money for elitist mental health sessions."

CHAPTER 26
Painted Black

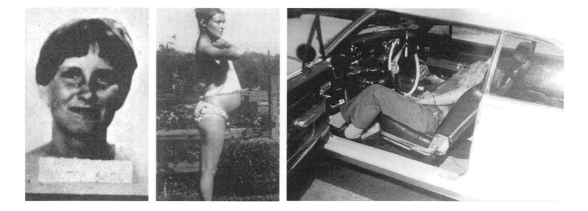

Legend in Hollywood lore is the tragic death of movie producer Paul Bern, husband of screen siren, Jean Harlow. Although Bern's death was formally ruled suicide, a lingering shadow still hovers over the incident, which some now believe was a murder cover-up by the movie industry to avoid a resultant scandal.

A couple years prior to the Tate/LaBianca murders, Jay Sebring rented a mock-Tudor mansion further up Benedict Canyon from the Polanski residence, at 1960 Easton Drive. After witnessing a series of spooky apparitions and strange, nocturnal sounds, Sebring became suspect that the house was haunted. Soon after, he learned that his home was the very same one where Paul Bern had died. This information subsequently freaked Sebring out, and he refused to sleep there at night. While considering what to do with his apparently haunted house, Sebring sought refuge at Polanski's pad.

Aside from the Bern suicide, sometime in the past another guest at the house had committed suicide, and a third man apparently drowned in the swimming pool. Several years after Sebring's death, a maid working at the estate hung herself. One night in 1965 – while Sharon Tate was staying there – she awoke to the figure of a "creepy little man" standing at the foot of her bed. Sharon blinked her eyes, and the image disappeared. Her next course of action was to pour herself a stiff drink. The next morning, Sharon was positive she had seen Paul Bern's ghost.

Hollywood producer, Milos Frank, owned the Bern house during this period, and remembered Sebring as "a real oddball... He kept making alterations to the house, but we didn't object because his lease gave him an option to buy." Bern's so-called "death-closet" had been converted into a bedroom, but Sebring used it as a gymnasium. "I called him after we heard that he had painted the bedroom black and the gym purple. He did that without asking if it was okay. Sebring suggested that my wife, Sally, and I have lunch with him the next day to talk it over and he would bring film actress Sharon Tate along. We thought he was going ahead with his option to buy the property." More likely, Sebring was planning to break off the lease, but as fate would have it, the meeting with Milos Frank never took place. That very night, Sebring went to see Sharon Tate at 10050 Cielo Drive. Soon after, Frank learned that the two had been murdered.

While Manson was in Big Sur with Stephanie Schram, a dope-dealing associate of Woytek Frykowski's from Toronto was whipped and "video-buggered" at 10050 Cielo Drive. Shortly before his death, Jay Sebring complained to a receptionist at his hair salon that someone had burned him for $2000 worth of cocaine and that he wanted revenge.

In a 1970's interview with Truman Capote, Bobby Beausoleil claimed that "Sharon Tate and that gang... burned people on dope deals... They picked up kids on the strip and took them home and whipped them. Made movies of it. Ask the cops; they found the movies. Not that they'd tell you the truth."

Dennis Hopper, in an *LA Free Press* interview, had this to say about these alleged videos: "They had fallen into sadism and masochism and bestiality – and they recorded it all on videotape, too. The L.A. police told me this. I know that three days before they were killed, twenty-five people were invited to that house to a mass whipping of a dealer from the Sunset Strip who'd given them bad dope."

One of the more controversial Tate/LaBianca theories suggests that Manson was the ring leader of a hit squad dispatched to 10050 Cielo Drive to execute a contract taken out on Frykowski and Sebring. Another theory suggests that certain members of the Manson clan were victims of the video whippings in question, and that an enraged Manson sent his goon squad to Cielo Drive on a mission of righteous revenge.

Shortly after the murders, an L.A. artist named Witold Kaczanowski – also known as Witold K., a Polish friend of both Polanski and Frykowski – phoned a New York friend claiming that he knew the killers identities, and that because of this, feared for his life. Later, Witold K. told police that Frykowski had been offered an exclusive Los Angeles MDA dealership, but subsequent friction developed, and one of the suppliers threatened Frykowski's life. The men in question were apparently the same group who created a ruckus at the Polanski housewarming party: Pic Dawson, Ben Carruthers, Tom Harrigan, and Billy Doyle, all frequent visitors to the Cielo Drive address. It was two members this group – both Canadians – that Witold K. identified as supplying Woytek and Gibby with the bulk of their drugs. Afterwards, an all-points-bulletin was issued for the apprehension of the two Canadians fingered in Woytek's short-lived drug dealing enterprise. They subsequently surrendered, but after questioning were cleared of all charges. In Ed Sanders' *The Family*, the dope-dealing Canadian identified as being "video-buggered" at 10050 Cielo Drive was Billy Doyle.

Pic Dawson – who at one time dated Mama Cass – moved in with Gibby and Woytek at their Woodstock Drive house. Witold K. was living there at the same time, and once – during an argument – Dawson tried to strangle the artist. When Woytek learned of this incident, he threw Dawson out, and an enraged Pic swore: "I'll kill them all and Woytek will be the first." John and Michelle Phillips also believed that one or more of the men – Dawson, Carruthers, Harrigan, or Doyle – might have been involved in the Tate murders. The Phillips passed on their suspicions to the police, claiming that on one occasion they witnessed a member of this group pull a gun on Frykowski.

During the Tate/LaBianca trial, Susan Atkins testified that the motive for the murders was two-fold: 1) To get Bobby Beausoleil off using their madcap copy-cat murder plan and, 2), because Linda Kasabian had been burned on a MDA drug deal. In trial transcripts, Atkins quoted Kasabian, who complained that she had been burned at the Polanski residence: "You remember the thousand dollars I had? I told her yeah – and she said, 'Well, I went up to some people in Beverly Hills for some MDA' – some new kind of drug... MDA. Oh anyway, she went up there to buy something and they burnt her for the bread."

On August 8th, Charlie – with Stephanie Schram riding shotgun – came rolling into Spahn Ranch. However, the reception awaiting him there was not the usual bright and beaming faces. Palpably evident was a tension in the air, and – sensing the need for a serious rap session with his Family's inner core – Charlie called together a pow-wow consisting of Leslie, Mary, Squeaky, Sadie and Linda, who informed him of Bobby's recent arrest. Linda recounted her phone conversation with Beausoleil, about the charges brought against him, and what he had told the police. After the phone call, the girls held their own meeting, and discussed the best way to help Bobby out of his dilemma. It was at this time that they came up with their copy-cat murder scheme.

When Charlie heard the copy-cat plan the girls were planning to hatch, he told them that the cops would never go for such a crazy scheme. In response, Sadie blurted out, "It *will* work, Charlie. At Gary's house, we wrote things on the wall like 'Political Piggie' and drew a panther's paw and that kind of stuff. We can do it again and they will think the niggers did it. It will be Helter Skelter!" To Charlie, Sadie's ominous utterances were reflections of what he himself had been feeding his Family for months, but the difference – according to Charlie in *Manson In His Own Words* – was that he had never actually wanted to start a war, and that his main concern was for defense and awareness, but Sadie had thrown his own words back at him. Manson reiterated that he thought they were nuts for even considering this copy-cat idea, and that if they tried to pull it off, it would probably land him back to prison. With that, Manson said he was gonna make some tracks, and get out while the gettin' was good. Just load up his Hostess Twinkie Truck and hit the bricks – with sweet Stephanie Schram by his side – leaving all this bad craziness behind in a cloud of Spahn Ranch dust.

"No, you can't go," Squeaky pleaded, "Love is one! We are one!" Once again, they had thrown Charlie's words back in his face. "If one goes," the pixie red-head continued, "we go together!" Sadie joined in the chorus, "Don't go, Charlie," as did the other girls: "Don't leave us, Charlie, stay here, we need you! We can do whatever is necessary and we won't send you back to jail!"

Charlie knew that staying was the wrong decision, but after all he'd been through with this band of runaways and outcasts, he felt there was no other choice than to see them through this crisis. After all, they'd given him the first real love and sense of belonging he'd ever known. "All right," Manson said, "I'll stay. But what you do is on your heads, not mine – understood?" Together, the whole bunch chimed in: "We understand, Charlie," amid a spontaneous outburst of smiles, hugs and kisses.

Charlie went out to the back ranch house where he found Tex, who was all hyped up on the recent news of Bobby's bust and the girls' copy-cat scheme to spring him from the slammer. In response, Charlie explained to Tex that whatever the girls did, they did on their own, and that he wasn't about to go back to jail on account of their crazy scheme. Charlie turned it around on Tex, saying, "You remember the black and what I told you when I came home from killing him?" (Charlie was still under the assumption that he'd actually killed Bernard Crowe.) Manson continued: "That life I took for you was your life," Charlie said, laying a heavy karma trip on Tex. "Bobby is my brother. He is your brother. And to save our brother, I'm asking you for the life you owe me."

Tex stood up straight, like a soldier preparing for war, and solemnly said, "I can handle it, Charlie. What have you got planned?" Charlie explained to Tex that it wasn't his plan, and that whatever went down was the girls' idea. The only reason Charlie wanted Tex to go with them was because he felt they needed a man along to do the dirty work.

Around 4 PM, Mary and Sandy used a stolen credit card at a Sears in San Fernando and were soon after arrested and hauled into Sybil Brand jail. Captured along with the two young ladies were several other hot cards and fake I.D.s. Later, Squeaky received a call from Sandy in jail, informing her of their predicament. When Squeaky passed on this news to Manson, he flew into a rage. "What the fuck is happening here, " he shouted. "One by one this fucked-up society is striping my young loves from me. I'll show them! They made animals out of us – I'll unleash those animals – I'll give them so much fucking fear the people will be afraid to come out of their houses."

According to Tex Watson's version of events – as related in *Will You Die For Me?* – Manson gave him detailed instructions to go to Melcher's old house and destroy everyone there, making it as gruesome as possible. They were to take rope and knives with them, Charlie instructed, as well as a pair of bolt cutters, which they'd use to cut the telephone wires going into the house. He told Tex that they should wear dark colors – creepy-crawly style – and to take a change of clothes with them, afterwards destroying the clothes they committed the killings in. Charlie also elaborated in depth on how he wanted the murders executed, specifically mutilating the victims and leaving messages scrawled in blood on the walls such as HELTER SKELTER and RISE. Tex said he wouldn't be able remember all that, but Charlie told him not to worry, the girls would know what to write. He handed Tex his .22 Buntline pistol, but instructed him to use knives whenever possible.

While Charlie went to round up the girls – Sadie, Linda and Katie – Tex crawled under the porch where he and Sadie kept a secret stash of speed, a Gerber jar hidden from Charlie, who didn't permit heavy drugs at the ranch. Sadie later confirmed that she and Tex were snorting the stuff at the time of the Tate and Hinman murders.

Many times before – with Manson conducting his dark symphony – Tex and other Family members practiced butchery in their heads, sitting around an empty chair in the ranch house, projecting grisly scenes upon an imaginary victim. But despite all these violent visualizations Charlie used to teach his disciples how to kill – how to scare the rich piggies shitless, then slit their throats – Tex was still reeling inside from the task awaiting him. To build his courage, he took a couple deep snorts of speed, then went to get the clothes, rope and bolt cutters.

After dinner, Manson pulled Sadie aside and told her to get a knife and a change of clothes. Next, Charlie told Linda to also get a knife, a change of clothing and her driver's license. With Mary arrested, Linda was the only person at the ranch with a valid license, so by default she was elected to drive Tex and the other girls to Benedict Canyon. Katie – lying down in the back house, trying to shake the effects of an afternoon acid trip – was next in line to receive her marching orders. She was awakened and, like the other girls, told to get a knife and change of clothes.

The death-mobile that delivered Tex and the girls to 10050 Cielo Drive was a yellow and white '59 Ford sedan with bogus license plates. As they began to pull out of Spahn Ranch on their appointment with destiny, Charlie stopped them, and leaned into the open window: "Leave a sign," he said. "You girls know what to do. Something *witchy*."

‡

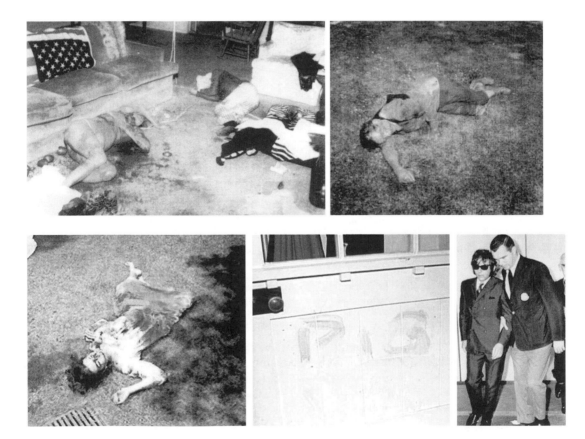

Charlie's shock troops pulled up to a gate at the end of a private drive, and Tex climbed onto the hood of the car, shinnied up the pole and cut the telephone line with bolt cutters. After the wires fell, he backed the car down the driveway to the street below and parked. The dark marauders climbed over the gate, dropping to the other side as suddenly a car appeared, heading their way. Tex told the girls to hide in the bushes, lie down and be quiet. The car's driver stopped and rolled down his window to push the button for the automatic gate. As he did so, Tex stepped from the shadows, a gun in one hand and a knife in the other. Through the open window, he jammed the Buntline special up against the driver's head, eighteen-year-old Steven Parent, who had been visiting the groundskeeper – William Garretson – in the guest cottage. Tex fired four quick shots. After Parent slumped in the seat, Tex reached into the white Rambler, shut off the lights and killed the engine, put it in neutral, and pushed the car back out of the way.

They creepy-crawled past a Porsche and Firebird, on up the walkway to the freshly painted window of an unfurnished nursery room on the north end of the house. Tex slit the screen with his bayonet and pulled it off the frame, crawled into the nursery and then entered the kitchen, on through the dining room and into the entrance hall, opening the front door and letting in the girls.

At first, the room appeared empty, although the stereo was blaring, but as they moved farther in they could see a blond man – Woytek Frykowski – asleep on a sofa draped with an American flag. He was wearing short boots, multicolored bell bottoms, and a purple shirt and vest. As they stood over Woytek – who was zonked-out under MDA's euphoric effects – Tex whispered to Sadie to go check the rest of the house. Frykowski stirred at the sound of Tex's voice, mumbling, "What time is it?" Tex replied, "Don't move or you're dead," holding the Buntline special in Frykowski's face.

When Woytek asked him who he was, Tex answered: "I'm the Devil and I'm here to do the Devil's business." Sadie brought a towel from the bathroom, which she used to tie Frykowski's hands behind his back. She then walked toward the hallway, to the two main bedrooms. In the room on the left, was a women in a white nightgown, Gibby Folger, laying on an antique bed, reading. When Gibby noticed Sadie, she smiled. Sadie returned her smile, and waved, then moved to the next room where Jay Sebring, with his back to Sadie, was sitting on a bed, talking to a pregnant blonde women in bra and panties, Sharon Tate. The two didn't notice Sadie, who – upon first sight of the pair – thought to herself, "Wow, they sure are beautiful people."

When Sadie returned, she told him about the three other people, and Tex instructed her to go get them at knife point and bring them into the living room. Sadie first brought back Gibby, and Katie held a knife on her while Sadie went back for the others. She returned with Jay and Sharon, who hesitated at the entrance of the living room. Tex leapt forward and grabbed Sharon's arm, jerking her in after Sebring. Tex instructed them to lie down on some pillows near the fireplace. At that point, Sebring lunged for the gun, and Tex shot him in the armpit. As he fell, Tex drop-kicked him on the bridge of the nose.

Tex – using the nylon rope he had brought along – wrapped it around Gibby and Sharon's throats, then lobbed the other end over the ceiling beam, instructing Sadie to pull down on the rope. With the free end, they knotted the rope around Sebring's neck to act as a dead weight. When Gibby and Sharon asked what he was going to do to them, Tex matter-of-factly stated they we're all going to die, repeating that he was the Devil.

At one point, Woytek freed himself and grabbed Sadie by the hair, pulling her to the ground. Sadie – escaping Woytek's clutches – swung her blade blindly, and managing to stab him in the back. Tex then joined in, shooting Woytek below the left armpit. Still he staggered on. Tex shot again, but the gun misfired, so he began to club Frykowski's face with the butt of his revolver.

Sebring, still struggling to free himself, was attacked again by Tex who ran over and began viciously hacking away on him. When it appeared, after several stabs, that Sebring was subdued, Tex ran up to Gibby, smashing her head with his gun butt, then stabbed her several times, her white nightgown turning blood red.

Meanwhile, Woytek staggered out on the porch where Tex caught up with him, delivering fifty stab wounds to his body. At the same time, Gibby stumbled outside, leaving a blood trail behind her, as Katie chased after, chopping the air with her knife. Gibby soon after collapsed. The whole time this sick scene was unfolding, Linda looked on, horrified, until at last she ran down the hill, climbed back over the fence, and lay down in the bushes, hyperventilating.

At some point, Katie went to see if anybody was in the guest cottage – then occupied by the nineteen-year-old caretaker, William Garretson – and apparently found it empty. Later, during the murder investigation, this proved to be one of the more puzzling aspects of the case: that Garretson neither saw nor heard anything that night, although he was present as the murders took place. The dogs he cared for became disturbed and barked on two occasions during the mêlée, but this apparently was not enough to alert him that Helter Skelter was coming down fast. Garretson claimed that he was watching TV and listening to his stereo at high volume during this time.

Sharon was the last to die, because – as Sadie later explained – she "had to watch the others die." That was a favorite Manson Family fantasy: to kill one victim, while another looked on in horror. "Please don't kill me," Sharon was reported to have said. "Please, I'm going to have a baby." Followed by Sadie's infamous reply: "Look, bitch! I don't care if you're going to have a baby. You'd better be ready. You're going to die." All told, Tex and Sadie stabbed Sharon sixteen times. Later, Sadie claimed it was the most exciting sexual experience of her life.

When the police found Sharon, she was laying on her left side, legs tucked up toward her stomach, in a fetal position, wearing a flowered bra and matching bikini panties, although the flower patterns were almost indistinguishable from all the blood. a rope was wrapped around her neck, one end of it extending over the rafter; the other end leading across the floor to dead Jay Sebring, looped twice around his neck, with a bloody towel covering his face.

To put the finishing touches on their Helter Skelter masterpiece, Sadie dipped a towel in a pool of blood on Sharon's chest, then walked over to the door and wrote PIG on it. Sadie later said that she felt compelled to drink the spilled blood of her victim. The sensation of blood on her hands was "slick and I brought my hand to my face and I could smell the blood. I opened my mouth and I licked it on my fingers…" She considered cutting the unborn baby from Sharon, then wrapping it up in the same bloody towel, and taking the baby to Charlie as a gift.

When all was said and done, a total of one hundred and two stab wounds were delivered to Sharon, Gibby, Jay and Woytek. In the aftermath, Sharon's black kitten padded through the debris of human wreckage, mewing. "They looked like zombies," Kasabian later noted, referring to the murderers. As Susan Atkins recalled: "Everything we did from the time he cut the poles to the time we got back to the ranch was spontaneous. *It was done with no thought…*" Now Charlie's philosophy of "no thought" had reached its zenith.

‡

On the drive back to Spahn Ranch, they tossed their bloody clothes over an embankment on Mulholland Drive, and Linda – appointed carrier of the weapons – threw the knives out haphazardly along the way. Tex flung the Buntline Special away himself, with his left hand, while driving. Once in the valley, Satan's minions stopped for gas, paying for it from the 72 dollars handed over by Gibby.

Back at Spahn's, Charlie was waiting for them, dancing naked in the moonlight with Brenda. Sadie – beaming with pride – ran up and threw her arms around him: "Oh, Charlie, we did it… I took my life for you!" The next morning, Sadie went to the only trailer at the ranch with a TV, to see if they'd made the news. The leading story was the Tate murders, which made her ecstatic. She ran and fetched Katie, Tex, Linda and Clem. As they watched the newscast, it blew their minds that the victims were such "Beautiful People."

At first, the main suspect in the Tate murder case was the caretaker, William Garretson. Initially, detectives had a hard time buying Garretson's story that he hadn't heard or seen anything that night, although neighbors some distance away heard screams and gunshots. However, Garretson was eventually cleared, after submitting to, and passing, a lie detector test.

Police at the Tate murder scene found several clues later suspected to have been planted as a false trail, one such being a pair of black horn-rimmed glasses. LAPD sent out flyers across the nation seeking information as to the owner of these mysterious specs, although no leads ever turned up. Charlie later claimed – in *Manson In His Own Words* – that he had visited the murder scene after the killings, and it is now believed by some that it was Manson who left the black horn-rimmed glasses. However, Manson now denies ever having visited the murder scene.

Several inconsistencies surfaced between the murder scene as described by Tex and the girls during the trial, as opposed to what was discovered by police the morning after the murders. One disturbing little touch apparently added to the scene was a towel draped over Jay Sebring's face, with the ends tucked under the rope-loops around his neck. This appeared to be some sort of macabre symbolism, as the rope had been thrown across the roof beam and looped around the necks of Sharon and Jay. The loops were far too loose to have caused death by strangulation, and the implication was that the couple was somehow linked together in death. Neither Susan Atkins – or any of the other murder participants – ever mentioned placing a towel over Sebring's face. The same goes for leaving behind any black horn-rimmed glasses. During the Tate/LaBianca trial, Ed Sanders – who was passing notes to Manson behind the scenes – asked him if he had gone to the Tate house after the murders, to which Manson replied: "I went back to see what my children did."

As related in *Manson In His Own Words*, Charlie visited the Tate murder scene to see if Tex and the girls had left a trail that would lead back to Spahn Ranch. When he arrived at 10050 Cielo Drive, Charlie carefully wiped Steven Parent's car clean of possible fingerprints, without disturbing his dead body. Once inside, Charlie and his helper – possibly Nancy Pitman (aka Brenda McCann) or Bruce Davis – used towels to wipe clean every place that fingerprints could have been left. Charlie then claimed he "placed the towel (he) was using over the head of the man inside the room," thus explaining Jay Sebring's mysterious death shroud. Next, Charlie and his accomplice took the pair of black horn-rimmed glasses they'd brought along with them, wiped the glasses free of fingerprints, then dropped them on the floor to mislead the police. (Ironically, a pair of eye-glasses was the key clue in Polanski's *Chinatown*.)

Afterwards, a police detective stated that the murder scene "looked ritualistic." The *LA Times* hit the stands with this front page headline:

FILM STAR, 4 OTHERS
DEAD IN BLOOD ORGY
Sharon Tate Victim
In "Ritual" Murders

The impact of the murders on the film industry was one of immediate shock, as rumors ran rampant through Hollywood that they were in some way related to "celebrity." A double murder occurred the night after the Tate murders and the following day, William Lennon – father of the Lennon Sisters singing group – was shot dead. Soon after, Sinatra split town and Jerry Lewis installed an alarm system at his Bel Air estate complete with close circuit TV, hiring around the clock bodyguards. Sonny and Cher bought a watchdog, and *Rosemary's Baby* star, Mia Farrow, went into hiding, because – as a relative explained – "She is afraid she will be next." A number of other Hollywood stars began packing heat and two hundred guns were sold in one Beverly Hills store over a two day period. It's interesting to note that Susan Atkins targeted some of the above-mentioned celebrities in the notorious "Manson Family Hit List" that later surfaced.

A group of stars who had been friends of the Polanski's – including Peter Sellers, Warren Beatty and Yul Brynner – offered a $25,000 cash reward for information leading to the arrest of the killers. But not only did celebrity types become concerned about their lives, paranoia concerning drugs also escalated. Jay Sebring's home was flushed of drugs by high profile pals before police had a chance to search the premises. As one local said, "Toilets are flushing all over Beverly Hills... the entire L.A. sewer system is stoned!"

After receiving news of Sharon's death, Roman Polanski flew back from Europe, only to face a barrage of questions from the press regarding reports that their rented home was the scene of drug and sex orgies, and that the Polanski's were involved in homemade porno films with their fast-lane Hollywood friends. During follow-up investigations at the Polanski residence, police discovered several films and videotapes in the main bedroom closet. Some of these films, it has been rumored, involved an elite underground Hollywood group who swapped smut of each other. One item discovered was a videotape of Sharon and Roman making love, although police never considered it pertinent to the case. During the Tate/LaBianca trial, defense attorneys were approached by the representative of a "rising movie actress" who had apparently left a roll of undeveloped film of herself in compromising positions at the Polanski residence, and was inquiring if Manson Family members had the film in their possession. Many years after the Tate/LaBianca murders, Manson told an interviewer, "Don't you think those people deserved to die?... They were involved in kiddie porn." Like Manson's *Hollywood Star* revelations, one must wonder about these allegations of Polanski making money from kiddie porn, as Charlie's claims pre-dated Polanski's late 1977 rape case of an under-aged girl.

Manson later told a Hollywood tabloid that "Dennis Wilson gave me a $5,000 videotape, TV thing for tapes that fit only to an elite bunch (porno ring) that was worldwide." At one point, two reporters approached the Manson defense team informing them that certain individuals in Hollywood were worried that the case might cause a film industry scandal. The reporters said that lots of porno – mainly of the hand-held, home-made variety – had been discovered during the Tate murder investigation, and that many influential people had put in pleas to the district attorney to lower the charge against Manson to manslaughter, as a way to keep him quiet.

One private investigator informed Ed Sanders that some associates had acquired a "porno ski epic" featuring a famous film comedian shot in Squaw Valley in the fall of 1968, featuring a "cast of thousands" including a well-known actress. In *Doris Day: Her Own Story*, Terry Melcher was quoted that the "murders had something to do with the weird film Polanski had made, and the equally weird people who were hanging around the house. I knew they had been making a lot of homemade sadomasochistic-porno movies there with quite a few recognizable Hollywood faces in them. The reason I knew was that I had gone out with a girl named Michelle Phillips, one of the Mamas and Papas, whose ex-husband, John Phillips, was the leader of the group. Michelle told me she and John had had dinner one night, to discuss maybe getting back together, and afterward he had taken her up to visit the Polanskis in my old house. Michelle said that when they arrived there, everyone in the house was busy filming an orgy and that Sharon Tate was part of it. That was just one of the stories I had heard about what went on in my former house."

With Polanski's return to L.A., jitters grew within the ranks of the Hollywood jet-set, as police began paying unexpected visits to Roman's movie star friends. Soon, information surfaced suggesting a possible link between the Cielo Drive residents and their murderers. A *Time* magazine article – which focused on Polanski – compared the Cielo Drive murder scene to "as grisly as anything depicted in Polanski's film explorations of dark and melancholy corners of human characters. The theories on sex, drugs and witchcraft cults (were) fed by the fact that Sharon and Polanski circulated in one of the film world's more offbeat crowds."

The LAPD asked Polanski to draw up a list of associates whom he considered possible suspects, one of whom included John Phillips. Polanski never completely explained his reasons for suspecting John Phillips, beyond the fact that Phillips was aware of a brief liaison between Polanski and his wife, Michelle Phillips. Polanski went so far as to go to Phillips' house one night to search his garage and check his cars for bloodstains. On another occasion, Phillips, accompanied by Polanski, was driving his Rolls Royce in L.A., when he was stopped by police for non-payment of traffic fines and taken down to the nearest precinct, leaving Polanski to drive the Rolls. Polanski – who made a thorough search of the vehicle – discovered a diary with entries written in capital letters, and he believed that the writing was similar to the word PIG scrawled on the wall at Cielo Drive. Polanski hurriedly photocopied a couple of the pages and sent them off to a handwriting expert to compare with a photograph of PIG taken from the murder scene, although nothing conclusive resulted from the tests.

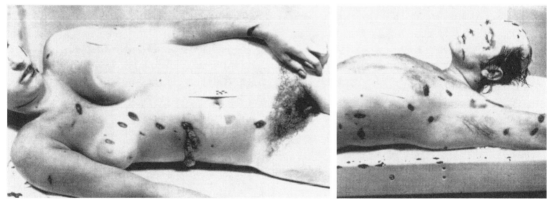

CHAPTER 27

Helter Skelter (Take 2)

After hearing how messy things went down at 10050 Cielo Drive, Charlie decided to show his children the "proper way" to bring about Helter Skelter. The evening following the Tate murders, he called Linda, Katie, Leslie, Sadie, Tex, and Clem together. It was gonna be the same as the previous night, Charlie told them – but this time they'd "do it right."

Charlie directed his disciples to put on dark clothing, and before leaving, gave each a tab of Orange Sunshine. As they prepared to leave, Charlie handed Tex a .45 automatic; for himself, a chrome-plated bayonet. Linda and Tex jumped in the front seat. Charlie and the rest climbed into the back and they pulled out of Spahn Ranch, laughing and singing, as if going to a party, happy and high as they started to come on to the acid.

From Spahn Ranch, they toured San Fernando Valley, then through Santa Monica, West L.A., Hollywood, and Pasadena, looking for the perfect venue to spread fear and panic among the masses. Finally – after driving around for three hours – Charlie directed them to an area south of Griffith Park, pulling up across the street from a home at 3301 Waverly Drive. Both Linda and Sadie recognized the house next door as having once belonged to a guy named Harold True. Previous to hooking up with Manson, Linda remembered visiting True's house, where she had imbibed peyote punch, while Sadie recalled attending an acid orgy there.

Linda asked Charlie: "I've been here before. You're not going to 'do' that house, are you?" Manson replied, "No, the house next door." Charlie got out of the car and snuck up the driveway, creepy-crawly style. A few minutes later he returned, telling Tex to follow him. Peering in the front window, Charlie pointed at a heavy-set fellow in his mid-forties, asleep on the couch. They went around to the backdoor, which was unlocked, and – as a big dog nosed them with friendly curiosity – Charlie and Tex crossed through the kitchen into the living room.

With the .45 automatic, Manson gently poked the portly pajama clad man – Leno LaBianca – awake. Leno asked what was going on, and Charlie told him everything was cool, that they'd just come to rob him, and no one would be harmed. He instructed Leno to roll over, then pulled out a leather thong and had Tex tie his hands with it. Charlie asked if there was anybody else in the house, and Leno told him that his wife, Rosemary, was in the bedroom. Charlie went into the bedroom, and returned a couple minutes later with Rosemary, who had pulled a blue dress over her pink nightgown.

Charlie asked if they had any cash, and Leno told him that the only money in the house was on his nightstand, along with whatever was in his wife's purse. Charlie sent Tex to retrieve the money, and when he saw the paltry sum he returned with, voiced his displeasure. Leno said he could get him more, but they would have to go to the store he owned.

They led Rosemary back into the bedroom, then stripped off the pillowcases, as Tex followed Charlie's instructions to gag them. In the living room, Tex put a pillowcase over Leno's head, then tied a lamp cord around his head and through his mouth. He returned to the bedroom and did the same to Rosemary. At this point, Charlie left, taking the gun and wallet with him. Before leaving, he took Tex aside and told him: "Make sure the girls get to do some of it... both of them."

Why Manson chose Tex, Leslie and Katie to execute the LaBianca murders one can only fathom, but according to Sadie and Linda, they both sent out silent witch-vibes indicating their desire not to partake in the carnage. Vibes, they say, Charlie picked up on, compelling him to exclude them. Manson summoned Leslie and Katie from the car, and charged them with their mission., telling them to "paint a picture more gruesome than anybody has ever seen... Make sure it's done so the pigs will put it together with Hinman and that pad last night. We're going to find another house. When you finish up, hitch back to the ranch and we'll see you there."

Carrying a change of clothes, Katie and Leslie entered the house. In the kitchen they choose their weapons: a carving fork and a serrated wood handled knife. Tex thought he was whispering when he asked the girls: "Did he say to kill them?" But his voice was louder than he thought, because as the girls nodded, Leno went ape-shit, screaming, "You're going to kill us, aren't you? You're going to kill us!"

While the girls were attending to Rosemary, Tex walked over to the sofa and drove the bayonet through Leno's throat, then stabbed him several times in the abdomen. Rosemary began screaming: "What are you doing to my husband?" There were sounds of a scuffle, so Tex ran into the bedroom to find Rosemary trapped in a corner with her pillowcase hood, swinging a large lamp (the wire of which was wrapped around her head) back and forth, keeping the girls at a distance. Tex, who had greater range with his bayonet, struck out several times, making contact with Rosemary's flesh, and continued to stab her after she slumped to the floor.

Katie – who had momentarily ran into the living room to check on Leno – returned, saying, "He's still alive!" His work unfinished, Tex – with his bloody bayonet, reached down and carved WAR on Leno's belly. Katie added to Tex's horrid handiwork by stabbing the dead man fourteen times with a carving fork she left wobbling in his stomach. Afterwards, Katie said she was fascinated by the fork. Having given it a twang, it vibrated, which she thought was cool. She then planted the serrated steak knife in Leno's neck, a disgusting allusion to the Beatles' "Piggies":

> "Everywhere there's lots of piggies
> Living piggy lives
> You can see them out for dinner
> With their piggy wives
> Clutching forks and knives
> to eat their bacon."

After Leno was finished off, Tex returned to the bedroom, encouraging Leslie to help Katie stab Mrs. LaBianca – even though she was already dead – following Charlie's orders to make sure both girls were complicit in the crime. Leslie did as she was told, stabbing Rosemary's buttocks, but with none of Katie's acid-fueled gusto.

Tex showered in the bathroom, washing the blood from his bayonet, as the girls did some interior decorating on the walls and refrigerator, writing RISE, DEATH TO PIGS and misspelling HEALTER SKELTER in blood – intended as a false trail to lead police astray and clear Bobby of the Hinman murder charge. Meanwhile, Tex changed into a pair of khaki pants and a shirt. Hungry, after all their hard work, the tripped-out trio helped themselves to some watermelon in the refrigerator. After making sure the girls had wiped everything for fingerprints, Tex led them out the back door, on the way out patting the head of the LaBianca's dog. Over the course of 48 hours, a total of 169 stab wounds had been amassed: 102 at the Polanski estate, and 67 at the LaBianca's.

‡

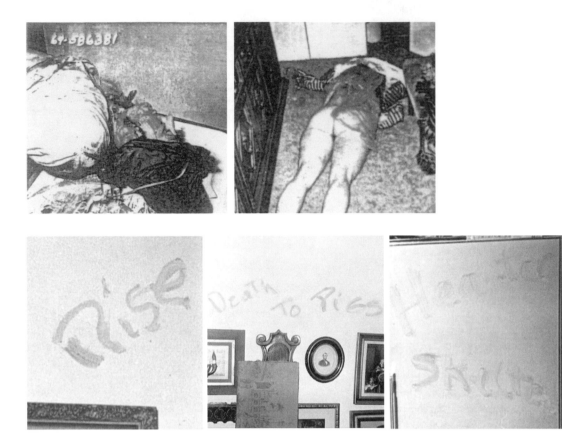

After leaving the LaBianca house, Charlie, Clem, Sadie and Linda headed out the Golden State Freeway, into the San Fernando Valley, to Sylmar and a Standard Gas Station to dispose of Rosemary's billfold. (Legend has it, Manson was under the impression that they were in a black neighborhood, and his intention was to plant another "red herring" clue leading the cops to the black panthers.) In the restroom, Linda deposited the billfold inside the toilet tank, above the flushing mechanism, where it remained for four months. From there they drove to a beach south of Venice, where Charlie and Linda went for a walk. Along the way, they met a policeman, with whom Charlie had a "very friendly conversation."

During their walk – according to Kasabian – Charlie asked her for the name of a "pig" she had recently met who lived nearby. The "pig" in question was actor Saladin Nader. Charlie had Linda take him to Nader's apartment complex, and when they arrived, Linda agreed to show him in which apartment Nader lived. Kasabian claims she took Manson to the floor below Nader's place, and pointed to the wrong door, hoping to save the actor from Helter Skelter's wrath. Before Charlie drove off in the car, he left instructions to do away with Nader.

Following Charlie's instructions, Linda returned to the apartment building with Sadie and Clem, equipped with a revolver. Linda went again to the wrong door, this time knocking on it. A man inside opened the door, just a crack, and asked, "Who is it?" to which Linda replied, "Oh, excuse me, wrong door" thus ending another chapter in the twisted history of Helter Skelter. Afterwards, they smoked some pot on the beach, as Clem buried the revolver in the sand. The three of them thumbed rides back to the ranch, singing "Piggies" along the way. That same night – Linda later testified – she began to make secret plans to escape from Charlie's Family.

‡

On August 9th, the LaBianca's had returned home from Lake Isabella, arriving home around 1 AM. Rosemary's fifteen-year-old son, Frank Struthers, had stayed over night in Lake Isabella with a friend, Jim Saffie, and the two youths returned to Los Angeles the next evening, when Saffie dropped off Struthers at around 8:30 PM. Carrying his camping gear up the driveway, Struthers noticed that the speedboat they had taken to Lake Isabella was still on the trailer behind Leno's Thunderbird, which seemed odd because his stepfather never left the boat out overnight. Frank noticed that the window shades inside the house were drawn, and that a light was on in the kitchen, which also seemed unusual. When Frank knocked on the door, and called out, there was no answer. At that point, he walked over to a nearby hamburger stand and phoned the house. Again, no answer. Frank then called his sister, Susan Struthers, and told her something was wrong. Susan and her boyfriend, Joe Dorgan, arrived at the hamburger stand at 9:30 PM, and from there drove over with Frank to the LaBianca's house.

Rosemary had hidden a set of keys in the garage, which they found and unlocked the back door. In the living room they found Leno, a carving fork protruding from his stomach. Having seen enough, Dorgan drove Frank and Susan to a nearby apartment, where he phoned the police. A few minutes later, two officers arrived at the LaBianca's house and – having a quick look inside – called for backup and an ambulance. Only after the ambulance arrived was Rosemary's body discovered.

That same day, while autopsies were being performed on the Cielo Drive victims, Sergeants Whitely and Guenther of the L.A. Sheriff's Department contacted Sgt. Jess Buckles – an LAPD detective assigned to the Tate murder case – and the two officers informed Buckles that on July 31st they'd been dispatched to Topanga Canyon to investigate the Gary Hinman homicide, which in their estimation, resembled the Tate murders. In addition, a message had been left on the wall – POLITICAL PIGGIE – written in the victim's blood. Whitely informed Buckles that Bobby Beausoleil had been arrested for Hinman's murder and was in custody at the time of the Tate killings. However, Whitely suspected that Beausoleil was not the only one involved in Hinman's murder.

Whitely informed Buckles that Beausoleil had been friendly with a bunch of hippies at an old movie ranch in Chatsworth, and was known to have stayed there on occasion. For some reason, Buckles lost interest with the mention of "hippies", informing Whitely and Guenther that his investigation had already arrived at a motive for the crimes. "It is a retaliation concerning a big dope transaction," said Buckles, choosing to ignore the many similarities between the two murders.

Although the LaBianca killings were supposedly random, former Manson Family member Catherine "Gypsy" Share – in an unpublished tell-all – recalled that just days before the murders, Sadie and Clem creepy-crawled the LaBianca residence. Around this time, Leno LaBianca wrote his oldest daughter, indicating that furniture had been mysteriously moved around inside their house during the middle of the night. Rosemary and Leno had also discovered – on more than one occasion – their dogs in the yard, when they should have been inside. Manson researcher Bill Nelson believed that the reason that the LaBianca canines were docile on the night of the murders was because they were familiar with Charlie Manson, lover of all creatures great and small.

In the 1990's, Sharon Tate's mother, Doris, presented evidence that Sharon had planned to be gone from 10050 Cielo Drive on the night of the murders, and that Charlie had foreknowledge of this. Apparently, someone noticed that Sharon's Ferrari was not parked at the Polanski residence on the afternoon leading up to the murders, and assumed she was gone with it. Actually, the Ferrari was being repaired at an auto shop. In addition, Sharon had planned to visit a friend's house that night, but for some reason these plans fell through. Thus Manson was alerted by an inside source that Sharon would be absent. After being informed of this, Charlie – as the theory goes – set his psychedelic shock troops into action.

In a 1994 interview, caretaker William Garretson told researcher Bill Nelson that on the evening of August 8th – as he was walking down the hill from the Polanski residence to the Sunset Strip – he noticed a VW van on the side of the road with some people in it that he thought "looked out of place." Around 10 PM, Garretson claims he was picked up hitchhiking on Sunset Strip by this same van occupied with a male and two females. Oddly enough, when they arrived at 10050 Cielo

Drive, Garretson asked to be let out, but they told him it was OK, "We're going up to the Tate house for a party." Although Garretson thought this curious, it didn't stop him from opening the gate for them. As they were parking the van, the "hippies" asked Garretson who the car near the garage belonged to. "Abigail Folger", he informed them. At this point, Garretson says he memorized the van's license plate in case the Polanski residence ended up getting robbed. Later, when detectives canvassed the neighborhood to determine if any strange people were seen hanging around prior up to the murders, a local, Emmett Steele, remembered that in recent weeks someone had been racing a dune buggy up and down the hills late at night, although he never got a good look at the driver or its passengers.

Garretson informed Nelson that – on two previous occasions – he had seen the same male in the "hippie" van. One time, on the Sunset Strip, the hippie dude had stopped him and asked for money, and Garretson gave him a dollar. According to Garretson: "He was *scary*." Another time, Garretson saw this "scary" fellow at the Polanski residence, although he never informed police about this individual, or of his ride in the van. From this information, Nelson concluded that Manson Family members were staking out of the Polanski residence prior to the murders, which might explain why Charlie's Family wasn't expecting to find Sharon Tate there that night. If true, this supports the theory that the murders may have been drug related, and that the main targets were Gibby Folger and her dope-peddling boyfriend, Woytek Frykowski, as well as Jay Sebring, another alleged dealer.

Frykowski – as noted – had been set up in wholesale drug distribution by Canadian connections. According to journalist Maury Terry, Frykowski is alleged to have established a drug ring outside the chain of command of his Canadian suppliers, and became a "renegade dealer", which angered the Canadian organization. Woytek also crossed the line by becoming a heavy user, another breach of drug protocol. The subsequent hit at the Polanski residence was in retaliation for these transgressions, and Sharon Tate (as with Steven Parent) just happened to be in the wrong place at the wrong time, and – as the theory suggests – got caught in the cross-fire.

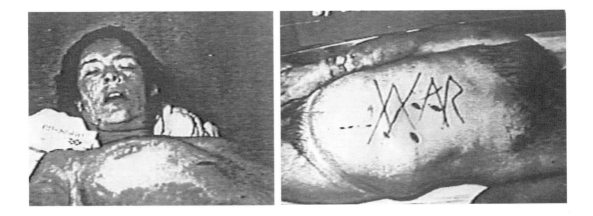

CHAPTER 28
Rosemary's Baby

During a *Hard Copy* interview, Manson admitted having asked Leno LaBianca to hand over a "little black book", a revelation which has led many investigators to speculate about a mafia hit contract taken out on LaBianca. When *Realist* editor Paul Krassner asked Manson about this black book, Charlie wrote: "The black book was what CIA and mob market players had, Hollywood Park (race track) and numbers rackets to move in the governor's office legally."

After the killings – Leno's former wife, Alice LaBianca – was cleaning up the pools of blood and writings scrawled on the walls at the LaBianca house when she came across the "little black book" and turned it over to LAPD Sgt. Frank Patchett. There are also rumors that Manson and Leno LaBianca once had a hostile confrontation in Harold True's front yard.

In the weeks following the murders, detectives found themselves weaving through the complex maze of Leno's financial affairs. According to a police report, Leno was a "...chronic gambler..." with a "...$500.00 dollar a day habit..." At the time of his death – it has been alleged – Leno was in debt to the tune of $30,000 to Frankie Carbo's Mafia organization. Manson, it should be noted, previously hung around with Carbo in prison. As he admitted to Geraldo Rivera: "I knew Frankie Carbo. Frankie Carbo knew Leno LaBianca."

Leno gambled heavily in Las Vegas, and apparently part of the mob debt he owed was from high stakes poker. Frankie Carbo was a known associate of Mafia boss Frank Costello, who had holdings in Las Vegas. As previously noted, Charlie was an "apprentice" of Frank Costello at the Chillicothe Federal Reformatory. These connections eventually led independent investigators to suspect that the LaBianca murders were mob contracted and that Manson carried them out to raise money to bail out Bobby Beausoleil and pay for his defense. According to Maury Terry:

> "I don't think that the black book contained a hit list, per se. I think more likely it was a ledger of who owed what to who and it perhaps contained some incriminating evidence that could have been used for blackmail. I also believe that when Manson went into that house and asked Leno about the book, that Leno – in pleading for his life – might have said that 'the book is up at a safe at my business,' and that he was killed anyway – because we do know that before the police got there the safe had been opened and all its contents removed...."

LaBianca served on the board of directors for a Hollywood bank that police believed was Mafia connected. As a result of the LaBianca murder investigation, several bank board members were later convicted of fraud, and a friend of Leno's told officers that he thought the LaBianca murders were Mafia related.

The weekend before Leno was killed, he was scheduled to meet with fellow board members of the Gateway Grocery chain, but for some reason failed to keep his appointment. Previously, LaBianca was asked to resign from the chain, as his partners in the corporation – including his mother – suspected him of embezzling funds. After LaBianca's death, it was discovered that $200,000 was missing from the Gateway Market coffers.

Prior to her death, Rosemary LaBianca had accumulated an estate valued at nearly three million dollars. A former divorcee with two children, Rosemary had worked as a car hop and cocktail waitress before hooking up with Leno in 1959. After marrying LaBianca, she became a partner in a dress shop, The Boutique Carriage, and began investing in the stock market. To muddy the waters even more, in 1987 a source informed Maury Terry that Rosemary had been involved in LSD distribution. Coupled with this allegation, researcher Bill Nelson discovered that Rosemary had purchased a shipment of wigs from Mexico that came to her shop accompanied by drugs. During this same period, Tex Watson sold wigs in the same area, which may be another connecting point linking Watson, the LaBiancas and Jay Sebring, who sold wigs in his own business, and allegedly dealt drugs.

In the early 1990's, Bill Nelson interviewed Alice LaBianca, who spent time cleaning up at the LaBianca house following the murders. One unsettling thing Alice discovered there was the placement of six logs on the floor, in front of the fireplace, lined up in perfect order. On another occasion, Alice found a brass door knob – taken from the back bedroom – inside the refrigerator. During Nelson's investigation, he consulted Dr. Howard Davis, a self-proclaimed expert on the Zodiac murder case, the infamous serial killer of the late 1960's and early 1970's.

After joining forces, Nelson and Davis began piecing together clues which seemingly connected the Zodiac and Manson Family murders. In this context, Nelson elicited Davis' opinion as to the curious clues left behind at the LaBianca's. In regards to the six logs, it was Davis's contention that these were a message, the meaning of which could be directly connected to Satanism. As for the brass doorknob, Davis regarded is as a form of "judgment" that could also be considered a warning. Although the obvious suspects for these "warnings" were at first thought to be Manson Family members, Nelson later fingered Susan Struthers-LaBerge – Rosemary LaBianca's daughter – as the culprit.

During this period, Alice LaBianca received a threatening phone call one day that persuaded her, and the surviving family members, to move out of the Waverly Street house. From unidentified sources, Nelson was informed that Susan Struthers was the individual who placed this phone call, although it's unknown what was discussed. At this time, Struthers was living with Joe Dorgan of the Straight Satans biker gang. Later, Manson was asked by a BBC reporter if he knew Dorgan, to which Charlie replied, "Sure, I knew Joe Dorgan, he rode with us."

As Nelson probed deeper into Susan Struthers' shadowy past, he interviewed one of her high school classmates who informed him that Susan's mother – Rosemary – had dabbled in black magic. This informant knew Rosemary and Susan during the period they lived near Sunset and Hollywood Boulevards and believed that Rosemary had "...brought it back on herself (the murders), and opened it all up with Black Magic."

Nelson interviewed Struthers' ex-husband, Chuck Wolk, who claimed that Susan possessed "special powers of darkness", citing two incidents, the first which took place in Nevada County on a hot day when Wolk felt a sudden chill and began shivering. Unaware of what was going on, he turned around to see Susan staring back at him with an evil leer. As Wolk rubbed his arms to bring back warmth to them, Susan sinisterly smirked and walked away. On another occasion, Wolk claims he actually saw an object levitated from a mantle, with Susan letting loose a weird demonic laugh, and then, once again, walking away, as the object dropped back down. Soon after, Chuck and Susan were separated.

In the late 1990's, an incident occurred between Struthers (now Susan LaBerge) and a person sharing property with her in Ventura, California. Apparently, the two had a dispute, and afterwards LaBerge was seen walking around her neighbor's house – with her children in tow – performing some sort of ritual with sticks, which they pointed towards the neighbor's house, repeating a chant. During this same period, LaBerge appeared on Pat Robertson's *700 Club* on behalf of Charles "Tex" Watson, proclaiming her love for Jesus Christ, and forgiveness of the man who killed her mother. Bill Nelson speculated that LaBerge and Watson knew each prior to the Tate/LaBianca murders, and that they have maintained a sinister friendship over the years.

‡

Another adherent to the Manson-as-mobster theory is Bill Scanlon Murphy, former Beach Boys session musician and friend of Dennis Wilson. Shortly before his death, Wilson told Murphy: "I know Manson didn't do it. He was an asshole and a criminal, but this Family shit is all wrong. I know." Although Wilson wouldn't elaborate, Murphy's curiosity was piqued, and he decided to launch an investigation that spanned over ten years and brought him into contact with a motley coterie of West Coast porn stars, mobsters and drug dealers.

Murphy's thesis contends that the Tate murders were an attempt by a band of late 60's petty criminals to muscle in on the Mafia's drug-dealing turf. From Mafia contacts, Murphy learned that Jay Sebring was "Hollywood's main candy man", and that his drugs were Mob-supplied. In addition, Murphy claimed to have proof that Tex – and other Manson Family members – visited the Polanski house on drug related business prior to the murders. On the night of August 8th, Sebring was allegedly carrying $40,000 in drugs, and because of this Tex and his cohorts paid a surprise visit to 10050 Cielo Drive to rip him off. Unfortunately, everything got messy when Sebring and his friends attempted to flee, resulting in the subsequent carnage. In Murphy's version of events, Tex Watson was the mastermind and ringleader, painting a portrait of Watson in stark contrast to the knife-wielding mind-controlled Manson Family killer, as he has been so often portrayed.

"This wasn't a gaggle of counter-cultural weirdos," suggested Murphy. "The so-called Manson Family were petty gangsters with big dreams... when they told Charlie what happened, he freaked. He started swearing, saying 'I'm just out of the fucking can and you are gonna put me right back inside, you assholes'."

Due to his investigations, Murphy claimed that he had been threatened by Manson supporters and the Mafia, harassment due in part to information obtained from sources within the California State Attorney's Office and the L.A.P.D. suggesting that authorities knew the real motive behind the Tate/LaBianca murders, but chose to prosecute it as a sham "serial killer cult trial" to cover-up the involvement of Hollywood bigshots and the Mob.

"I have it from the killers that they realized getting tried for mass murder as part of a psycho cult was bad, but pure bloody murder for financial gain was a sure way to get a ticket to the gas chamber."

CHAPTER 29

The Raid of Spahn Ranch

For many years, Sharon Tate sought superstardom. Suddenly – over the course of three days – she attained her earthly ambition, albeit in ghostly form. On Tuesday, August 12th, Sharon's name moved from headlines to theatre marquees, as *Valley Of The Dolls* was re-released, opening in more than a dozen Los Angeles theaters, followed soon after by *The Fearless Vampire Killers* and other films in which she had appeared. The only difference now was that Sharon was given star billing. That same day, LAPD officially ruled out any connection between the Tate and LaBianca homicides. According to the *L.A. Times*, "Several Officers indicated they were inclined to believe the second slayings were the work of a copycat."

On August 16th, the L.A. Sheriff's Office raided Spahn Ranch and arrested twenty-four members of Charlie's Family. The architect behind the raid was Malibu LASO Sgt. Bill Gleason, who had been informed of the arsenal of weapons cached at Spahn ranch, in addition to an incident in the spring when Manson allegedly raped a girl.

The day before the raid, several Straight Satans visited Spahn Ranch, presumably to wrestle Danny De Carlo from Manson's clutches, and to reclaim the club sword which "86 George" had previously bestowed upon Charlie. As one of the Straight Satans later informed Vincent Bugliosi: "A lot of the guys in the club were going to go up there and beat his ass, teach him not to brainwash our members…" The Straight Satans wanted Danny to leave that day, but for some reason DeCarlo talked them out of it. They gave Danny until five o'clock the next day to get his ass back to their Venice Beach headquarters, after which time they threatened to burn down Spahn Ranch.

Why the Straight Satans were so pissed-off at Manson is not entirely clear. Certainly it couldn't have been over the DeCarlo defection alone. Their beef with Manson had perhaps more to do with the ceremonial sword, which – after it was taken back into club protection – was broken up and hidden at their club headquarters. One can only assume that the bikers had become aware of the grim deeds linked to the weapon, such as the Hinman murder, and thought it best to destroy the evidence. However, the sword pieces were never disposed of and were later discovered and taken into possession by LAPD.

During the Straight Satans August 14th visit, a fight nearly broke out between the club and Charlie's Family, but was averted when Manson called down his girls from the nearby hills, which apparently did much in the way of changing the bikers' surly attitudes, as the fucking, drinking and drug-taking went on late into the night. Afterwards, the front driveway was littered with Olympia beer cans, a uncommon sight for Spahn Ranch, as Charlie normally forbid his group to consume alcohol.

Early the next morning, around 4 AM – after the Straight Satans left and everyone had gone to sleep – a sudden commotion ensued, as helicopter rotors whirred overhead, and doors were kicked in by cops. During the mass confusion, Charlie grabbed his clothes and slipped out the back door of the saloon, diving under the porch and bellying his way as far out of sight as possible. As he lay there – contemplating all the commotion going on – it was now evident that he had been set up. And if there was one thing Charlie couldn't abide, it was a snitch. Whatever the case, he'd probably never get a chance to plug the little weasel, as Manson figured the reason for the raid was on account of the Tate/LaBianca murders.

The raid had all the trappings of a massive military maneuver, one of the first of its kind, a civilian land-air operation. In photos of the raid, some of the officers appeared to be out of uniform, wearing a combination of Marine Corps fatigues and regulation LASO clothing. The suspects were placed sitting in a circle in the driveway and included Gypsy, Katie, Sadie, Squeaky, Ouisch, Leslie, Sandy, Clem, Brenda, Kitty Lutesinger, Little Larry, Vern Plumlee, Herb Townsend, Simi Valley Sherry (Cooper), Barbara Hoyt, Cappy Gillies, Little Patty, a young runaway named Laura, Stephanie Schram, Spahn ranch-hand David Hannon, Danny DeCarlo, and Straight Satan member Robert Rinehard.

"Where's Jesus?" officers asked when they noticed Manson missing. Charlie was finally discovered when the cops beamed their flashlights into a space beneath the saloon floorboards, spotting Manson lying face down about thirty feet from the back porch, and instructed him to come out. Charlie complied, and when he reached the edge of the porch, a deputy grabbed him by the hair and led him the rest of the way out. When Christ stood up, a folder of credit cards tumbled out of his shirt. Charlie was handcuffed and carried over to the circle, where they dumped him, barefoot and buck-skinned.

Everyone rounded up in the raid was arrested for grand theft auto. In addition, Manson was charged with the credit card theft. Danny DeCarlo was charged for assault with a deadly weapon when he went for a .45 automatic. Out of the twenty-four arrested, seventeen used pseudonyms. Little did the LASO know but some of those arrested were murderers, who would be released a mere 72 hours later when all charges were dropped, due to an invalid search warrant.

A few days after being released, Charlie and Stephanie Schram were in the outlaw shacks when deputies barged in and arrested the pair. Going through Manson's pockets, a half-smoked roach was discovered. Charlie was charged with possession; Schram with indecent exposure. The lovebirds were subsequently taken to the Malibu station and booked.

Charlie was pissed, convinced that someone had snitched him off. Prior to this incident, the cops barely knew about the outlaw shacks, much less when Manson was going to be there. Plus, he hadn't been carrying any dope, so he assumed that someone must have planted the stuff. At the police station, a lab check was run on the roach, and it tested negative for THC, so the dope rap against Charlie was dropped, as was the indecent exposure charge against Schram. In addition, Charlie was able to skate on statutory rape charges since Stephanie denied fornication ever taking place. Whoever had tried to set Charlie up had botched it, and after giving the situation some thought, Manson decided that the snitch was a certain Shorty Shea.

Throughout 1969, a German émigré, Frank Retz, was buying up land around Spahn Ranch, and by July had purchased the entire property. Once Retz became sole owner, he informed George Spahn – in Squeaky's presence – that he intended to have Charlie's Family moved out completely. Retz mentioned to Spahn that he needed a security guard to keep watch over the place, to insure that once he got Charlie's Family out, they stayed out. Spahn recommended Shorty Shea for the job, which in the long run proved fatal for Shorty.

Shea had worked on and off as a cowhand at the ranch, but his main ambition was to became a Hollywood actor. He was, in fact, on the verge of some modicum of screen success when the Grim Reaper swung his bloody scythe. In the summer of '69, Shorty had landed a small part in a movie to be filmed several months in the future. That being the case, he accepted the Spahn Ranch security guard job to tide him over, which in retrospect was an ill-fated decision, as on August 26th – the night Charlie was released from the Malibu jail – Shorty was killed by Manson Family members, although the facts of his demise, to this day, remain obscured.

For many years it was believed that several Manson Family members – including Charlie, Clem, Bruce, Bill Vance, Larry Bailey and some of the girls – had tortured Shorty and played mind games with him prior to hacking him to pieces, then burying his remains at Spahn Ranch. Legend grew around Shea's death, until it became an apocryphal tale embellished upon to ridiculous proportions. One version had the girls masturbating Shorty, as one of the men chopped his head off at the exact instant he climaxed. This part of the legend was later disputed when Steve "Clem" Grogan (directed authorities in the mid-1970's to the Shorty's burial site. Once exhumed, Shea's remains were discovered intact.

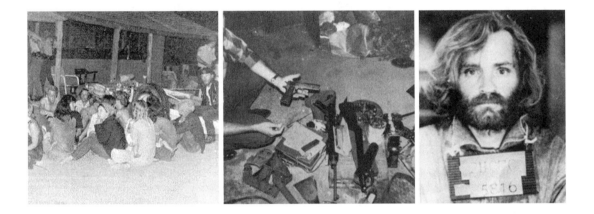

CHAPTER 30
Roman's Return

In late August, *Life* magazine writer Tommy Thompson contacted Polanski and suggested that he might want to "set the record straight" regarding the many decadent rumors surrounding the lifestyles of his deceased wife and friends. Roman agreed, and one afternoon he, Thompson and photographer Julian Wasser visited 10050 Cielo Drive, the first time Polanski had been back to the house since the murders. Also along was famed psychic Peter Hurkos, who had worked with police on the Boston Strangler case. Friends of Jay Sebring had asked Polanski if he had any objections to Hurkos attempting a "reading" at the scene which might help identify the murderers, and Polanski consented.

Upon arrival, Polanski sarcastically announced, "This is the world famous orgy house." At the front doorstep, they noticed that the word PIG, scrawled in blood on the door, was still apparent, although starting to fade. Polanski posed for photographs, even sitting on the blood-splattered porch where Frykowski's made his last stand. When Thompson asked how long Frykowski had lived there, Roman answered, "Too long, I guess. I should have thrown him out when he ran over Sharon's dog." Meanwhile, Hurkos crouched down in the blood-stained living room, tuning in on the dark vibes.

Afterwards, Hurkos announced to the press that "three men killed Sharon Tate and her three friends – and I know who they are. I have identified the killers to the police and told them that these men must be stopped soon. Otherwise, they will kill again." The killers – Hurkos added – had gone berserk under massive doses of acid. The killings, he suggested, erupted during a black magic ritual known as "goona goona."

This *Life* article, supposed to "set the record straight", turned out to be not much more than media voyeurism, and did nothing to dispel the many rumors of strange happenings leading up to the murders. Thompson reported that "Roman did not know what was going on at the house while he was away. All he knew was that one of his beloved Poles (Frykowski) was staying there. Sharon probably knew but she was too nice or too dumb to throw him out. If any creeps or weirdos went up there it wasn't on Sharon's invitation."

Peter Hurkos made the Tate murders his last case, as the stress of psychically reliving the gory events left him a physical wreck for sometime afterwards. Apparently, Hurkos' was under police orders to keep the results of his psychic readings secret until all of Manson's appeals had been heard by the higher courts, but a story was leaked with Hurko's psychic reading – done before the arrest of Manson and the girls – to the effect that that the murderer was a bearded man named Charlie with initials "D.W." Could this perhaps have been Charles D. "Tex" Watson?

During the Tate murder investigation, LAPD began questioning psychics in the prospect of turning up new leads. At that time, researcher David St. Clair interviewed an anonymous psychic who claimed that three officers came to her house displaying grisly photos of Sharon Tate and the other Cielo Drive unfortunates. The psychic tuned her vibes onto the photos and received the name "Charles Mason."

John Phillips even got into the act when he and a reporter, Min Yee, visited a voodoo astrologer, who informed them that midnight of August 8th-9th was the perfect time for a voodoo sacrifice. It had been suggested that Frykowski's Canadian drug dealing associates – who had been involved in Jamaican dope-peddling – were part of a Jamaican voodoo group somehow connected with the murders, and that there were indications that one of these voodoo practitioners had threatened Frykowski a few days before the murders. A short time later, Polanski and Phillips flew to Jamaica to continue an investigation into drugs and voodoo, according to Mr. Yee.

CHAPTER 31
A Worthy Opponent

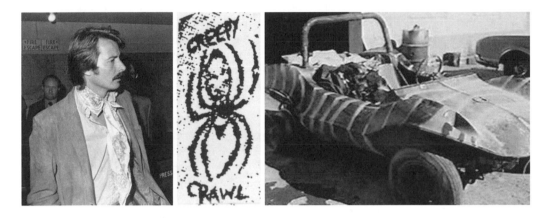

Several days after the murders, Manson showed up at Dennis Wilson's apartment demanding $1,500 in cash to help finance his Family's move out to the desert. When Dennis nonchalantly asked Manson where he'd been of late, Charlie told him, "I been to the moon." Dennis gave Charlie all the money he had on him – which was very little – and Manson left, disgruntled. By this time, Charlie had learned that Terry Melcher was living in Malibu at his mother's beach house. One morning, Melcher awoke to find that a telescope out on the deck was missing, the result of possibly another of the Manson Family's creepy-crawls into the homes of Hollywood's rich and famous. One day, Manson called Gregg Jakobson and asked if Melcher owned a green telescope. When Jakobson said he did, Manson replied, "Not anymore." Ed Sanders later wrote that Charlie's Family set up this telescope on a ridge during the latter days at Spahn Ranch as a lookout when they feared a Black Panther invasion.

John Phillips was another apparent rich and famous Manson Family creepy-crawls victim. At his Bel Air home one night in late 1968, when Phillips heard sounds in his garage, he grabbed a shotgun and went downstairs to investigate. There he found six people, dressed in black tights and leotards, who "tiptoed away like penguins." When Phillips went back upstairs and told his wife, Michelle, what had occurred, she gave him a Valium and told him to go to bed, thinking his imagination had gotten the better of him, no doubt on account of all the drugs Phillips had been ingesting during this period. Later, Michelle Phillips realized they'd been victimized by a Manson Family creepy-crawl.

In early September, Charlie's Family – now numbering around 30 – moved to Death Valley, and it was during this period that the vibes began to take on a decidedly darker hue. Upon Stephanie Schram's Death Valley, Charlie handed her a knife, and instructed Stephanie how to slit throats. All of Charlie's children – even when nude – wore hunting knifes strapped to their waists in anticipation of Helter Skelter. One of Charlie's plans was to take over the nearby desert towns of Shoshone and Trona. He also talked about terrorizing the local police force. First he would kill the pigs, remove their clothes, then leave their uniforms, shoes and hats neatly arranged in piles on the desert ground, as if their bodies had somehow vanished.

Torture, it seems, weighed heavily on Charlie's mind, as many of his fireside rants were comprised of gory subject matter. Manson, it has been said, became "feral beyond description" during this period. According to Kitty Lutesinger: "He got wild when he was out there... he was just beating on Snake all the time – or everybody." One night Kitty committed the unforgivable sin of falling asleep during one of Charlie's sermons. To teach her a lesson, he punched her in the face.

In Death Valley, life for Charlie's Family was stripped down to the basics, and their existence – in many respects – was no different from the desert animals. As has been noted, Manson's respect for desert creatures was boundless; he had no fear of them, either. Charlie was famous for letting rattlesnakes crawl across his naked body.

Coyotes became the official Manson Family mascot. Like coyotes, Charlie's Family ran around in packs, constantly on guard against enemies. *Coyotenoia* took hold, as paranoia became a higher form of awareness. On the morning of the Barker Ranch raid, Charlie was camping out with a couple of the girls when a "big coyote came across the flat and up to me. He stopped just in front of me and was looking dead ahead with no fear. He kept it up for maybe half a minute, and a few times he kept looking back over in the direction he had come. And then I was looking out that way and I saw some rangers. They were coming across the desert floor. The big coyote was warning me!"

A siege mentality took hold. They carried knifes and ate with the dogs, ever wary of the long arm of the law. Sex, as well, became more violent and primitive; they humped on rocks, or in the bushes, just like animals – hiding by day and roaming at night. As one Family member noted: "In Goler Wash, even an insect or a scorpion that is deadly, that crawled up and sat on your arm... if you brushed it off you were going against what Charlie wanted, he said you have to let them crawl on you and you have to learn from them. They are the same as you. We're all here together...

"I remember Charlie, " another Manson Family member related, "how he'd sit sometimes for hours at a time, just looking into the face of one of the dogs, feeling their teeth with his fingers and talking to them. Whispering... None of us were really ourselves in the desert. We were just reflections of Charlie. We were him and it was impossible for us to think of life without him."

One day, Charlie commanded Simi Valley Sherry to give Juan Flynn a blow-job. When she refused, Manson beat her up. Next, he ordered Bo Rosenberg to perform the same act. In fear, Bo complied. After this bad scene went down, the girls decided to sneak away, barefoot down Goler Wash's entire rugged length. When Manson discovered they had left, he became furious. The next morning, Charlie roared down the gulch in his dune buggy, and found them eating breakfast at the Ballarat General Store. Manson stood outside the door and flashed the girls one of his secret signals, which Mrs. Manwell – the store's owner – described as some sort of rolling eye-whirl, indicating that he wanted them to come outside. There the girls informed Charlie that they were leaving him. Always unpredictable, Manson calmed down, gave them twenty bucks, then split. Mrs. Manwell took the girls into Trona where they each bought a pair of tennis shoes and caught a bus back to Los Angeles. Later, Manson sent Clem to L.A. to look for them.

Toward end of September, Charlie was making numerous forays throughout Death Valley, locating strategic hideouts, such as caves to store his ever-growing supply cache in preparation for Helter Skelter, all the while searching for the magic hole. Traveling in dune buggy caravans, these expeditions lasted several days at a stretch, as he left Clem, Bruce and a few girls back at Myers Ranch to keep an eye on things.

The only thing preventing a total Manson Family takeover of Goler Wash was Paul Crockett, who had previously extricated Paul Watkins, Brooks Poston and Juanita Wildebush from Charlie's mental control and, because of this, had become a respected adversary. Crockett, Poston and Watkins were then living in a shack at Barker Ranch, and it was believed that Crockett had placed a psychic force-field around the surrounding area, preventing Charlie's Family from entering.

One day, Bruce Davis showed up at Barker Ranch in one of the Family's dune buggies to deliver the message that Charlie was down at the mouth of Goler Wash, requesting Crockett's permission to come up. Curious at last to confront Manson, Crockett agreed. Soon after, a gathering was convened in the Barker main house to witness this epic confrontation, and Charlie immediately began bragging about the vast amount of food, camping gear, stolen dune buggies and weapons he'd amassed in preparation for Helter Skelter. When he saw that Crockett was unimpressed, Charlie walked over to Brooks Poston, pulled his head back and held a knife to his throat.

Ultimately, a stand-off was reached. Charlie – after filling the hot, desert air with just the right amount of tension – left with his gang, heading back to Myers Ranch. After their departure, Crockett, Poston and Watkins talked late into the night about whether to leave. There was still plenty of mining to be done, and Crockett wasn't buying in to Charlie's orchestrated fear antics. As there was still work to done, Crockett decided to stay at Barker Ranch awhile longer.

According to Tex Watson, Paul Crockett was the first person he'd encountered – during his Manson Family days – who Charlie perceived as a direct threat to his authority. Manson – usually the master at messing with people's minds – was at a loss on how to deal with Crockett.

Crockett, like Manson, was a former Scientology student. But where Manson used Scientology as a vehicle to further his own agenda, Crockett – by drawing from his own knowledge of Scientology – was able to take Charlie to task when Manson incorporated Scientology catch-phrases and concepts into their verbal sparring matches. In this manner, Crockett was able to effectively counter-punch, often leaving Charlie standing flat-footed, or sometimes even back-peddling, a position to which he was totally unaccustomed.

In fact, most of Manson's disciples were unaware of Charlie's past association with Scientology, and considered many of his concepts original. For the most part, Charlie's Family consisted of young and impressionable kids, whose first in depth exposure to any sort of philosophical, metaphysical or religious discipline (that varied from traditional organized religious thought) came to them directly from the mouth of Manson. Thus Charlie was cast in the light of a truly original thinker, while in fact much of his philosophy was borrowed from such divergent sources as Scientology, eastern religions, and The Bible.

Charlie engaged Crockett in verbal sparring matches that lasted for hours, but Crockett always responded in a way as to not provoke Manson's anger, merely expressing opinions which left Charlie scratching his head. Crockett later confessed that he and Manson shared many of the same opinions, but that Charlie "had a hole in his humanity."

As could be expected, Manson felt himself at odds with the world-wise Crockett, due to the fact that Crockett had "deprogrammed" three of his former followers. Tex Watson claimed that Manson considered the idea, at one time, of killing Crockett.

During this period, Charlie's Family steered clear of Barker Ranch, although occasionally they'd show up, build a bonfire, sing and smoke dope. During one of these outings, Paul Watkins claimed that Charlie bragged about all the people he had killed, although no mention was made about the Tate/LaBianca murders.

Around this time, Manson had a falling out with Juan Flynn and Charlie threatened to carve him up, so Flynn split, moving to Barker Ranch where he joined Crockett and the others. Meanwhile, Charlie had been sending his womenfolk down for periodic Barker Ranch visits in the prospects of luring his lost brethren back into the fold. When these enticements didn't work, Charlie tried another ploy, brandishing shotguns with Tex and Clem and discharging them around Barker Ranch. Crockett simply shrugged off these demonstrations, and Manson's inability to rattle him left Charlie visibly peeved.

One night as Crockett, Poston, Watkins and Flynn were sleeping in the Barker Ranch bunkhouse when they heard a rustling outside. Flynn grabbed a shotgun and they walked outside to investigate, discovering Charlie, Clem and Bruce skulking about in the shadows, doing their creepy-crawl routine. A couple of nights later they were awakened again by Charlie and his creeping chums. "He doesn't give up does he?" Crockett remarked, as they then observed Charlie slowly open the bunkhouse door and crawl inside on his hands and knees.

"Lose something, Charlie?" Crockett inquired.

"One of these nights," a frustrated Manson shot back.

At this point, Crockett suggested they go down to the main house, have a pow-wow and try to defuse the tension existing between their two camps. In this setting, Manson and Crockett squared off for a monster three day rap session. Afterwards, the two established a wary truce. Nonetheless, Crockett remained on guard, sensing that Manson was someone it wasn't wise to turn his back on.

The Thing That Crawled Out Of The Cupboard

The raid that led to Manson's arrest for the Tate/LaBianca murders was set in motion when he and other Family members set a Park Service skip loader on fire in the Panamint Mountains. According to Kitty Lutesinger, Manson torched the equipment because he thought the authorities were deliberately digging holes in the desert so that his Family would crash their dune buggies into them. Later, Manson claimed that he torched the loader because he thought it was harming the environment.

Park Ranger Richard Powell investigated the fire and determined the cause was probable arson due to a pack of matches found at the scene bearing the logo of Ralph's Supermarket, a favorite Manson Family dumpster-diving venue. Three days later, on September 22nd – in Hail and Hall Canyon, located near the skip loader's charred remains – Ranger Powell stopped a red Toyota pickup carrying four scantily clad females and one "hippie type" male. Powell was unable to run a make on the vehicle – as was normal procedure – due to the position of the Panamint mountains, which blocked his radio transmitter signal from reaching the Death Valley National Park dispatch office.

Later, when Ranger Powell ran a vehicle check on the Red Toyota, he traced it to Gayle Beausoleil, wife of Bobby B., then in custody for Gary Hinman's murder. Given this information, Powell contacted Dennis Cox of the Inyo County Sheriff's Office, suggesting a joint trip to Hail and Hall Canyon.

On September 24th, Cox and Powell headed for his last known point of contact with the hippies in red Toyota truck. When they reached Hail and Hall Canyon, the "hippies" were long gone. Instead, they met an old prospector, Ballarat Bob, who informed them that the bunch had left a few hours after Ranger Powell had first spoken to them. The prospector went on to denounce the long-haired lot, stating they were part of a larger hippie contingent that had taken over some abandoned mining shacks in the area, and were intimidating the locals.

At this time, the Inyo County Sheriff's office was reluctant to commit further manpower towards the search, due to the logistical challenges involved. Normal protocol for such an endeavor would be to pair up officers with at least two four-wheel drive vehicles, in case one of the vehicles broke down or got high-centered on the rough, undeveloped road leading into Goler Wash.

On September 29th, Ranger Powell acquired a new ally, Highway Patrol Officer James Purcell, and the two conducted a follow-up investigation. At Barker Ranch, the officers discovered two teenage girls, who told them that the person who lived there had gone to Ballarat. Not long after, the officers encountered Paul Crockett and Brooks Poston delivering a truck full of supplies up Goler Wash to a group of hippies. Crockett and Poston went on to outline the group's bizarre activities, which consisted of drug and sex orgies, and far out tales of a twisted cult leader who fancied himself a modern day Christ.

A quarter mile up Goler Wash, Purcell and Powell came across some semi-nude women hunkering in the sagebrush. Powell instructed them to put some clothes on, and they led the officers farther up the wash to another gaggle of scantily-clad gals. As they approached, a male (Charlie) ran away, back down to Barker Ranch, where he grabbed a double-barreled shot gun, then climbed up on the ridge, assuming a position overlooking both Myers and Barker Ranch. Charlie fired the shotgun three times, dodging behind rocks and shouting, attempting to rattle the officers. At this point, the officers thought it best to regroup. They returned to headquarters, then later that night held a meeting with other local law enforcement officials to determine how to deal with this crazy hippie and his cadre of skimpily attired acolytes.

On the evening of October 2nd, Fillipo Tennerelli – a Gypsy Jokers biker gang member and known Manson Family associate – was found shot dead in a room in Bishop. At first, the coroner suspected suicide, but three days later the California Highway Patrol recovered a blue 1969 Volkswagen over a cliff off Highway 190, between Lone Pine and Death Valley. In the vehicle, registered to Tennerelli, the CHP's discovered blood on the seats and floorboard.

Earlier that day, Crockett and Poston hiked out of Goler Wash to a mining camp near Warm Spring. From there, the two caught a ride to Shoshone, and at the Sheriff's Office informed Deputy Don Ward that they had left had Barker Ranch in fear of their lives. The next day, the Deputy Sheriff interviewed Crockett and Poston, who related mind-blowing tales of sex orgies, satanic worship rituals, and a modern version of Rommel's Desert Corps, using dune buggies instead of panzers. Poston stated that on one occasion, Charlie had given him a knife and told him to go to Shoshone and kill Deputy Ward.

On the night of October 9th, a contingent of Inyo County sheriff's officers, National Park Rangers and California Highway patrolman assembled near Barker Ranch for a raid to commence early the next morning. At around 4 AM, as the officers hiked down a gully near Barker Ranch, they spotted two males – Clem and Hugh Todd (aka Rocky) – sleeping on the ground with a sawed-off shotgun. The men were subsequently arrested for possession of the sawed-off shotgun, arson and grand theft auto. Another male, Robert Lane (aka Soupspoon) was apprehended on a hill over-looking Barker Ranch where he had been posted as a lookout, but had fallen asleep. The officers came across still another lookout post with a tin roof hidden by brush. Inside were Leslie, Gypsy and Katie. The police discovered mattresses in the bunker, in addition to a telephone set-up, with field wires running to another lookout post about 300 feet up the hillside, equipped with Terry Melcher's stolen telescope.

Next, the officers descended on Barker Ranch, arresting Sadie, Squeaky, and Little Patty. At Myers Ranch officers arrested Sandy, Ouisch, Brenda and Diane Van Ahn. All told, ten females and three males were apprehended, ranging from sixteen to twenty-six years of age. All but two of the women were armed with knives and appeared very casual about the whole situation, taking off or exchanging clothes in an offhand manner, and urinating in the officers presence. Two babies were with the group: one-year-old Zezozose Zadfrack Glutz – son of Sadie – who had scabs over his nose and under his left eye. The other child was one month old Sunstone Hawk, son of Sandy Good, who had a badly sun-burned face.

Officers remained in the area for the better part of the day, turning up a number of hidden vehicles, mainly stolen dune buggies, in addition to a .22 Ruger pistol, several knives, caches of food, gasoline and other supplies. Also discovered were more sleeping bags than people, indicating the possibility of additional group members still in the area. At dusk, the three men, ten women and two babies were chained together and escorted down Goler Wash. Before leaving, Sadie approached the officers and – pointing to Clem – requested that they "unhook him." When the officers asked why, Sadie replied, "I want to take him behind the buildings and make love to him one more time. He's the best piece I've ever had, and I may never see him again."

‡

On October 12th, a second raid was executed just after dusk. When the cops burst into the Barker Ranch house, Manson Family members – most of whom were sitting around a table – were ordered outside, lined up, and searched. Among those arrested were Snake, Collie Sinclair, Simi Valley Sherry, Bruce Davis, John Philip Haught, Kenneth Brown and Lawrence Bailey. Missing, however, was their most sought after prize, Jesus Christ himself, who had thus far eluded the officers.

Officer Purcell decided he would recheck the ranch house, which was completely dark inside, except for a single candle burning. Taking the candle, Purcell searched through the rooms and, on entering the bathroom, he was forced to move the candle around to discern objects. As Purcell lowered the candle toward the wash basin – and noticed a small cupboard below it – he saw long hair protruding from the partially open cupboard. To Purcell, it seemed impossible that someone could squeeze into such a tiny space, measuring 3' x 1½' x 1½'. Without a word, a gnome-like figure emerged from the cupboard, unfolding himself. After Purcell recovered from the initial shock, he advised the strange little man – who he now recognized as Charlie Manson aka Jesus Christ – to continue on out, and not make any sudden moves. Once out, Charlie – bedecked in buckskins – simply said, "Hi." Inside the house, Purcell discovered another male, who identified himself as William Rex Cole (aka Bill Vance). After being handcuffed during the first sweep, Vance had somehow snuck back inside.

On the hike out of Barker Ranch, Manson informed the officers that he had left his backpack, and requested help locating it. When the officers looked about and couldn't find the backpack, Manson asked if they might be so kind as to unlock his handcuffs, so that he could take a look himself. Wisely, Manson's request was refused. As to the pack in question, it was later found by one of the officers, and booked with the rest of the property seized from the raid. As the police report stated, it was an "army type pack" containing – among other things – sixty-four movie star magazines, one canvas money bag marked "Federal Reserve Bank of Dallas" and a paperback copy of Robert Heinlein's *Stranger in a Strange Land*. Ed Sanders later theorized that the movie magazines had been brought in by Charlie to stir up hatred for all the "Beautiful People." It was during this period, Sanders claimed, that Charlie's Family compiled their famous Hollywood "Hit List."

As the prisoners reached the mouth of Goler Wash – followed by the headlights of the police vehicles – Country Sue (aka Susan Bartell) and Cappy Gillies were arriving in a black Oldsmobile with $500 worth of groceries. The girls were arrested and taken into custody, as was the food, to supplement the jailhouse diet of this weird Jesus and his disciples.

During the ride back to Independence – location of the Inyo County Jailhouse – Manson laid down his Helter Skelter rap, informing the cops how the blacks were going to rise up and overthrow the country, and that he and his group were only looking for a peaceful, quiet place to sit out the forthcoming unrest. According to Officer Purcell, "...two things happened which indicated to me the leadership exerted over the group by subject Manson. At least twice Charlie made statements that would cause the others to say 'amen' two or three times in unison. Also, a few times when the others would become involved in whispered, giggly conversations, Charlie would simply look at them and immediately they would fall silent... The amazing part of the stare was how obvious the results were without a word being spoken."

During the raid, Stephanie Schram and Kitty Lutesinger were found a few miles from Barker Ranch, attempting to escape. LASO Detectives Whitely and Guenther had been looking for Lutesinger ever since learning she was Bobby Beausoleil's girlfriend. Notified of her arrest, detectives drove to Independence and interviewed her on October 13th. At that time, Lutesinger stated that she had heard that Manson had sent Bobby and Sadie to Hinman's to get some money, and when Hinman didn't come across with the cash, he was killed.

The next day, Whitely and Guenther questioned Susan "Sadie" Atkins. Sadie informed them that she and Beausoleil had been sent to Hinman's house to get some money Hinman had inherited. During the officer's interrogation, Sadie admitted participation in Hinman's murder, in addition to blabbing about the Shea murder. Sadie's statement – unlike Lutesinger's – did not implicate Manson.

Two days later, on a return visit to Barker Ranch, officers searched areas where soil had been overturned, digging a trench across a bonfire area where Lutesinger alleged that Charlie's Family had conducted Satanic rituals. Previously, there was a report that Charlie and Tex had taken a girl for a walk in the area, and – after being gone for less than an hour – returned without her. However, there was no indication of a grave at the site.

After being booked for Hinman's murder, Susan Atkins was transferred to Sybil Brand Institute, a women's detention facility in Los Angeles. At Sybil Brand, Atkins gained quite a reputation, not only on account of her weird nickname "Sadie Mae Glutz" – but also due to assorted crazy antics, which included spirited singing and torrid go-go dancing to the music piped into the cells. Atkins became known to other inmates as "Crazy Sadie." Most made fun of her, but two inmates – Ronnie Howard and Virginia Graham – befriended Atkins.

Atkins was assigned to a dormitory bunk opposite Ronnie Howard, a former prostitute awaiting trial on a charge of forging a prescription. The same day Sadie moved into the dormitory, so did Virginia Graham, another ex-call girl. Although they hadn't seen each other for several years, Ronnie and Virginia had gone out on "calls" together in the past, and Ronnie had married Virginia's ex-husband.

For work assignments, Atkins and Graham were given jobs as runners, carrying messages back and forth for prison officials. During slow periods when there wasn't much to do, the two sat on stools in a control area – the "message center" – and talked. It was during these moments that Sadie began spilling the beans about the Hinman, Tate and LaBianca murders.

At night, after lights-out, Atkins and Ronnie Howard also talked; not only about the murders, but about such subjects as psychic phenomena, and Atkins' stint as a topless dancer in San Francisco. It was in San Fran – Atkins told Howard – that she met a man named Charlie who had changed her life, transforming her from Susan Atkins to "Sadie Mae Glutz." Virginia Graham remarked that she didn't consider that such a great favor.

To Atkins, Charlie was the strongest man alive; he had been in prison for many years, but had never been broken. Sadie said she followed his orders without question, as did the other kids who followed him. She said he was going to lead them into the desert, to a hole in Death Valley, where they would all live in a literal land of milk and honey. Charlie – Atkins confided – was Jesus Christ.

Atkins said she had dropped acid hundreds of times, and had done everything there was to do; there was nothing left; she had reached a stage where nothing shocked her anymore. In time, Atkins grew to trust Graham, and eventually admitted her role in the Tate murders. More than anything else, Sadie's bedtime bunkmate confessions would prove the true undoing of Charlie's Family, as Howard and Graham soon informed authorities of these conversations. The DA's office felt that these statements alone would not be enough to convict Manson and the rest of the girls, so they offered Atkins a deal: if she would repeat her story to the grand jury, the D.A. would not seek the death penalty in her case. Sadie agreed, and on December 4th, 1969, confessed to participation in the murders.

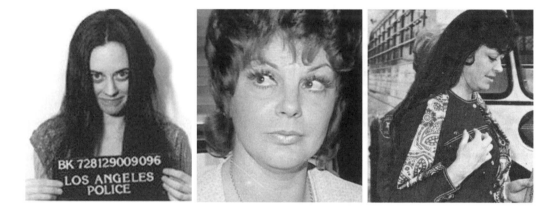

CHAPTER 33

The Family That Preys Together, Slays Together

Several unsolved murders have been linked to Charlie's Family. One with all the markings of a Manson Family hack-job was that of seventeen-year-old Marina Habe, whose body was discovered on New Year's Day, 1969, in the underbrush off Mulholland Drive. Habe received contusions to the eyes, and multiple stab wounds to the chest and neck. In addition, she'd been raped and burns inflicted on her nude body. Investigators later learned that Habe had associated with Charlie's Family.

On November 3rd, 1969 – as Charlie and the girls were being held in Los Angeles pending trial – the body of another young woman was discovered in almost the exact location as Habe's body. A brunette in her late teens, the woman had been stabbed one hundred and fifty-seven times.

On November 5th, 1969, a suicide call was placed from a Venice beach house. When police arrived, they discovered Manson Family member John Philip Haught – aka Zero – on a bedroom mattress, a fatal bullet lodged in his head. According to those present – Bruce Davis, Little Patty, Country Sue and Cappy Gillies – Haught had been playing Russian roulette and lost. But unlike the traditional method – with a single bullet in the chamber – Zero was playing with all chambers loaded, except one. Although Haught's death appeared suspicious, police ruled it suicide, officially closing the case.

A week after Manson's involvement in the murders broke, an *L.A. Times* reporter, Jerry Cohen, was contacted by a young man who claimed he had been present when Haught was murdered. The witness asserted that Haught had not been playing Russian roulette, but was shot by one of the girls present. At a later Manson Family gathering, this same girl sat staring at him for three hours, fingering a buck knife. The frightened young man borrowed $25 from Cohen to travel to Northern California, tentatively agreeing to testify at a later date. Unfortunately, Cohen never learned the young man's name, or ever saw him again.

On November 21st, two Scientology members – fifteen-year-old James Sharp and nineteen-year-old Doreen Gaul – were found dead in a Los Angeles alleyway, each stabbed in excess of fifteen times. When LAPD Detective Earl Deemer arrived at the murder scene, his first reaction was: "The people who did this, did Sharon Tate." This murder was later attributed to the Zodiac killer.

Prior to her death, Gaul had moved into a Los Angeles Scientology commune house at 1032 South Bonnie Brae, where Bruce Davis had formerly lived. Reports placed the Manson Family bus parked on this street on several occasions. While Davis has admitted to living in this "Scientology commune", he denies ever having met Doreen Gaul.

Joel Pugh – Sandra Good's former alleged husband – flew to London in late 1968, accompanied by Bruce Davis. On December 1st, 1969, Pugh's decomposing body was discovered in London's Talgarth Hotel. His throat had been cut with razor blades, there were slash marks on both wrists and his blood had been used to inscribe backwards writing on a mirror in the room. Scotland Yard ruled the death a suicide, but later when Inyo County D.A. Frank Fowles learned of the death, official inquiries were made through Interpol to check Davis' visa to determine his whereabouts. Officials confirmed that Davis had been in London in April, and at a later date, as well. Davis was next reported in Los Angeles in February 1970. After Davis was indicted by a grand jury in the Hinman murder, he disappeared again, surfacing next on December 2nd, 1970, four days after Manson Defense Attorney Ronald Hughes' disappearance. After Squeaky Fromme and Sandy Good vacated a hotel room in Independence, authorities found a letter written by a former Manson Family member, stating that "I hope what happened to Joel Pugh doesn't happen to me."

On December 1st – the same day Joel Pugh's corpse was discovered in London – Los Angeles Police Chief Ed Davis announced that his department had solved the Tate murder case, and that warrants had been issued for Tex Watson, Patricia Krenwinkel, and Linda Kasabian. Davis said that indictments would be issued for five more individuals, and that the Tate and LaBianca murders were linked. This last revelation came as a surprise, since LAPD had maintained from the start that there was no connection between the two cases.

Earlier, on September 1st, ten-year-old Steven Weiss found a .22 caliber Hi Standard Longhorn revolver behind his home, located near the Polanski residence. Steven handed over the gun to his father, Bernard Weiss, who immediately called the LAPD. Not long after, patrol officer Michael Watson arrived at the Weiss residence and took possession of the revolver and, in so doing, left finger and palm prints on the weapon.

On December 16, Bernard Weiss discovered – from a *Los Angeles Times* story – that a .22 caliber revolver had been used in the Tate/LaBianca murders. Weiss notified the LAPD – who apparently had been asleep at the wheel – and soon after the headlines read:

POLICE FIND GUN BELIEVED USED
IN SLAYING OF THREE TATE VICTIMS

Meanwhile, LAPD began digging around Spahn Ranch, searching for Shorty Shea's remains, a laborious process that at times involved bulldozers, and which would not produce any results for another eight years. In early December, Mary Brunner informed authorities where to locate Shea's '62 Mercury, which had been left for several months not far from the Yellow Submarine House. Inside the car, police discovered Shorty's blood-caked boots, in addition to a foot locker covered with Bruce Davis' fingerprints, evidence that would ultimately lead to his conviction.

In October – when Tex Watson returned to his hometown in Denton, Texas – locals observed a "change in Tex." One friend remarked that he seemed to "have a tornado in his head." In late November, the long arm of the law finally caught up with Watson, and he was placed in custody by his second cousin, Tom Montgomery, the Sheriff of Denton. When the LAPD attempted to extradite Watson, Bill Boyd, Watson's attorney, was able to fend off extradition for several months. This, in turn, caused a separate trial for Watson, as authorities were unable to return him to Los Angeles in time for the first Tate/LaBianca trial.

CHAPTER 34
Headless Chickens

In late 1969 through early 1970, Manson Family members moved into a Van Nuys house, and it was at this time that Little Paul Watkins temporarily rejoined the group. Although Watkins – with Paul Crockett's help – had seemingly extricated himself from Charlie's programming, evidently this separation had not been complete. After all they'd been through together, Watkins felt he owed Charlie's Family his support during the difficult period leading up to the Tate/LaBianca murder trial. As well, Watkins still had an affinity for his former guru, for it was he – Little Paul – who Charlie had groomed as his successor. Over the next several weeks, Little Paul met Charlie in jail, discussed defense strategy, and helped his girls secure lawyers. Meanwhile, at the Van Nuys house, Watkins reinstated therapy sessions, indoctrinating new recruits into the art of LSD sex, carrying on Charlie's lysergic legacy.

In February 1970, Bruce Davis was arrested in Inyo County on auto theft charges and as a result, Little Paul was subpoenaed to testify. Watkins hitchhiked to Inyo County with new Family member Jenny, who just happened to be carrying twenty-four tabs of acid with the intent of slipping some to Davis. This plan, Little Paul assumed, was a way of testing him, because Charlie suspected Watkins of being a spy. During the proceedings, Watkins took the Fifth Amendment, refusing to answer on grounds of self-incrimination. Inyo County District Attorney, Frank Fowles, was livid, as without Watkins testimony they'd be unable to convict Davis. At one point, new Manson Family member, Jenny, tried to slip Bruce a tab of the aforementioned acid. Bruce dropped it on the courtroom floor, but before anyone could react, he scooped it up, and gobbled it down. Meanwhile, a cop seized Jenny's purse, and discovered another acid tab. She was held for two days, then released.

In March, Inyo County authorities learned that Paul Watkins' name had been added to the infamous Manson Family "Hit List." Three days later, Watkins was rescued by a friend from a burning Volkswagen van and taken to Los Angeles General Hospital with scorched lungs and burns to his face, arms and back. Needless to say, Watkins steered clear of Charlie's Family from that point forward.

In the spring of 1970, Manson sent some of his girls down into the L.A. sewer tunnels to see what it would be like to live there. Later, Bruce Davis – after being indicted for the Hinman murder – fled into the sewers to escape the law, until he surrendered later that year. The Mansonoids even had a plan to break Charlie out of jail and flee into the sewers, which – as wacky as it sounds – might actually have worked.

In May, Paul Crockett, Brooks Poston and Paul Watkins were in Shoshone when they ran into Clem and Gypsy. Clem told Watkins that: "Charlie says that when he gets out of jail, you all had better not be around the desert." On May 31st, Death Valley Rangers discovered the body of a "hippie" in the sand dunes northeast of Stovepipe Wells. The dead man was dressed in overalls, with long black hair, and carrying no identification. The decomposing body was never positively identified, nor was the actual cause of death established. While there's no proof that this person was a Manson Family associate, Charlie's Family had been present in Death Valley at this time.

Later that year, the National Park Service learned that Gypsy and other Manson Family members were in Goler Wash with two young film makers, Robert Hendrickson and Lawrence Merrick, working on a Manson documentary. Since commercial photography companies operate under Park Service permits – and because no such permit had been issued – Rangers approached Gypsy and the film crew, informing them of the policy violation. In response, Gypsy launched into a vociferous tirade that culminated with: "You are the hunters and we are the hunted, but you've got a mark on your head and some day we'll be the hunters and you'll be the hunted."

The end result of the Merrick/Hendrickson collaboration, *Manson* – released in 1973 – featured several segments with Squeaky, Brenda and Sandy brandishing buck knifes and firearms in "urban guerrilla hotpants." In one suggestive scene, Squeaky fondled a rifle and cooed, "You have to make love with it. You have to know every part of it. To know you know it is to know it, so that you could pick it up at any second and shoot!" In 1977, Merrick was shot dead at his Hollywood film school by an unknown assailant.

Following the Tate/LaBianca trial, a slew of Manson Family related B-movies were released in an effort to cash in on the tragedy. One such was *The Deathmaster*, featuring a band of California hippies who become mesmerized by the evil powers of a long-haired vampire named Khorda, adopting him as their gory guru. Another, *I Drink Your Blood*, depicted a group of blood-sacrificing hippies infected with rabies, attempting to wipe out a town. An adult movie, *The Commune* featured a Manson-type character fucking a headless chicken. A biker flick – *Angels Wild Women* – shot at Spahn Ranch, featured William Bonner as a Manson figure, with other actual Manson Family members appearing as extras. Troy Donahue starred as a Manson-like manipulator in *Sweet Savior*, while *The Manson Massacre* was really a repackaged softcore porn feature.

Easily the classiest production to emerge out of this deluge was Wade Williams' *The Other Side of Madness*, a fairly straight-forward re-enactment of the tumultuous days leading up to the Tate/LaBianca murders. In 1970 – prior to the film's release – Roman Polanski and Warren Beatty attempted to buy all existing copies and destroy them, although copies of the film still exist.

‡

In 1971, Charlie's old jailhouse pal, Phil Kaufman, released Manson's LIE LP, comprising overdubs of demos recorded in 1968. The album's cover photo was lifted from the infamous *Life* magazine issue of December 1969, featuring Charlie on the cover; a 1968 mugshot of Manson on acid. The record's co-producer, Al Swerdloff, lifted the "F" from LIFE, hence the title. "The idea was that the entire press was lies," Kaufman told reporters at the time. "We tried to find the most offensive of the yellow journalism and present it... But it was also to let you know it was a lie, and that's the idea of the LIE cover." The back cover included verse written by Squeaky, as well as an interview with Charlie published in the underground newspaper, *Tuesday's Child*.

Kaufman approached RCA, Capitol and Buddha records to release the album, but all declined. Calling it a "moral obligation", Kaufman pressed the record himself, whose sales at $4.25 each – he said – would finance the release of further records, and help pay for Charlie's defense fund. At the time, the album didn't sell particularly well, due mainly to the fact that they couldn't find a distributor. Kaufman pressed 3000 copies, although the investors – who included Harold True – never recouped their money, as half the copies were later stolen by Manson Family members.

During this period, Kaufman believed his old jailhouse buddy incapable of murder. In fact, it was Kaufman who set up Manson's *Rolling Stone* interview, so that Charlie could state his case to the public. Kaufman still contends that there was never any physical evidence connecting Manson to the murders. Nonetheless, Kaufman suspects that Charlie "planted the seeds" and directed the thought traffic of his murderous minions. Manson may have cut off Gary Hinman's ear, says Kaufman, but he was too smart to ever personally kill anyone. Kaufman looked after some of Charlie's girls following Manson's arrest, mainly because he thought they were innocent of the crimes. Later, when the names of the perpetrators were released to the public – he realized he'd had sex with each of the Manson murderesses.

It was Kaufman's observation that – after Charlie and the girls were sentenced – remaining Manson Family members became fragmented, as there was no one there to direct their "mental traffic." Everyone still part of the group began running around in different directions, presumably performing the will of Man Son's, although in reality none of them really knew what Charlie wanted, and so were like a bunch of headless chickens, involved in various crazy schemes, void of rhyme or reason.

During this period, Einstein Eddy, a fellow who lived on Kaufman's property, alerted Phil to some strange going-ons that had taken place during his absence. "Some people are crawling over the wall, and every night at midnight, they crawl to your house, and then they leave."

Kaufman – who figured it was probably Charlie's Family behind these midnight creepy-crawls – decided on his first night back to stay up, and sure enough, at the stroke of midnight, the Mansonoids came scrambling over the fence. When Phil inquired as to what the fuck they were doing, the creepy-crawlers replied that Charlie'd sent them on a mission to re-claim his sacred music. Just then, Einstein Eddy came running down the driveway, bare-ass naked, carrying a loaded shotgun. When the Mansonoids saw this weird guy, with his balls swinging to and fro, they asked, "Are you gonna fuck us or shoot us!?" Kaufman told them to get the hell off his property, and to go out the way they came: crawling. As they started across the lawn, Eddy fired a shot just to make them dance. They had never seen people crawl so fast!

Undaunted, the Manson creepy-crawlers continued to stalk Kaufman's pad. The next time, the girls surrounded his house: "Phil, Phil, give us the music, give us the music," sang the plaintive chorus of Manson Family chicks. Kaufman called the police, who came and hauled off the girls.

Around this time, Squeaky paid Dennis Wilson a visit, and told him that if he didn't give up the tapes Charlie had recorded at Brian Wilson's, she was going to kill him. Dennis informed Squeaky that he'd already turned over the tapes to the D.A., which was, in fact, a lie. What actually happened was that Beach Boy Manager Nick Grillo – after hearing about the murders on TV – locked the tapes in a vault, where they've reportedly remained all these years.

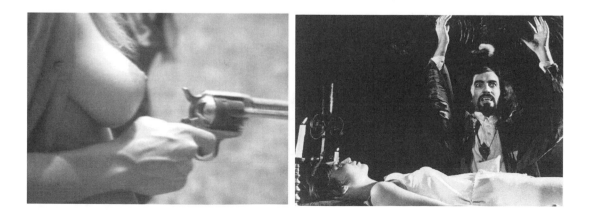

CHAPTER 35

Performance Theatre of the Absurd

> From the start of the trial, wraith-like figures out of some theater of the insane have been
> floating in and out of the heavily guarded courtroom: Occultists, astrologers, necromancers,
> self-styled witches who depart cackling, "I got the vibes. I got the vibes from Charlie."
> –*Newsweek*, April Fool's Day, 1971

On December 10th, 1969, Judge William Keene issued a gag order, forbidding anyone connected with the Tate/LaBianca case from discussing it with the media. However, Keene's order was imposed too late to prevent Susan Atkins' attorneys from selling publication rights of her confession. Journalist Lawrence Schiller had approached Atkins' attorney, Richard Caballero, to set up the deal using tapes of her confession. *L.A. Times* reporter Jerry Cohen wrote the text, and the rights were sold worldwide. These newspaper articles were later made into a quickie mass market paperback, *The Killing of Sharon Tate*.

On December 17th, Manson requested permission to fire the public defender, Paul Fitzgerald, assigned to his case, and be allowed to represent himself. Judge Keene arranged for Joseph Ball – former Warren Commission Chief Counsel – to meet with Charlie and determine if he was competent to act in his own defense. Ball reported back that Manson had "a very fine brain" and was indeed able to defend himself.

On December 19th, Manson appeared on the front cover of *Life* magazine, captioned as "Charles Manson, cult leader" and accompanied by the heading "The Love and Terror Cult: The man who was their leader, The charge of multiple murder, The dark edge of hippie life".

On Christmas Eve, Keene granted Manson the opportunity to act as his own attorney.

On January 17th 1970, Manson represented himself pro per, presenting some rather unusual motions. "Charles Manson, also known as Jesus Christ, Prisoner;" was assisted by other pro per prisoners working under the name of "The Family of Infinite Soul, Inc." Filed under a habeas corpus, the group charged the L.A. County Sheriff of depriving Manson of his civil and spiritual liberties in an unconstitutional manner out of harmony with the laws of man and God. Charlie requested to be freed at once!

On March 6th, Manson asked the court to incarcerate the Deputy District Attorneys Stovitz and Bugliosi for the same length of time, and under the same circumstances, as he. Charlie further requested that he be free to travel in preparation for his case. In response, Judge Keene removed Manson's pro per status, appointing Charles Hollopeter to act as his attorney. "Go wash your hands. They're dirty," Charlie spat back at Judge Keene after losing his right to self-representation.

On March 19th, Hollopeter made the following motions: 1) That Manson be given a psychiatric examination, and 2) that his case be separated from that of the other defendants. Enraged by Hollopeter's request, Manson attempted to fire him. When asked whom he wished for representation, Manson replied, "Myself." Judge Keene denied the change. In response, Manson picked up a copy of the Constitution and, saying it meant nothing to the court, tossed it in a trashcan.

In May, Charlie acquired the services of attorney Irving Kanarek. Concurrently, Judge Keene – who had presided over the preliminary trials – was replaced by Judge Charles Older. On June 15th, 1970, the trial got under way, as Charlie assumed the position of crucifixion, with his three girls mimicking him, yelling, "Why don't you kill us now?"

From the outset, Manson and Charlie's girls did everything in their power to disrupt the proceedings, such as shaving their heads, firing their lawyers, making funny faces and loudly ridiculing the judge and the prosecutors. As Patricia Krenwinkel later admitted: "The whole trial was scripted by Manson." Near the trial's end, Charlie arrived one morning with a bloody X carved into his forehead, as outside the Hall of Justice his followers distributed a typewritten message on behalf of their misunderstood messiah: "I have X'd myself from your world. I am not of you, from you... I stand opposed to what you do and have done in the past... You make fun of God and have murdered the world in the name of Jesus Christ... My faith in me is stronger than all of your armies, governments, gas chambers, or anything you may want to do to me. I know what I have done. Your courtroom is man's game. Love is my judge." The following weekend, Sadie, Katie and Leslie lit matches, heated some bobby pins red-hot, and burned x-marks on their foreheads. A day later, Sandy, Squeaky, Gypsy, and several other Manson Family members followed suit. As new followers joined Charlie's Family, the forehead X-marking became a rite of initiation.

‡

During the trial's initial stages, there was a honeymoon period when Manson was courted by the counterculture and underground press. Yippie leader Jerry Rubin visited Charlie in jail, and was quoted, "I fell in love with Charles Manson the first time I saw his cherub face and sparkling eyes on national TV." In *We Are Everything*, Rubin recounted a three-hour rap session in which Manson told him," I've spent all my life in prison. When I was a child I was an orphan and too ugly to be adopted. Now I am too beautiful to be set free." During their meeting, Rubin felt himself being hypnotized by Manson's penetrating eyes.

Radical underground group The Weathermen declared 1970 to be the "Year of the Fork" in Manson's honour, referring to the sharp implement emdedded in Leno LaBianca's belly.

The underground newspaper, *Tuesday's Child*, hailed Charlie as *Man of the Year*. Conversely, *Rolling Stone* designated Manson *the most dangerous man alive*. When Charlie decided he wanted his life story told, he sent for the stars of *Easy Rider*: Dennis Hopper, Peter Fonda and Jack Nicholson. Eventually, Manson's lawyer's arranged a meeting with Hopper – Charlie's first choice to portray him on film – a two-hour session on the eighth floor of the Hall of Justice. Meanwhile, Nicholson attended daily trial proceedings. Hawkers soon were cashing in on Manson mania, manufacturing buttons, black light posters and T-shirts with his photo, or bearing the slogan *Free Manson*.

‡

By late February, Susan Atkins had backed out of her deal to testify against Charlie, so the district attorney brokered a deal with Linda Kasabian's attorney, promising that if she testified fully and truthfully, all charges against her would be dropped against her. Without hesitation, Kasabian agreed to these terms.

Meanwhile, Paul Fitzgerald began constructing his defense for Patricia Krenwinkel based on the argument that she had been transformed into a doped-up zombie killer under Manson's hypnotic command. Fitzgerald went on to predict that Tate/LaBianca would be the first in a succession of "acid murders" to spread across the country.

According to Assistant District Attorney Aaron Stovitz, Manson's "M.O. is very simple. He says to a new girl 'You want to feel good? Here take one of these.' He gives her acid and takes one himself. Pretty soon she's feeling great. Then Charlie says: 'You want to feel even better? Here. Take another one'. Only this time Charlie pretends to drop some acid with the girl. After he's done this three or four times she's so far out that he can get her to do anything. Especially if he repeats the treatment a number of times."

Fitzgerald's "LSD Defense" was designed to convince jurors to dismiss Kasabian's testimony as the mutterings of a drug-addled juvenile delinquent in pixie pony-tails, disguised as a pure-bred Pollyanna. Fitzgerald's claimed that Kasabian had dropped acid hundreds of times, which disqualified her as a reliable witness. Furthermore, it was his position that Manson Family members as a whole were not normally in control of themselves, thus could not be held morally responsible for their crimes. This was particularly evident in the behavior of the three female defendants, who seemed oblivious to the entire proceedings, as they paraded through the Hall of Justice on their way to courtroom each day, singing songs and swinging their hips, smiling blissfully and flashing secret hand signals along the way. But where once – around the campfires at Spahn or Barker Ranch – the singing of the girls seemed starry-eyed and full of innocence; the sound of their sweet voices now echoed eerily, as they sang Charlie's lyrics for the world to hear:

Always is always forever,
As one is one is one.
Inside yourself for your father,
All is none, all is none, all is none.

Throughout the course of Kasabian's testimony, Manson's defense team did their best to rattle her, although with little success. More than any other witness, Linda did the most to hammer the figurative nails into Charlie's wrists; his crown of thorns in the form of the x carved on his forehead in protest of what he felt was a violation of his civil liberties, executed in a modern day Circus Maximus.

From the very beginning of the trial, Charlie and the girls tried to catch Linda's eye, in order to intimidate her. They ran fingers over their lips, to signify Linda was a blabbermouth, and ran their fingers up and down their noses to indicate when a lie was being told. On the second day of her testimony, Manson was heard to say, "You're lying, Linda. You lied three times." To which Kasabian answered clearly, "No, I'm not, Charlie. And you know that."

Despite the intimidating antics of Charlie and the girls, Linda laid it down for all to see. The drugs and orgies; the control and manipulation; and Manson's *no sense makes sense* philosophy that he used to break down egos, filling the empty soul-holes of his followers with bad craziness, ultimately transforming former Sunday school teachers and high school homecoming queens into murderous zombies.

When Kasabian described Manson's directions to the group on the night of the murders, Charlie put his hand up to his throat and, with one finger extended, made a slitting motion. Undeterred, Linda forged ahead. At one point, defense attorney Ron Hughes asked her:

Q: Now, Mrs. Kasabian, you testified that you thought Mr. Manson was Jesus Christ. Did you ever feel anybody else was Jesus Christ?
A: The biblical Jesus Christ?
Q: When did you stop thinking that Mr. Manson was Jesus Christ?
A: That night at the Tate residence.

CHAPTER 36
Man's Son

REWARD FOR INFORMATION LEADING TO THE APPREHENSION OF JESUS CHRIST
WANTED – FOR SEDITION, CRIMINAL ANARCHY – VAGRANCY AND CONSPIRING TO
OVERTHROW THE ESTABLISHED GOVERNMENT
DRESSES POORLY. SAID TO BE A CARPENTER BY TRADE, ILL-NOURISHED, HAS VISIONARY IDEAS,
ASSOCIATES WITH COMMON WORKING PEOPLE THE UNEMPLOYED AND BUMS. ALIEN – BELIEVED
TO BE A JEW. ALIAS: 'PRINCE OF PEACE, SON OF MAN' – 'LIGHT OF THE WORLD', ETC.
PROFESSIONAL AGITATOR RED BEARD, MARKS ON HANDS AND FEET THE RESULT OF INJURIES
INFLICTED BY AN ANGRY MOB LED BY RESPECTABLE CITIZENS AND LEGAL AUTHORITIES.
　　　–THE YOUNG

　　　–Taken from a sign posted at Spahn Ranch during the Tate/LaBianca trial, written
around a picture of Jesus Christ.

Manson alternately claimed to be Christ, God or Satan. Whether he genuinely believed himself to be any of the above mentioned is open to debate, although I don't believe that Charlie was delusional. I suspect the real reason Manson took on these roles was to use them as imprinting devices. Simply stated, if Manson could convince his flock that he was the earthly embodiment of Christ, then whatever pronouncement issued forth from his divine lips would be the undeniable Truth and the Way.

　　　Conversely, if such a person could convince his followers that he was alternately Satan, then he could likewise instill immense fear and blind loyalty, perhaps even transforming former cheerleaders and homecoming queens into homicidal, knife wielding maniacs or obedient sex slaves.

　　　When Krenwinkel's lawyer, Paul Fitzgerald, was asked how Katie could have performed the abhorrent act of sticking a fork into Leno LaBianca's stomach – and receiving such a kick from this experience when she tapped it with her finger and the fork went 'twang' – he replied, "She thinks that Charlie is Jesus Christ... I mean that literally. They actually think that Charles Manson is the second coming; they are absolutely convinced that he is Jesus Christ." This was amplified in testimony by the prosecution's darling, Kasabian:

Q: Did you disagree with his (Manson's) philosophy in some respects?
A: Yes, I did.

Q: And you told him that you disagreed with it when he told you?

A: No. Because I was always told, "Never ask why."

Q: Were you told that you couldn't disagree?

A: The girls used to always tell me that. "We never question Charlie. We know that what he is doing is right."

Q: Were you afraid?

A: Yes.

Q: What were you afraid of?

A: I was just afraid. He is a heavy dude – man.

Q: What is a heavy dude?

A: A dude is a man. Heavy. He just had something, you know, that could hold you. He was a heavyweight, you know. He is just heavy, period.

Q: Did you love Charlie?

A: Yes, I did. To be truthful I felt... I felt that he was the Messiah come again; you know, the second coming of Christ.

To live up to his legend, Manson was required to perform a miracle upon occasion. One apocryphal tale passed down was the time he levitated the Family's bus up Goler Wash to rest in a spot above Barker Ranch, where it sits to this day, a testament to Manson's mystical powers. While most level-headed humans believe that Charlie actually drove the bus to its resting-place – as opposed to some paranormal feat – it's not an easy proposition to explain how it got there. Negotiating Goler Wash's rugged terrain is an extremely difficult task under the best conditions, even for four wheel drive vehicles. Of course, the means of levitation employed by Manson might have been inspired by chemical enhancement. As an LAPD officer remarked after having interrogated Charlie's Family: "Man, if we were at three thousand feet, they were at six. They were *flying*." So when the subject of levitation was brought up by the Family, it needed to be taken in a certain chemically related context.

According to Ed Sanders, the Mansonoids discovered a secret clearing on the outskirts of Spahn Ranch, located near a rock out-cropping. On one side of the clearing was a hill ceremoniously dubbed The Hill of Martyrdom, and it was here that mock Manson Family crucifixions took place, with Charlie acting out the role of crucified messiah – strapped to the cross – as everyone blazed on acid. At these divinely inspired events, one chosen female follower would play the role of Mother Mary, kneeling at the foot of the cross. Afterwards – following Charlie's resurrection – they'd fuck with holy fervor, high on bad religion and drugs.

CHAPTER 37
Nixon Vs. Manson!

On August 3rd, 1970, newspapers around the country featured headlines proclaiming President Nixon had declared Manson guilty of the Tate/LaBianca murders. The previous day, at a law enforcement convention, Nixon described Manson as "a man who is guilty, directly or indirectly, of eight murders. Yet here is a man who, as far as the (media) coverage is concerned, appeared to be a glamorous figure."

When the story broke, Irving Kanarek moved for a mistrial, but Judge Older denied the motion. Manson immediately replied to the press with this statement: "Here's a man who is accused of murdering hundreds of thousands in Vietnam who is accusing me of being guilty of eight murders." The next day, violating the judge's order to keep newspapers out of the courtroom, Daye Shinn – Susan Atkins' attorney – brought in a copy of the *L.A. Times*. Manson, seizing the opportunity, stood suddenly and turned to the jury box, holding up the front page of the newspaper:

> Manson Guilty,
> Nixon Declares

The following day, Sadie, Katie, and Leslie rose, and asked the judge: "Your Honor, the President said we are guilty, so why go on with the trial?" Thus began speculations in the press that Nixon's remarks might lead to a mistrial, or a reversal of any conviction. Ultimately, Manson's ploy proved unsuccessful. Each juror was questioned separately to determine if they'd seen Charlie display the headline, and it was determined that few had actually seen it. The trial proceeded with Judge Older ruling that the jury had not been unduly prejudiced, and that Manson had invited the error.

‡

On September 5th, 1970, Barbara Hoyt was contacted by some of the Manson girls, who offered her an expenses paid Hawaiian vacation in lieu of testifying. Hoyt accepted and, under assumed names, she flew with Ouisch to Honolulu where they booked a penthouse suite at the Hilton.

After several days, Ouisch said she had to return to California, but that Barbara was to stay in Hawaii. The two girls took a cab to the airport, arriving just before noon, and Ouisch suggested that they get a bite to eat. While Hoyt paid the cashier, Ouisch laced Barbara's hamburger with ten hits of acid, then bid *aloha* and boarded the flight, just before Hoyt launched off on a little flight of her own. Unaware she'd been dosed, Hoyt flipped out and starting running through traffic. She soon after collapsed and was transported to a hospital. Police – after finding Hoyt's I.D. – called her father, who promptly flew to her rescue. Barbara went on to testify at the trial. During examination, Bugliosi asked her what Manson had instructed her to do to Juan Flynn. "The oral watchmacallit", Hoyt replied. After Bugliosi established that she meant "orally copulate", he established that Hoyt only performed oral sex on Flynn while Charlie was present, and ceased when Manson left, further evidence of Charlie's purported power to make people perform his will.

The four Manson Family members who had conspired to blow Barbara's mind – Clem, Squeaky, Gypsy, and Ouisch – were initially charged with conspiracy to commit murder, and three other charges related to the psychedelic burger caper. These charges were eventually reduced to misdemeanor, and the four were sentenced to 90 days in jail, indicted for conspiracy to prevent and dissuade a witness from attending a trial.

‡

On September 16th, several Manson Family women – including Squeaky, Ouisch, Gypsy, Sandy, Mary and Brenda – set up camp on the corner of Temple and Broadway, outside the Hall of Justice. Like urban guerrillas, they wore sheathed hunting knifes, slept in the bushes, then later in a van they parked nearby. To demonstrate their unique brand of political performance theater, a "Crawl for Freedom" was staged covering nearly fifteen miles along Sunset Boulevard, from the beach to downtown L.A., on their hands and knees. Covered by the media, the stunt gave Squeaky – now the official Manson Family spokesperson – a chance to state their cause to the world.

On September 18th, Tex Watson – after having been extradited from Texas – appeared in the spectator section of the Tate/LaBianca courtroom. Gaunt and subdued, he resembled an emaciated Mr. Spock, as the three female defendants giggled and blew him kisses. Watson had dropped over fifty pounds while purportedly vegetating in his Texas jail cell. Apparently, Tex could no longer communicate with others, barely managing a feeble smile, and was unable even to feed himself, eventually having to be fed with tubes. Finally, Tex became so weak that only injections could sustain his life. Medical examiners described him as "catatonic" and "in an acute psychotic state." A formal hearing was conducted to determine Tex's sanity, and the presiding Judge ruled Watson incompetent and sent him to Atascadero State Mental Hospital for further observation. According to one ex-inmate at Atascadero, Tex was faking the whole thing as a ploy to get declared unfit to stand trial. Manson, in the presence of several witnesses, offered to bring Tex out of his funk. Said Charlie: "Just give me twenty minutes with him alone and I'll bring him back."

On November 19th, the defense attempted to rest its case, but as the attorneys made their motion, the three female defendants stood up, shouting that they wanted to testify. Calling counsel to chambers, Judge Older wanted to know what was going on. Fitzgerald explained that there had been a split between the defense attorneys and their clients. The girls wanted to testify, but the attorneys were opposed to this. The girls' sudden desire to take the stand was to testify that they had planned and committed the murders without Manson's direction. Bugliosi suggested to Judge Older that he take the matter to the Supreme Court, however Older decided that even though the attorneys had rested their case, the girls' right to testify superseded "any and all other rights." Older asked Manson if he, too, wanted to testify, and Charlie replied, "No," then after a moment's hesitation, added, "That is, not at this time anyway."

The following day, Manson surprised the court when he requested to go on the stand before the girls. Manson was sworn in and, rather than have Irving Kanarek question him, Charlie requested and received permission to make a statement. The following are excerpts from Manson's testimony:

> These children that come at you with knives, they are your children. You taught them... I didn't teach them. I tried to help them stand up. Most of the people at the ranch that you call the Family were just people you didn't want, people that were alongside the road, that their parents had kicked out, that did not want to go to Juvenile Hall. So I did the best I could and took them up on my garbage dump and I told them this: that in love there is no wrong...
>
> I told them that anything they do for their brothers and sisters is good if they do it with a good thought...
>
> I was working at cleaning up my house, something that Nixon should have been doing. He should have been on the side of the road picking up his children, but he wasn't. He was in the White House sending them off to war...
>
> I have killed no one and I have ordered no one to be killed. I may have implied on several occasions to several different people that I may have been Jesus Christ, but I haven't decided yet what I am or who I am. I was given a name and a number and I was put in a cell, and I have lived in a cell with a name and a number. I don't know who I am. I am whoever you make me, but what you want is a fiend; you want a sadistic fiend because that is what you are. You only reflect on me what you are inside yourselves, because I don't care anything about any of you and I don't care what you do...
>
> I don't understand you, but I don't try. I don't try to judge nobody. I know that the only person I can judge is me... But I know this: that in your hearts and your own souls, you are as much responsible for the Vietnam war as I am for killing these people...
>
> I can't judge any of you, but I will say this to you, you haven't got long before you are all going to kill yourselves, because you are all crazy. And you can project it back at me...but I am only what lives inside each and every one of you.
>
> My father is the jailhouse. My father is your system... I am only what you made me. I am only a reflection of you...
>
> I have ate out of your garbage cans to stay out of jail...I have wore your second-hand clothes...I have done my best to get along in your world, and now you want to kill me, and I look at you, and then I say to myself, you want to kill me? Ha! I am already dead, have been all my life. I've spent twenty three years in tombs that you built.
>
> Sometimes I think about giving it back to you; sometimes I think about just jumping on you and letting you shoot me... If I could, I would jerk this microphone off and beat your brains out with it, because that is what you deserve! That is what you deserve...
>
> You expect to break me? Impossible! You broke me years ago. You killed me years ago.
>
> You can do anything you want with me, but you cannot touch me because I am my love. If you put me in the penitentiary, that means nothing because you kicked me out of the last one. I didn't ask to be released. I liked it in there because I like myself...

To conclude his oratory, Charlie angrily asked, "What about your children? You say there are just a few? There are many, many more, coming in the same direction. They are running in the streets – and they are coming right at you!"

After Manson left the stand, he passed by the girls and told them: "You don't have to testify now." Eight days later, Manson attorney Ronald Hughes disappeared after being driven to Sespe Hot Springs by Manson Family associates James and Lauren Willet. Hughes' decomposing corpse was discovered five months later in Sespe, wedged between two large boulders, the apparent victim of a flash flood. One strange anecdote, surrounding the discovery of Hughes' corpse, was the retrieval of a postcard downstream, free of water damage, addressed to Sharon Tate.

In his January 15th, 1971 closing argument, Bugliosi referred to Charlie as "the dictatorial master of a tribe of bootlicking slaves," while Sadie, Katie and Leslie were "a closely-knit band of mindless robots." At one point, Bugliosi was interrupted "when Judi Shapiro, nineteen, a shapely blonde who described herself as an 'apprentice witch' stood up in court and yelled, 'I have proof that key prosecution witnesses were coerced, bribed and threatened.'" Shapiro was removed, and later that day the jury began deliberations. On January 25th, the four defendants were convicted on twenty-seven counts of murder.

On March 4th, Manson trimmed his beard to a neat fork and shaved his head. As he explained to newsman, "I am the Devil and the Devil always has a bald head." On March 29th – with shaved heads and bloody crosses on their foreheads – Charlie and the girls entered the courtroom for the verdict. The penalty, in each case, was death. Afterwards, the four were filled with fury, as Sadie shouted out: "Better lock your doors and watch you own kids!" The Family members on vigil outside also shaved their heads in solidarity, and continued protesting. Ten months later, in February 1972, the California death penalty was overturned, and their sentences reduced to life imprisonment.

CHAPTER 38
The Hawthorne Shoot-Out

In the summer of 1971, Manson formed an alliance with the Aryan Brotherhood (A.B.) at Folsom Prison by arranging visits between A.B. members and his girls, who – following Charlie's orders – gave the A.B.-ers hand jobs and lap dances in the Folsom Prison visiting room. Charlie swung a deal with the A.B. where they would protect him against prison beatings and homosexual assaults on the inside and, in return, Charlie's girls would look after A.B. members on the outside.

The first A.B. member to join the Manson fold was Kenneth Como, who led a group of Manson Family members on a ten-minute shootout during an attempted robbery of the Western Surplus Store in Los Angeles on August 21st, 1971. This incident later became known as "The Hawthorne Shoot-Out." Others involved in the robbery included Mary Brunner, Gypsy, Charles Lovett (aka Chuckleberry), Little Larry and Dennis Rice.

Shortly after closing time, the Mansonoids burst into the store and ordered a clerk and two customers to lie down. They then began carrying out rifles, shotguns and pistols to a van parked in the alley. Around 140 guns had collected when they were spotted by a police patrol car, and LAPD immediately sealed off the alleyway. The gang of six came out with guns a-blazing – Gypsy leading the charge – and in a ten-minute gun battle, the Family's van was riddled with over fifty bullets. In return, Manson Family members sent twenty bullets of their own into the black-and-whites. Amazingly, no one was killed, although three Family members received slight wounds.

After the arrest of the Manson Family Six, it was learned that this same group had been responsible for the August 13th robbery of a Covina beer distributorship. The motive behind these robberies was to collect an arsenal of weapons to break Manson out of prison. According to Vincent Bugliosi, their madcap plan included using the stolen weapons to hijack a 747 and kill one passenger every hour until Manson – and all other incarcerated Family members – were released.

On October 20th, Kenneth Como escaped from the Hall of Justice. Dangling a rope of bed sheets from his cell window on the thirteenth floor, Como was able to descend five floors and kick in the window of the very same courtroom where the Tate/LaBianca trials had been held. From there, Como made his way down a stairwell to the street where he found a waiting for him, and sped away to momentary freedom. At a previously agreed upon location, Como switched vehicles, hopping into a van driven by Sandy Good. Unfortunately for Como, Good crashed the van trying to outrun police, and he was recaptured.

Como in due time became a clan leader in his own right, as those Manson Family members who had followed him into armed battle now became his followers. Gypsy declared herself to Como, along with Mary Brunner, Charlie's first Manson Family convert. This resulted in a dispute between Manson and Como that soon came to a head, leading to the subsequent breakdown of the pact between the Aryan Brotherhood. and Charlie's Family.

CHAPTER 39
The Parts Left Out of the Manson Case

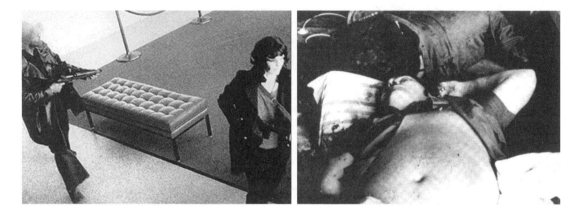

Another counterculture personality who entered the Manson Family sphere was Paul Krassner, editor of *The Realist*. Krassner had written Manson in prison, seeking material for a book he was working on called *The Parts Left Out of the Manson Case*. "Call Squeaky," Charlie replied. To break the ice, Krassner brought along several 300-mic tabs of acid , which he, Squeaky, Brenda and Sandy dropped. Coming on to the stuff, the girls sang along to the Moody Blues, as well as a new tune that'd just hit the charts: "A Horse With No Name." The song's lyric, Squeaky explained, was pregnant with meaning, speaking of oceans beneath the desert floor; the same revelation that Charlie rapped about during his many acid fueled Death Valley rap sessions.

Sandy and Squeaky invited Krassner to join them in a bathtub *ménage à trois*, but he declined because he couldn't get the shower scene from *Psycho* out of his mind. Instead, the girls let him try on Charlie's ceremonial vest. Krassner sat fully clothed on the toilet, while the two girls bathed nude in front of him. At one point, Brenda asked Krassner for another hit of acid to send to Charlie in prison. She pulverized the tab and affixed the residue to a piece of paper with vegetable dye, inscribing "Words fly fast," on it, explaining that Charlie would know exactly what that meant.

During the course of Krassner's research, he became aware of Charlie's involvement with Scientology, and that there had been an E-Meter at Spahn Ranch. Krassner learned that Charlie had visited the Scientology Celebrity Center in L.A., mingling with rich and famous Scientologists. Krassner also obtained a copy of the original Scientology log entry, which read: "7/31/68, new name, Charles Manson, Devt., No address, in for processing + Ethics + Type III." Apparently, the classification "Type III" identified the subject in question as "psychotic."

Seeking more information, Krassner visited Warren Hinkle, the editor of *Scanlon's*, who was working on an article about Manson. Hinkle pointed Krassner in the direction of Hal Lipset, an L.A. private investigator, who informed him that not only did LAPD seize pornographic videotapes from the Polanski house after the murders, but that certain LAPD officers were selling these videos on the black market. Lipset talked with one source within the LAPD who told him exactly which porno flicks were available: a total of seven hours selling for a quarter of a million dollars. Among these videos, the most notorious allegedly featured Greg Bautzer – an attorney for Howard Hughes – fornicating with the former wife of a certain former governor. Also included in this video collection was Sharon Tate with a popular singer; Sharon Tate with Steve McQueen; and another featuring Tate with two black bisexual men.

Lipset informed Krassner about a videotape involving Cass Elliot in an orgy with Yul Brynner and Peter Sellers. Brynner and Sellers, it might be recalled, were part of a group offering a $25,000 reward for the capture of the Tate killers. This disclosure regarding Mama Cass particularly upset Krassner, as he and the late singer had been good friends. Later, Krassner tracked down a reporter who told him that the LAPD had shown her video porn starring Susan Atkins and Woytek Frykowski. When Krassner posed the question to Manson: "Did Susan sleep with Frykowski?" Charlie replied: "You are ill advised and misled. Sebring done Susan's hair and I think he sucked one or two of her dicks, I'm not sure who she was walking out from her stars and cages, that girl *loves* dick, you know what I mean, hon. Yul Brynner, Peter Sellers..."

In an interview with Ronald Reagan Jr. in the early 1990's, Manson stated that his conviction for Tate/LaBianca had nothing to do with the actual murders, but was really about missing video tapes, which showed Peter Sellers and Yul Brynner "gobbling on each other's knobs."

In *5 to Die*, authors LeBlanc and Davis wrote:

> Reporters who were scouring every possible source for film of the Manson Family in later days said they were cautioned that if they ever ran into a certain footage of motion picture film, in which numerous statutory laws concerning oral copulation, sodomy, and all around lascivious conduct were flagrantly violated in a succession of scenes featuring the same cast of a dozen men and women, the law would be deeply indebted for the return of the film. According to the story, to cinch its investigation of the wild criminal activities going on at the Spahn Ranch hippie colony, the law had sent in an undercover man the last few days before the raid. The undercover man was convincing enough as a hippie, with his shaggy hair and fragmentary beard, but Charles Manson's initiation processes forced the man into a difficult position. Either he join them in a sex orgy and break every known sex law himself, or he would give himself away as an outsider, aborting his mission. Unfortunately, perhaps influenced by LSD-laced drinks, he chose to stay and play, and doubly unfortunately, this particular orgy, whether by chance or due to a suspicious hunch that clicked in Manson's keen mind, was filmed in its entirety, the participants identifiable. Could it be that the fear of such a film popping up in the hands of the defense made the District Attorney's Office decide, in the interests of justice, that the (raid) case not be prosecuted?

Prior to the Tate/LaBianca murders, Krassner met an individual named Billy Doyle through Mama Cass. At the time, Doyle had just arrived from Jamaica and during breakfast one morning, Doyle, Cass, and Krassner sat around talking about the music scene, drug use and political activism. Doyle liked to act tough and portray an air of mystery. "We know all about you," he finally told Krassner. "You better watch your step."

Later, Krassner came across Doyle's name in Sanders' *The Family*. Doyle, it has been alleged, was Frykowski's main drug connection. Sanders wrote: "Sometime during (the first week of August) a dope dealer from Toronto named Billy Doyle was whipped and video-buggered at (the Tate residence). In the days before his death, Sebring had complained to a receptionist at his hair shop that someone had burned him for $2,000 worth of cocaine and he wanted vengeance. Billy Doyle was involved in a large-scale dope-import operation involving private planes from Jamaica." According Sanders' account, Sebring and Frykowski tied Doyle to a chair, whipped him, then sodomized him while video-taping the event before an audience. Police later eliminated Doyle as a suspect in the case. According to Mike McGann, a detective assigned to the murders: "We investigated the incident. It hadn't taken place at Cielo Drive, but at Cass Eliot's house, and didn't involve either Sharon Tate or Jay Sebring."

According to Jay Sebring's hair salon receptionist – a lady named McCaffrey – her boyfriend, Joel Rostau, delivered cocaine and mescaline to 10050 Cielo Drive on the night of the murders. Later – during the Tate/LaBianca trial – several Sebring associates were murdered, among them Rostau. In this regard, Krassner suspected that the Manson Family had served as an underworld hit squad.

In the last week of life, Woytek Frykowski appeared out of control. One day he showed up at John Phillips' house, demanding to be let in. According to Phillips, Woytek seemed, "slightly incoherent and had a bizarre presence about him. I wouldn't let him in, but he insisted. I just didn't feel right about it. He was rumored to have had weird drug connections and was part of the crowd that had been feeding off Cass. I apologized and closed the door in his face."

In *Papa John*, Phillips detailed the deterioration of Cass Elliot, who had fallen in with a bad crowd that "hung around (her) in the hills or around the house that Terry Melcher sublet to Roman Polanski up on Cielo Drive.... Among them were Jay Sebring... Woytek Frykowski... and the same boyfriend of Cass' who had been sought by Scotland Yard a year before."

While visiting Cass Elliot at Caesars in Las Vegas – on the opening night of her first solo performance – Phillips happened upon this same bunch. It was Phillips opinion that this group contributed greatly to Cass's deterioration, plying her with drugs and – like leeches – sucking her dry of her fame and fortune. Although she was supposed to perform that night, Cass was a total wreck. With her in the dressing room was an individual named "Billy", seated over an immense block of Iranian hash the size of a cheese wheel. When Phillips saw the huge hunk o' hash, he became enraged. In between sets, Phillips confronted Billy, blaming him for Cass' deterioration. "Billy" could perhaps have been Billy Doyle, or another shadowy character, whom we will soon discover, named William Mentzer.

In his obsessive pursuit to get to the bottom of the Manson murder mystery, Krassner hooked up with the noted conspiracy theorist, Mae Brussell. When asked if she knew anything about the Manson case, Brussell replied: "Of course. The so-called Manson murders were actually orchestrated by military intelligence in order to destroy the counterculture movement. It's no different from the Special Forces in Vietnam, disguised as Vietcong, killing and slaughtering to make the Vietcong look bad... Charles Manson was a patsy, identical with Lee Harvey Oswald, Sirhan Sirhan, James Earl Ray. The Manson thing was a hidden war against the youth culture. People sharing their housing, their food, their cars, recycling their old clothes. Make your own candles and turn off the electricity. It was an economic revolution, affecting everything from the cosmetic industry to the churches."

Brussell put Krassner in touch with Preston Guillory, a former deputy sheriff in Los Angeles, who informed him:

> A few weeks prior to the Spahn Ranch raid, we were told that we weren't to arrest Manson or any of his followers. We had a sheaf of memos on Manson – that they had automatic weapons at the ranch, that citizens had complained about hearing machine guns at night, that firemen from the local fire station had been accosted by armed members of Manson's band and told to get out of the area. Deputies started asking, 'Why aren't we gonna make the raid sooner?' I mean, Manson's a parole violator, we know there's narcotics and booze. He's living at the ranch with a bunch of minor girls in complete violation of his parole. Deputies at the station quite frankly became very annoyed that no action was being taken about Manson...
>
> My contention is this – the reason Manson was left on the street was because our department thought that he was going to launch an attack on the Black Panthers. We were getting intelligence briefings that Manson was anti-black and he had supposedly killed a Black Panther. Manson was a very ready tool, apparently, because he did have some racial hatred and he wanted to vent it. But they hadn't anticipated him attacking someone other than the Panthers. You have to remember that Charlie was on federal parole all this time from '67 to '69. Do you realize all the shit he was getting away with while he was on parole? Now here's the kicker. Before the Tate killings he had been arrested at Malibu twice for statutory rape. Never got (imprisoned for parole violation). Manson liked to ball young girls, so he just did his thing and he was released, and they didn't put any parole on him. But somebody very high up was controlling everything that was going on and was seeing to it that we didn't bust Manson.

Throughout the 1960's, *agent provocateurs* were used to infiltrate and sabotage radical activist groups at the behest of the FBI, LAPD, and other law enforcement and intelligence agencies. The Black Panther Party (BPP) was the primary target of these operations. Other radical groups, such as the Yippies and Weather Underground, were targeted by the FBI's COINTELPRO, also known as Counter-Intelligence Program. Manson may have very well been used in this manner, as an *agent provocateur*.

COINTELPRO was created as a means of monitoring Communist activity in the U.S., but quickly came to encompass radical groups like the Panthers. COINTELPRO used questionable tactics to secure information, including wiretaps, fabricated publications and false letters to agitate radical leaders, infiltration of group meetings and the leaking of information to the press for the purpose of creating opposition among various radical groups. At its height, COINTELPRO agents raided safe houses and activist headquarters, jailed and killed prominent leaders in the youth movement, particularly members of the BPP.

COINTELPRO activities extended to other black leaders like Martin Luther King, who the FBI attempted to frame in a sex scandal. MLK was allegedly assassinated by James Earl Ray, another probable patsy of intelligence agency tomfoolery. Also in on the act was the CIA's Domestic Operations Division, who – as far back as 1967 – had begun a surveillance program against the Panthers.

During the early 1970's, Vacaville Medical Facility – later to house Manson – was designated a "Maximum Psychiatric Diagnostic Unit"; a behavior modification operation that allegedly produced mind-controlled assassins programmed to kill prominent blacks, including BPP leaders Huey Newton and Bobby Seale. According to researcher Alex Constantine, CIA agent Colston Westbrook was in charge of this program which produced the group of prisoners who formed the Symbionese Liberation Army (SLA). This group included Donald DeFreeze, who kidnapped Patty Hearst and led the SLA to a fiery demise. According to Constantine, DeFreeze "described his incarceration on the prison's third floor, where he was corralled by C.I.A. agents who drugged him and said he would become the leader of a radical movement and kidnap a wealthy person. After his escape from Vacaville (an exit door was left unlocked for him), that's exactly what he did."

In recent years, similar evidence has come to light suggesting that Jonestown was a possible CIA mind control experiment that self-destructed, and when many of Jones' followers refused to swallow the poison Kool-Aid cocktails proffered, they were assisted in their "mass suicide" by bullets and/or hypodermic needles filled with death-inducing drugs, delivered courtesy of Jones' goon squad.

Jim Jones entertained a long association with the U.S. Intelligence Community. To a lesser degree, Manson may have been playing the same shadowy role. If mass mind control experiments exist on the level that some suggest, then to conceal and protect the true participants involved in these crimes, scapegoats must be offered up on The Nightly News' sacrificial alter. Enter Jim Jones, Donald DeFreeze, Dave Koresh, etc. Or, in a similar vein, James Earl Ray or Lee Harvey Oswald; patsies, one and all, offered in sacrifice to placate the dumb-downed masses. Manson might have been just one such construct; a myth created to explain the creation of zombie automatons programmed to kill.

Mae Brussell's contended that such incidents as the Tate/LaBianca murders – or Waco – were part of a "strategy of tension", the end result of which was to create an atmosphere – via the test-tube creation of mass murderers and killer cults – where the political spectrum of the country is moved farther to the "right." This, in turn, would lead to an erosion of civil liberties, justification for stripping away our constitutional rights and eventually the construction of a police state. Some would say that we've come a long way on the road toward fascism since Helter Skelter came down fast on August 9th, 1969. Others would even suggest that we've reached the point of no return, and that the forthcoming placement of the Mark of the Beast on our foreheads is but a formality.

Brussell – in an article titled "Why Was Patricia Hearst Kidnapped?" – outlined the "strategy of tension" in which such groups as the SLA participated, whether witting or unwitting. The SLA's role – according to Brussell – was that of *agent provocateurs*, baiting members of radical groups to join the "revolution", trying to draw these groups into violent action, which in turn would justify the subsequent assassinations of radical leaders at the hands of The Establishment.

In the mid 70's, a brief alliance between Charlie's Family and the SLA was formed, the design of which was to engineer Manson's escape from prison. Sacramento police detectives estimated that Manson Family members and SLA associates in jail had accumulated 1.5 million dollars over the course of two years using a sophisticated credit-card scam in California, Oregon, Nevada and Arizona.

Theoretically, Charlie's Family were utilized in the same manner as the SLA; to create a "strategy of tension" thus inciting a race war in the U.S. that would, in turn, provide a rationale to dismantle the Constitution. Brussell listed several goals to be achieved by the creation of such an elaborate conspiracy:

* Create a national fear of terrorist organizations, and of future kidnappings, accompanied by increased bombings.

* Discredit communes.

* Escalate domestic race war between blacks and whites.

* Increase public and private police forces and security agents.

* Turn the population into informers, who turn each other in.

* Link demons and the Devil to communists, radicals, leftists and other deviants from the official Government line, and virtuous, right-thinking Christianity to strong-arm police tactics.

CHAPTER 40
The Motive

In 1971, Ed Sanders was working on a follow up to *The Family*, called *The Motive*, a project he later decided to drop in fear of his life. When Paul Krassner asked him what was "the motive", Sanders cryptically replied, "Ask Peter Folger," Abigail Folger's coffee tycoon father. While researching *The Family* – Sanders told Krassner – he had received the Mafia "kiss of death" from Peter Folger's lawyer. Given these circumstances, Krassner began to suspect that Abigail Folger's death might have been on account of her political leanings, as she had been an ardent Tom Bradley supporter – the first black mayor of Los Angeles – despite protestations of her father, a reputed racist. When Sanders advised him to "ask Peter Folger", Krassner at first assumed that Folger had conducted his own murder investigation, and that he had answers. Later, Krassner suspected worse: that Folger might have actually had his daughter murdered due to her support of minority causes, as well as shacking up with a drug dealing foreigner. Granted, this was a far-fetched theory, but the deeper Krassner looked into the Tate/LaBianca murders, the weirder things got.

As Krassner's research took ever more bizarre twists, he began analyzing Folger's television commercials, and became convinced that Peter Folger was using them to program viewers with racism, depicting blacks in a negative light.

The juiciest lead in Krassner's research came when Mae Brussell informed him that a Naval Intelligence agent named Nathaniel Dight had associated with Tex Watson prior to the murders. "Aha!" thought Krassner: L. Ron Hubbard had been with Navel Intelligence. The Committee to Investigate Assassinations had also linked Lee Harvey Oswald with Naval Intelligence! Even the infamous Zodiac killer had left obsolete Naval Intelligence ciphers. Dight, Brussell claimed, was a Postgraduate at the Navy's Monterey Language School – where only intelligence officers were admitted. Dight, she said, had used the cover of a "hippie artist" while working as an undercover agent provocateur to infiltrate Charlie's Family.

According to Brussell, Dight was the Manson Family's main drug supplier. After the murders, Dight, "...cut his hair, put his shoes back on..." and returned to the Monterey Language School, setting aside his hippie guise, which had served its purpose. Prior to shedding these hippie trappings, Dight had done artwork for an "underground" magazine that, Brussell asserted, "...was a conduit for CIA funds for medical research in mind control, intelligence money for electrode implants and for LSD experiments, according to documents I got from the Pentagon."

Mae Brussell was alluding to MK-ULTRA, the CIA's covert mind control experiments started in 1953 under a program exempt from congressional oversight. Agents and "spychiatrists" involved in MK-ULTRA tested radiation, electric shock, microwaves, and electrode implants on unwitting subjects, including prisoners at Vacaville State Prison, Manson's future home.

MK-ULTRA's ultimate goal was to create sleeper agents that could be awakened by post hypnotic command à la *The Manchurian Candidate*. To this end, the CIA tested a wide range of drugs to find the perfect chemical compound in which to achieve their goals. In 1953, the Agency attempted to purchase the entire world supply of LSD from Sandoz Laboratories in Switzerland. In fact, for many years the CIA was the principal source for LSD. Ken Kesey, Allen Ginsberg and Jerry Garcia were all turned on to acid via CIA funded projects sponsored by such conduits as Stanford University.

After a "Manchurian Candidate" has been used in an assassination – or assassination attempt – s/he often retains no actual memory of the event, which might explain the irrational behavior of Charlie's girls; how at one moment they could be harmless little flower waifs skipping arm in arm, tossing daisies over their shoulders; then in the next instant knife-wielding nutcases with no hint of moral accountability. This is not to say that mind controlled assassins always compartmentalized the act of murder. In some cases, the memory of murder or assassination may seem a dream-like recollection. This type of mental state is similar to that exhibited by Tex and the girls during the murders when everything slowed down and turned almost surreal, like an altered state of consciousness.

In the late 1970's – as the CIA and other intelligence agencies came under greater congressional scrutiny – MK-ULTRA experimentation moved out of the laboratories and into the streets where it would be harder to trace. Religious cults soon became the new MK-ULTRA breeding grounds for spychiatrists to ply their trade, recruiting future Manchurian Candidates from counterculture communes and covens. One such scenario has been applied to Jonestown by conspiracy researcher John Judge. In this same manner – it could be conjectured – the Manson Family was a similar experiment in group mind control.

Paul Krassner soon discovered that trying to connect Nathaniel Dight to Charlie's Family would be no easy task. Preston Guillory, for one, didn't recognize the name, nor was Manson copping to knowledge of Dight. The only corroborative evidence was a former neighbor, who – when presented with Tex Watson's photo – placed him at Dight's residence. Other than that, Krassner thought he'd hit a dead end; that was, until he was presented with the opportunity of visiting the Manson girls – Katie, Leslie and Sadie – in jail. There he asked them if they had ever met Nathaniel Dight. "Oh yeah," Sadie replied. "Tex took me to sleep with him. And he gave us dope."

In Folsom Prison, Charles Manson asked Tim Leary – when the two were located in cells next to each other – why he didn't "use acid to control people?" According to John Judge, Charlie's question revealed a basic contradiction, as LSD – in his estimation – would be useless as a control agent, except to create a state of confusion. For anyone who's experimented with LSD, it quickly becomes evident that – as a mind control tool – it's a highly unstable. This was discovered during MK-ULTRA's early days when it was tested on numerous unwitting human guinea pigs – including some of the CIA's own agents – without consent, provoking unpredictable behavior, including suicides.

Judge theorized that the type of "acid" the Mansonoids were using was a military version, unlike the stuff found on the streets. Although called "acid", it was actually an MK-ULTRA version; a psilocybin derivative identified as EA1729. According to Judge, this is the same "acid" that David Berkowitz was given by while in the Army, when placed in a special program reportedly for profiled candidates. Mae Brussell was convinced that Berkowitz was another in a long list of MK-ULTRA patsies, referring to him as "son of Uncle Sam." By the mid 1960's, at least 1,500 army personnel are documented as having been used in Chemical Corps LSD experiments.

In 1975, Paul Krassner wrote an article for *Rolling Stone* titled "My Trip With Squeaky" which included a paragraph about Nathaniel Dight, and Dight's alleged Tex Watson association. As a result, Dight sued *Rolling Stone* for libel because, as he claimed, he had never been affiliated with Naval Intelligence. This required Krassner's sources to give dispositions. The neighbor who said she had seen Tex Watson at Dight's house was, by this time, committed to a state mental hospital. As detailed in a psychiatric evaluation: "Her feet are encased in the most unusual pair of slippers constructed of layers of garbage, including coffee grounds, bread crumbs, tea bags and lettuce and socks stiff with age and then plastic bags. The patient denies that this garb is out of the ordinary. In fact, she indicates that she was planning to use this foot gear as a pattern for a pair of slippers...she has related to the staff that she has been entered by the spirit of (Watergate burglar) James McCord and that she must die in order to free herself from this hex." Realizing that the deponent would damage an already shaky case, Krassner decided against requesting her deposition. His only other source was Susan Atkins, who was deposed at the California Institute for Women:

> Q: Charles Manson, on occasion, he asked you or ordered you to sleep with men, whoever they might be, just men in general?
> A: Many times.
> Q: And Tex Watson did the same?
> A: No, he never ordered me to sleep with anybody.
> Q: So, on the occasion when you went to visit this friend of Tex Watson's with Tex, it was not at Tex Watson's request that you slept with this fellow?
> A: No. There was a mutual attraction.
> Q: So that was Charles Manson's function, and no one else had that prerogative?
> A: Yes, I guess you could put it on that basis. I was kind of used...Not kind of, I was used as a ploy to get guys to stay at the ranch. (She is shown a photo of Dight, whom she doesn't recognize.) Can I say something? I don't find him attractive at all to me, and I have this thing with men about overbites. I don't like men with overbites...

Eventually, *Rolling Stone* settled the Dight case out of court, and Krassner published a letter of retraction. Nowadays, Krassner writes off the whole incident as a "paranoid freak-out" he suffered after dipping his toes too deeply in the conspiratorial abyss. In contrast, Mae Brussell felt that Krassner sold out when he began to fear for his life, in much the same way that Ed Sanders went into hiding, and that is why his follow-up to *The Family* – titled The *Motive* – never saw the light of day. Brussell carried on with her mission, broadcasting the truth, as she saw it, on her weekly radio program, and, in the end, this might have been her undoing.

Sometime in mid 1975, Brussell received a threatening letter and notified the authorities, who then passed it on to the FBI. Released under the Freedom of Information Act, the letter appeared to have been signed, but the name was blacked-out. It read:

"Mae, you are thinking yourself in a circle of madness. Charles Manson has been 28 years in prison and all that B.S. you are running is a reflection of what the news and books have programmed your soul's brain mind to... You are looking for attention. It seems as if you are looking for your death wish in the Family." An unrelated FOIA document dated five years later referred back to the incident and states that "during October and November of '75 she received threatening letters from (blacked out) member of the Manson Family."

In 1988, Mae Brussell died under – what some would term – mysterious circumstances, just a few months after canceling her long running radio program in response to a death threat. Researchers have speculated that Brussell's death was on account of her then topic of concern: satanic cults in the military. Although Brussell's doctor stated that the terminal cancer she succumbed to was unremarkable, this didn't dissuade conspiracy buffs, who suspected that her cancer had been artificially induced.

CHAPTER 41

MK-MANSON

Manson was released from prison in 1967, and under parole stipulations reported to Roger Smith at the Haight Ashbury Medical Clinic, a facility sponsored by the National Institute of Mental Health (NIMH). In recent times, it has been revealed that the NIMH was a MK-ULTRA conduit. Some have suggested that the Haight-Ashbury district was a "human guinea pig farm" and that Dr. Louis Jolyon West – an infamous figure in the MK-ULTRA annals – ran a safe house in the Haight during this period where he conducted LSD testing on unwitting dupes.

In the 1990's, West – a renowned as an expert on cults – became director of the American Family Foundation (AFF), which states its official position as an organization dedicated to protect the public from cults. AFF was the mother organization for the Cult Awareness Network (CAN). Adding another twist to this already puzzling picture, CAN – during the late 1990's – was taken over by Scientology in a libel suit settlement which included all of CAN's assets and records on cults, one of which was Scientology. Now, if you phone CAN, you will in essence be reaching a Scientology representative.

Rabbi Maurice Davis – another AFF director – worked as a chaplain for the NIMH, then later moved to Indianapolis and sponsored the career of Rev. Jim Jones, late of Guyana poison Kool-Aid fame. The bulk of AFF funding was channeled through the same New York Law Firm that represented the Process Church in their libel suit against Ed Sanders over his book, *The Family*. It's a small world after all...

‡

The most in-depth story on Manson as a product of MK-ULTRA is *Test-Tube Murders: The Case of Charles Manson* by Carol Greene, published in Germany and unavailable in English. Greene's thesis is that the "Summer of Love" was not a spontaneous phenomenon, but was, in actuality, an exhaustively planned behavior modification experiment aimed at subverting the cultural and moral values of the 1960's youth movement, with the Manson Family the end product of this experimentation.

Greene suggests that Manson's parole officer, Roger Smith, and Haight-Ashbury clinic director, David E. Smith, played pivotal roles in molding the madness that eventually erupted in Helter Skelter. In Greene's final summation, she contends that the Manson Family unleashed a wave of subsequent "copy-cat" serial killers and related sociopathic behavior among a population that received the same sort of indoctrination as Charlie's Family; i.e. sex, drugs and New Age mumbo-jumbo. During this period – asserts Greene – the FBI assembled a database of individuals who had shown a propensity toward such violence. Greene described this list as a "Who's Who" of America's potential fascist scene, and believes that if The Establishment continues upon its present course, they may find it necessary to deploy some form of "friendly fascism" upon its citizenry. Greene is alluding to a squadron of mind controlled patsies who could be used to implement a war not only upon dissidents, but whoever it deems "dangerous." Greene says, in closing:

> This book was written because we believe that in the United States, as in Germany during the Third Reich, the majority of the population is against such a development. This majority must now wake up and act. What came to pass under the Nazi regime was believed by most of those who helped bring them to power, in a desperate economic and social situation, to be simply not possible. And yet it was possible, and it is today again possible.

It is noteworthy that Greene brings up the Third Reich in relation to present day United States, as the seeds of MK-ULTRA were planted by Nazi concentration camp experimentation during World War II. Under a shield of U.S. Government protection, many of these very same Nazi concentration camp doctors – as well as high level Nazi spies – were secreted into the United States at the war's end, continuing their work under the umbrella of "democracy."

‡

Manson grew up in Charleston, West Virginia, within close proximity to Sarah Jane Moore, who – in 1975 – attempted to assassinate then President Gerald Ford. In the mid 1980's, a local store owner was interviewed and confirmed that Manson and Moore knew each other as kids, and often came into his store together.

It seems more than mere coincidence that Manson was associated with two women who later attempted to assassinate Ford. The other, of course, was Squeaky Fromme. At the time of Squeaky's unsuccessful assassination attempt, she was living in Sacramento, California with Sandy Good where the two waged a radical campaign against the Establishment, having moved there to be closer to their "master and mentor" at San Quentin. The girls spent their days writing letters to Charlie, and their nights performing magic rituals and entertaining Aryan Brotherhood members.

During this period, Squeaky found herself a "Sugar Daddy" in sixty-five-year-old Manny Boro, who showered Fromme with gifts and shuttled her and Sandy around town in his Cadillac, in return for Squeaky's affections. Concurrently, Manson formed "The Order of the Rainbow," a religious sect for his rapidly dwindling coven of nuns – or as Charlie referred to them, the Nuness. Squeaky became Red, and Sandy, Blue. He also assigned colors to the girls in prison, although at this point the Tate/LaBianca female murder trio was less than receptive to Charlie's new spiritual direction, and, in fact, refused to join his order.

There were seven degrees of initiation in Charlie's new religion, that of witch, queen, goddess, aliken, and three others. As Squeaky stated in a letter dated May 1974, "One degree in nuness can be gotten by sleeping in an open grave at the graveyard. No violence. Only completion of Old Christian fears."

Charlie's new rules were strict. He wrote to Squeaky: "NO MEAT, NO SMOKING, NO MAKEUP." On ceremonial occasions the women were to wear nun habits in the appropriate colors Charlie had assigned. Like Muslims, Charlie suggested that they cover their faces in public with veils. Unlike the days of free love at Spahn Ranch, now the women were instructed that there was to be "no fornication, or showing your ass, and the morality is the highest on earth. Laws behind the veil as much as it was at the ranch. Outside the veil, we will obey the laws of the land... Oh yeah," added Charlie, "no movies with violence that sets thoughts to death and confusion." The message was clear: if Charlie wasn't able to have sex with his remaining female Family members, than neither could anyone else; except, of course, somebody like Manny Boro, who Squeaky was using much in the same manner as she had once used old George Spahn, as a sugar daddy. Nor did it prevent the girls from posing nude for the camera when they needed publicity.

Charlie's new "religion" seemed just like one more way of retaining control of his women from inside prison walls. It was through overindulgence in sex that he had been able originally to gain control of their minds. Now, by forcing them to abstain, he would once again attempt to assert that control, which proved effective with Squeaky and Sandy. Another reason for this change from sexual promiscuity to chastity might also have had something to do with a falling out with the Aryan Brotherhood around this time, and this was Charlie's way of terminating the agreement he had previously made with the group, in regards to sexual access to his women.

During the "Order of the Rainbow" period Charlie was transferred to the California State Medical Facility in Vacaville, where prison officials gave Red and Blue permission to correspond with him. Vacaville authorities closely monitored these correspondences, which at first seemed merely to involve discussions of philosophy, religion and ecology. In November 1974, however, prison officials discovered hidden messages in the letters containing instructions for a prison break, bringing to a close this short period of correspondence.

The "Order of the Rainbow" evolved into ATWA (Air, Trees, Water, Animals) – Manson's Earth First-like movement intent on saving the Earth... even if it meant killing everyone on the planet to do so! Into this endeavor, Squeaky and Sandy sometimes recruited psychotic young men, including a fellow named Vandervort, who Squeaky tried to persuade to phone corporate executives, and threaten them – in his meanest tough guy voice – that if they didn't clean up their act, there would be hell to pay. In the end, Vandervort backed out of this half-baked scheme when his mom discovered that he was associated with Manson Family women.

Dressed in a little Red Riding Hood outfit, Squeaky made occasional visits to Sacramento area news bureaus, delivering wrathful press releases attributed to Manson, along with baskets of fresh baked cookies. "We're waiting for our Lord and there's only one thing to do before He comes off the cross and that's clean up the earth," Squeaky elucidated. "We're nuns now... Our red robes are an example of the new morality... They're red with sacrifice, the blood and sacrifice."

Squeaky and Sandy's most madcap plan was the creation of the "International People's Court of Retribution", an alleged worldwide environmentalist terrorist organization. According to the pair, this covert cabal had formed in the 1950's in federal penitentiaries at Terminal Island, California, and McNeil Island, Washington, which just so happened to be the same institutions where Manson was incarcerated during that time. As the spurious story went, the International People's Court of Retribution (IPCR) had grown during the Cuban missile crisis, with major expansions in Florida and Mexico, consisting of two thousand members worldwide.

After several decades underground, said Red and Blue, the IPCR was now ready to emerge and kick some corporate ass. However, when making these pronouncements to the press, Squeaky and Sandy added the disclaimer that they were not affiliated directly with the IPCR, but merely communicated on their behalf. Later, an FBI agent testified at Sandy's 1975 trial that the bureau possessed no knowledge whatsoever regarding an "International People's Court of Retribution."

In July 1975, an anonymous female – who prosecutors later identified as Sandy Good – phoned the *San Francisco Chronicle* and read the following statement:

> The International People's Court of Retribution is a new justice movement for the balance
> of the earth. All state, federal and private money interests are now warned: Stop whaling.
> We consider all wildlife to be part of ourselves and will move viciously to defend our lives.
> Anyone caught killing wildlife, polluting or cutting down trees will be maimed, poisoned or
> chopped in a similar manner. A whaler without arms cannot swim.

Squeaky and Sandy's next press release was titled "Manson is Mad at Nixson", blaming the former President (his name intentionally misspelled) for the conviction of Charlie on account of his famous

"Manson is Guilty" proclamation. Along with other condemnations made against society, the rant read: "If Nixon's reality wearing a Ford face continues to run this country against the law, your homes will be bloodier than the Tate/LaBianca homes and My Lai put together."

On another occasion, Sandy and Squeaky – attired in crimson cloaks embroidered with swastikas – took reporters on a midnight photo shoot at the Sacramento Cemetery where the two hooded women pointing forebodingly at a tombstone.

Around this time, Squeaky went on a series of "missions" throughout California, one which included a thwarted meeting with Led Zeppelin guitarist Jimmy Page at the Continental Hyatt House in Los Angeles. Instead of directing Squeaky to Page's room, the desk clerk passed her on to the band's publicist, Danny Goldberg. Squeaky informed Goldberg that something terrible was soon to befall Page, assuring him that the last time she'd had a similar vision, someone was shot dead right before her eyes. Goldberg told Squeaky that Page was unavailable, but that he would deliver the message on her behalf. An agitated Squeaky finally agreed to write a note, then left in a huff. That night, at a Led Zeppelin concert in Long Beach, Page was struck on the head with a roll of toilet paper.

Another rock star that Manson's nuns attempted to convert to the "Order of the Rainbow" was Keith Moon, who was first approached – while on tour in San Diego – by six Manson nuns adorned in red robes. When he finally figured out that the girls were more interested in preaching the word of Charlie than "putting out", Moon bid the barmy babes farewell and left that night for a San Francisco gig, presumably giving Squeaky and her fellow nuns the bum's rush.

The next night, Moon was taken aback when he answered his motel room door to find the very same Manson nuns from San Diego. Security was called and the women in red promptly ushered out. After San Francisco, The Who played a concert in Oakland and following the gig – as the group was partying in their dressing room – Manson's nuns once again materialized, and started proselytizing about how "...Keith and the band should join the Manson sect and follow the devil and all that caper." Once again, the women were ushered out and as their next gig was in Portland, it seemed unlikely that Charlie's Nuns would follow Moon all the way there. But when The Who's airplane touched down in Portland, who should be awaiting them but "six look-alike chicks in cheap red dresses." At this point, Moon flipped out, as the women stared fixedly at him, trying to zap him with some Mansonoid spell. Quickly, Moon was hustled into a waiting limo and spirited away. Upon arriving back at the hotel, he encountered Manson girls once again, waving Bibles and Tarot cards, imploring him to join their act and declaring: "Charlie is the sun and you will be the Moon." Once again, Moon was able to give the girls the slip, as hotel security shortly after interceded, ushering out the red-hooded nuns. Fortunately, The Who's west coast tour finished that night, and Moon was bothered no more by the Nuns of Man's Son.

CHAPTER 42
Uncle Sam's Girls?

On September 5th, 1975 – as President Gerard Ford was being ushered across a park leading to the California State Capitol – Squeaky Fromme, adorned in her Little Red Riding Hood outfit, emerged from the crowd. Pulling a .45 caliber Colt from her robe, Squeaky squeezed the trigger, but it failed to fire. Squeaky was wrestled to the ground by Secret Service agents, and the weapon forced from her hand. Afterwards, it was discovered that the pistol was loaded with four live rounds in the clip, but none in the chambers. As there was no live ammunition, some have speculated that Squeaky never intended to assassinate Ford.

During interrogation, Secret Service agents concluded that Squeaky seemed "under the influence of either an intoxicant or a drug", although urine samples failed to detect alcohol or drugs in her system. Perhaps Squeaky's state of consciousness was due more to some form of mind control than actual drug intoxication. Later, under custody, U.S. Marshall's noted that Squeaky, on occasion, would fall into "LSD trances" and during these periods it was impossible to reason with her. After the failed assassination, Squeaky was asked why she wanted to kill President Ford, to which she replied, "I wasn't going to shoot him. I just wanted to get some attention for a new trial for Charlie and the girls."

The Colt .45 was traced to Squeaky's "sugar daddy", Manny Boro, who claimed that the gun had been stolen from him, although Squeaky claimed he'd given it to her. In media reports, Harold "Manny" Boro was identified as a draftsman, who worked at McClellan Air Force Base, near Sacramento, starting in 1941, but according to conspiracy researcher John Judge, Boro was a "draftsman" for only two years, following 28 years of service with Air Force intelligence.

According to Judge, Squeaky was a patsy in a plot that went awry. The actual assassins were arrested the previous night, and in their possession several high-powered weapons were found, as well as sewer maps for the street where the assassination attempt occurred. The first newswire stated that Squeaky was handed a gun by a "blonde woman in a polka-dot dress." Oddly enough, a similar "woman in a polka dot dress" first came to the attention of conspiracy researchers in 1968 during the RFK assassination. Newswires afterwards made no further mention of this elusive "woman in a polka-dot dress" that supposedly aided Squeaky.

Shortly after the assassination attempt, Sandy Good called a press conference, informing reporters about a coming "wave of assassinations across golf courses and bridge clubs throughout the country. And people in the news media, you better stop lying or you're going to get cut up, too. Your blood is going to be on the walls." She then thrust a wooden crucifix into the face of a woman reporter from *Newsweek*. "You, in your eyeshadow and dyed hair – trying to get your sensational story. Look at this." Sandy held the crucifix closer, and decried: "This is you, woman!" A hush came over the room, then Sandy changed her tone. Smiling, she said. "I know you're sincere…We've all put Charlie on the cross."

Sandy – calling herself "Hungry Knife" – mailed hundreds of letters during this period, issuing threats against businessmen, indicating that their families would be mercilessly butchered by the IPCR if they didn't stop polluting the Earth. Good was eventually jailed for these mail threats and later reunited with Squeaky in prisons. Arrested with Good was another Manson disciple, Heather Murphy, who managed to create a few colorful moments of her own during Squeaky's trial. One day, Murphy came into court dressed as a Catholic nun, habit and all. "I'm a sister in Manson's church," she said.

‡

In the 1980's, John Judge received correspondence from Patricia Krenwinkel, who stated her suspicion that she'd been a mind control victim, and requested Judge's help to discover the truth. However, he decided not to pursue the matter, fearing some kind of set-up. According to Judge, this was during a period when Charlie still had ties to the A.B., and he didn't want to become another Manson Family statistic.

According to Judge, Manson's girls all came from high ranking military intelligence families associated with MK-ULTRA type operations. Once the Helter Skelter scenario was set in motion, the women were fed mind control drugs, and Charlie was given control over them. Meanwhile, Manson's handlers led him to believe he was "king of the desert in his little shack", as they propped him up with the idea of an imminent race war, and that he would survive the Apocalypse and ultimately rule the world. After Charlie's arrest, he was quoted as saying, "I want to know who was peeing on my leash," which, in essence, meant that Manson understood he'd been let out a certain amount, then dragged back in once he had served his purpose.

An alleged MK-ULTRA outgrowth is Project Monarch. According to legend, Monarch programming begins at birth, and is carried out through the lives of its victims, as they are used by intelligence agencies and secret societies as sex slaves, drug mules and "Manchurian Candidate"-type assassins.

One alleged Project Monarch victim is Cisco Wheeler, who with co-author Fritz Springmeier in *The Illuminati Formula Used to Create an Undetectable Total Mind-Controlled Slave* identifies Manson as a "monarch slave and monarch slave handler" who received his initial mind control programming at the China Lake Naval Air Weapons Station, located 45 miles northwest of Barker Ranch. The authors suggest that Sharon Tate's murder was conducted in a ritualistic manner, which has been often speculated. The allusion given by Wheeler and Springmeier is that Tate was in some way a traitor to either the Manson Family or her Project Monarch handlers. As has been documented, the beautiful actress was left hanging in the No. 12 Tarot Card's "hangman position" from the house rafters on the night of the murders, representative of "a traitor's death", as pictured in the Tarot. It should also be noted that Sharon's father, Paul Tate, was a career military intelligence officer.

Many of these Project Monarch's revelations first came to light courtesy of psychologist Dr. Cory Hammond – former President of the American Society of Clinical Hypnosis – during a lecture delivered at the Fourth Annual Eastern Regional Conference on Abuse and Multiple Personality in Alexandria, Virginia in 1992. This lecture has become widely known as the "The Greenbaum Speech" wherein Dr. Hammond outlined his own personal Project Monarch discoveries, detailing the modus operandi used by mind control practitioners. In regards to Manson mind control connections, Dr. Hammond made reference to a new incarnation of The Process Church of The Final Judgment, which he identified as a mind control cult:

Remember the Process Church? Roman Polanski's wife Sharon Tate was killed by the Manson Family who were associated with the Process Church? A lot of prominent people in Hollywood were associated and then they went underground, the books say, in about '78 and vanished. Well, they're alive and well in southern Utah. We have a thick file in the Utah Department of Public Safety documenting that they moved to southern Utah, north of Monument Valley, bought a movie ranch in the desert, renovated it, expanded it, built a bunch of buildings there, carefully monitored so that very few people go out of there and no one can get in, and changed their name. A key word in their name is 'Foundation.' 'The Foundation.'

CHAPTER 43

Man's Son Of Sam

In *The Ultimate Evil*, author Maury Terry contended that Sam of Sam killer, David Berkowitz, was a member of "The Children", a Satanic cult based out of Venice, California, with links to the military and intelligence community. According to Terry, "The Children" was a splinter group of The Process Church of the Final Judgment, which – although officially disbanded over 30 years ago – continues to operate secretly in the U.S.

From his sources – among them, Berkowitz – Terry learned that one Son of Sam murder was videotaped, and that the cameraman, Ronald Sisman, was subsequently murdered when cult members went to recover this Son of Sam snuff film. Terry pinned this murder on a mysterious figure named Manson II, whom he later identified as William Mentzer, an "occult superstar" and hit man who moved through the same late 60's milieu of sex, drugs and porn as Manson, and who had been intimate with Abigail Folger. Terry quoted his source on Mentzer/Manson II as "someone in the intelligence community."

In high school, Berkowitz joined the New York Police auxiliary, and has stated that three Yonkers police department members were involved with "The Children" cult. Retired NYPD detective Sgt. Joseph Coffey testified that he was ordered to destroy a letter sent to Berkowitz by Police Commissioner Michael Codd. Another letter, suppressed by police for four years, read:

> This is a warning to all the police agencies in the tri-state area: For your information, a satanic cult (devil worshipers and practitioners of witchcraft) that has been established for quite some time has been instructed by their high command to begin to systematically kill and slaughter young girls or people of good health and clean blood.
> They plan to kill at least 100 wemon and men, but mostly wemon, as part of a satanic ritual which involves the shedding of the victim's innocent blood...
> Warning: the streets shall run with blood.
> I, David Berkowitz, have been chosen, chosen since birth, to be one of the executioners of the cult. He who hath eyes, let him see the dead victims. He who hath ears, let him listen to what I say.

Following his arrest, Berkowitz wrote several letters detailing the 1974 ritual murder at California's Stanford University Chapel of Arlis Perry, a devout Christian woman from North Dakota. The date of the murder coincided with Aleister Crowley's birthday, and was also the birthday of a young man named John Carr, a reputed Satanist and friend of Berkowitz.

In 1979, John Carr's corpse was discovered at his girlfriend's apartment at North Dakota's Minot Air Force Base, dead from a shotgun blast to the head. In shades of Helter Skelter, cryptic messages were left on the wall in the victim's blood, and "666" scratched on his hand. Carr was alleged to have been involved in Satanism since high school, and was in the Air Force until being discharged a few months prior to the beginning of the Son of Sam murders.

Maury Terry contended that John Carr was a Son of Sam murder participant, as his description closely matched that of a gunman in one of the slayings. A Son of Sam letter sent to newspapers included a reference to "John 'Wheaties' – rapist and suffocater of young girls." Carr – who went by the nickname of Wheaties – had a penchant for jail bait, and just so happened to have a sister named Wheat. Nonetheless, police overlooked these clues and pinned the slayings entirely on Berkowitz. In fact, John Carr's father, Sam, owned the dog that Berkowitz claimed had instructed him to commit the murders; or more accurately, it was Sam Carr – who Berkowitz claimed was really a six thousand-year-old man – that spoke to him through this supposed demon dog. Furthermore, John Carr was the true "Son of Sam."

Terry claimed that John Carr was involved with a Satanic cult headquartered in Bismark, North Dakota, and traveled back and forth between Bismark and Yonkers on cult "missions." Witnesses placed Berkowitz in North Dakota during the same period that Carr was active there. John Hinkley, Jr.– who attempted to assassinate President Ronald Reagan in 1981– stated that he met Berkowitz in Colorado during this same time frame. Once again the spectre of mind controlled assassins rears its ugly head.

Berkowitz also fingered John Carr's brother, Michael – a ranking Scientologist – as a member of "The Children" cult. Both Carr brothers died violently within two weeks after their names were handed over to Son of Sam murder investigators. In 1997 – a decade after the publication of *The Ultimate Evil* – a former Process member named Linda Harrison came forward claiming to have seen Michael Carr at a Process Church meeting in Chicago in 1970.

Witnesses at the Arlis Perry murder scene described a sandy-haired young man at the campus chapel shortly before Perry arrived. According to Terry, this description matched that of the shooter in the second Son of Sam slaying. Berkowitz later confirmed that these descriptions were of the same person, that being Manson II aka William Mentzer, a former bodyguard of Larry Flynt.

According to Terry, Mentzer worked as a contract hit man for "The Children" cult and was arrested in 1988 for the murder of Long Island show biz entrepreneur, Roy Radin. Radin was a notorious figure, fond of throwing drug orgies at his Long Island mansion, which were known to include, upon occasion, videotaped gang rapes, including one involving actress Melonie Haller of *Welcome Back, Kotter*. Terry suspected Radin was the "Mr. Big" that Berkowitz referred to as the godfather of "The Children" cult. According to Terry's sources, this individual commissioned the videotaping of one or more of the Son of Sam murders for a collection of snuff films for sale to a worldwide black market.

Mentzer had been associated with Mama Cass during 1968-1971 when the singer fell prey to a group of psychic vultures. In his 1986 autobiography, John Phillips wrote: "At home, (Cass) was surrounded by losers and cruel users...They were just hustlers, music industry leeches...They were sometimes drugged-out, belligerent (dope) dealers, in leather with weapons, chains and cycles...They were like muggers." One of these "leeches" was William Mentzer. In 1987, LAPD sources confirmed that information in their possession held that Mentzer was a member of "some kind of hit squad."

In a segment of A&E's *Investigative Reports*: "Son of Sam Speaks: The Untold Story", Berkowitz identified The Process Church as the unifying force tying together various Satanic cults, including "The Children." Berkowitz told Maury Terry – who produced the segment – that one of the conditions of joining the cult was turning over photos and personal info about his immediate family. Because of this, claims Berkowitz, he confessed to all the Son of Sam murders, playing the "lone nut" card on orders of the cult, as they had threatened to harm his family if he didn't cooperate.

According to the *Investigate Reports* episode, The Process Church occupied headquarters on

Manhattan's 1st Avenue from the late 1960's through mid-1970's, and at least one witness claims to have seen Berkowitz enter this building just days before his arrest. Jesse Turner – a so-called "Process hitman" currently in prison – claims that photographic artist Robert Mapplethorpe contracted him to kill the cameraman, Ronald Sisman, who had filmed a Son of Sam hit. Turner – who lived with Mapplethorpe in the early 1970's – added that the artist was not a Process Church member, although associated with the cult.

Berkowitz estimated that the cult had over a thousand members, and was segmented into several chapters across the country. Berkowitz informed a fellow inmate that Manson, who belonged to the Los Angeles chapter of the cult, was working "on orders" when he directed his Family to commit the Tate/LaBianca murders. In *The Ultimate Evil*, Terry placed Manson – two days after the Tate murders – driving a Mercedes-Benz belonging to a big-time LSD dealer, who, in Terry's description, was "said to have been a former Israeli who had strong links with the intelligence community." Terry took this to be one of the truly fascinating players in LSD history: Ronald Hadley Stark. In *The Ultimate Evil*, Stark is identified under the alias of Chris Jetz.

Although not an Israeli, Stark posed as one upon occasion, as he was fluent in several languages, and fond of assuming multiple identities. He first appeared on the psychedelic scene in 1969 with numerous cover stories and a seemingly endless bankroll, boasting that he had worked for the CIA. As part of his resume, Stark financed a Belgium lab that was, at one time, the single largest underground source for LSD

In *Will You Die For Me?*, Tex Watson said that Orange Sunshine was being used by the Manson Family prior to the Tate/LaBianca murders. Orange Sunshine was manufactured and distributed by a drug commune known as "The Brotherhood of Eternal Love" who operated out of Malibu, counting Ronald Stark as one of its major associates.

From an informant, Maury Terry learned that Manson, Abigail Folger, Shorty Shea and one other individual met at a restaurant near Golden Gate Park in 1967. It has always been assumed that Shea first met Manson at Spahn Ranch in late '68, but according to Terry, this was not the case. Terry's source indicated that Folger and Shea were later murdered on the instructions of the fourth person present at the restaurant. This same source confirmed that Manson originally met Abigail Folger at the home of Mama Cass.

"Gibby had more money than she knew what to do with," Terry's source stated. "She was into finding herself and new directions, and she was always investing in things... Not long before the murders, about six weeks, she got involved in putting up some cash for a small recording studio. It's possible that Terry Melcher, who knew Manson well, had a link into that studio..."

"That night in San Francisco, she loaned ten grand to a small theater, and she had also given money to Manson from time to time." Later on, Charlie and Gibby had a falling out, when she refused to continue giving him money. Also – Terry's anonymous source stated – Folger spurned Charlie when he came on to her for sex. This provided further impetus – Terry speculated – for Charlie to oversee the Cielo Drive butchery. "It made sense that Shea was killed after that," the source added. "He knew both of them, and he could tie things together that nobody wanted tied."

From another informant, Terry learned that during this '67 meeting with Manson, Folger agreed to advance $10,000 to the Straight Theater, coincidentally located on the corner of Haight and Cole streets, right in the heart of the Manson Family's Summer of Love stomping grounds. Charlie's then budding Family lived at 636 Cole. Meanwhile, The Process Church was collecting followers and waving capes at 407 Cole, just down the block. The connections once again start lining up like dark dominoes. Bobby Beausoleil took part in Kenneth Anger's "equinox of the gods" performance on September 21, 1967 at the Straight Theater.

Following these connections even further, Anger and LSD guru Timothy Leary – along with a host of other psychedelic entrepreneurs – were involved in the formation of The Himalayan Academy, a new age research center. According to Terry, Abigail Folger contributed money here, as well. "Folger donated to the place, and it was there that Manson was first exposed to The Process," Terry's informant claimed. "The academy was into all sorts of things and The Process was invited to speak there. That's how it happened."

As noted earlier, Folger attended Esalen Institute seminars. Process founder Robert DeGrimston lectured at Esalen, and Manson made at least one appearance there, crooning groovy tunes with his guitar to a less than receptive audience. Esalen and the Himalayan Academy shared basically the same agenda, and many of the same players gravitated to both camps, which is not to suggest that they knowingly harbored some kind of satanic hit squad in their midst. What I am suggesting, though, is that Esalen – like many another human potential center – was co-opted by the intelligence community, to one degree or another, just as Stanford and other universities – funded by the CIA – were using street shamans and anybody else they could get their hands on for experimental purposes, dispensing to them LSD and other drugs under clinical conditions at their research facilities.

At such human potential centers as Esalen, group "dissonance" or stress was introduced to destroy an individual's previous beliefs, and to replace the destroyed personality with a new-group oriented personality. These so-called "group encounter" and "sensitivity programs" were used in much the same way that Manson programmed his flock, systematically breaking down an individual's personality to be reconstructed along the lines of the group-mind. The enigmatic Ronald Stark – big-time LSD entrepreneur and possible MK-ULTRA operative – was an Esalen financial supporter. Keep in mind that many of the people involved in the human potential movement – who were often bankrolled by CIA front organizations like the Human Ecology Fund – brought good intentions into their endeavors, although there can be no argument that the intelligence community were using the likes of Tim Leary and others of his ilk as test subjects in behavior modification experiments.

In *The Ultimate Evil*, Terry claimed that a "jailed Manson killer" informed him that Process leaders hooked up with Charlie's Family at the Spiral Staircase House in 1968. In *Manson In His Own Words*, Charlie claims he met individuals at The Spiral Staircase who worshipped "multiple devils" – a probable allusion to The Process hierarchy worshipped by the group: namely Lucifer, Satan and Jehovah. In addition to these revelations, Terry claims he viewed a letter in Manson's handwriting in which Charlie recounts rubbing elbows with Process leaders at the Polanski residence.

The scene of many cult activities detailed in *The Ultimate Evil* transpired in Untermyer Park in Yonkers, New York, which was within close proximity to where the Carr brothers and David Berkowitz lived during Son of Sam. In addition, Process founder Robert DeGrimston lived near Untermyer Park in the mid-1970's. At this time, altars and black magic paraphernalia were discovered there, as well as the remains of skinned German shepherds used in apparent ritual sacrifices. Maury Terry associated the sacrificed canines with the Process Church, infamous for their German shepherd dog packs.

In regards to Manson, familiar names continued to resurface. Throughout 1979, Keith Richards of The Rolling Stones was living in a rented home in the immediate vicinity of the Untermyer Park, and John Phillips was a frequent guest there. Scorch marks were discovered on an isolated section of Richards' property at this time, indicative of ritual activity. Also, during 1979, a teenage boy was shot to death in Anita Pallenberg's bedroom on Richards' estate. Police ruled the death a suicide.

‡

In the fall of 2000, I came into contact with an individual calling himself Michael, who claimed to be a former Process Church member. Michael reportedly worked for William Mentzer (the alleged "Manson II") from the mid to late 1970's. Mentzer, Michael alleged, was also a Process member, although higher up in the organizational chain of command than he. During this association, Michael heard the rumor that Manson had been hired as a hitman by The Process to whack Woytek Frykowski. Furthermore, Michael alleged that Mentzer possessed foreknowledge of the Son of Sam murders.

According to Michael, the Process was into drug manufacturing and distribution, as was Frykowski, Hinman and possibly Rosemary LaBianca. In addition to these activities, Michael makes the same assertions as Maury Terry that the group was involved in producing pornography, prostitution, arms dealing and Satanic worship.

In the late 1960's/early 1970's, the Process supposedly went underground, branching off into splinter cults that changed their names, but continued playing the same games that Process hierarchy had previously paved the way for ala murder and assorted mayhem. When I inquired if the group Michael belonged to was Process offshoot – just using a different name – he replied that his group was indeed the one and only Process Church of the Final Judgment. Michael described group members as pure evil, although he says you'd never know it from their appearance, as most of these closet Processeans owned legitimate business fronts, such as car dealerships, insurance agencies, etc. When I asked Michael whether he was nervous going public with these revelations, he admitted that yes, he was because, "the organization continues to exist." When *The Ultimate Evil* was published in 1987, the mainstream media, by and large, dismissed the sensational allegations made therein of a vast Satanic Underground (reportedly involved in drug distribution, pornography, snuff movies and ritual murder) as nothing more than a dark fantasy spun to fan the flames of the "satanic panic" then running rampant through the tabloid media and segments of the religious right. To many, the apparently outlandish tales of human sacrifice, bizarre sex rites and blood guzzling were way too much for most civilized people to digest. Thus these stories were relegated to the status of urban legends and dismissed as the ravings of religious fanatics and conspiracy theorists.

In 1989, many myths were subsequently confirmed regarding ritual human sacrifice and its relation to large scale drug distribution and pornography rings with the arrest of Mexico's Matamoros cult. Basically, what Maury Terry laid out in the *Ultimate Evil* was confirmed by the revelations which unfolded in gruesome detail concerning the torture, mutilation and dismemberment of the cult's victims.

Although different alleged players and crimes were involved in Terry's *Ultimate Evil* scenario, the modus operandi of the Son of Sam Cult (aka "The Children") seemed alarmingly similar, in many respects, to what went down on the Mex/Tex border in Matamoros. Drug dealing – in addition to the sex and pornography trade – was a means of cult recruitment. After a prospective member was lured in, then the second phase of actual participation in occult rituals and activities began. All told, the Matamoros death toll totaled fifteen mutilated victims; a gruesome sight for police officers who raided the ranch, as the remains of victims were found in blood encrusted cauldrons, waiting to be devoured by the ghoulish crew.

The cult's motivations were several-fold. Human sacrifice was a method of bonding and initiation. Once a ceremony had been experienced – and with each successive sacrifice ritual – new members were plunged ever deeper into the occult hierarchy, sharing a common secret that not only bonded them to an oath of silence, but psychically empowered the participants involved in ritual sacrifices. The Matamoros cult believed that the soul of the sacrificed victim was released upon death, and subsequently captured by the cult members, bringing unto them great powers, such as being able to make themselves invisible to law enforcement authorities while running drugs across the border.

Another aspect of the Matamoros cult – paralleling the Son of Sam/Children cult – was the practice of blackmail used on those in positions of power, such as politicians, law enforcement officials and major players in the entertainment industry. Often such prominent people were placed in compromising positions, secretly filmed while performing sex acts of either a homosexual or bestial nature, or in the company of children. Films containing footage of politicians performing ritual sacrifice or buggering little boys could, quite obviously, go a long ways in furthering the aims of drug dealing blackmailers.

In 1989, the *Brownsville Herald* featured a story containing allegations that thousands of pounds of cocaine and marijuana had been moved across the border to supply high-ranking Chicago crime bosses, courtesy of the Matamoros cult, illustrating the links between Satanism and organized crime. Satanism, it appears, is nothing more than a means of recruitment. Berkowitz believed he was serving a devil worship cult, when in reality that all might have just been a front; a method of controlling dupes in a larger crime syndicate. What binds these disparate elements together is a black market of drugs and pornography, some of the same influences that appear to have motivated the Manson Family.

Another thread in this tangled web is serial killer Henry Lee Lucas, who claimed membership in a nationwide Satanic cult known as the Hand of Death. According to Lucas, both he and his partner, Ottis Toole, worked as contract killers for this shadowy group, which was involved in drug dealing, murder-for-hire and children smuggling into Mexico. Curiously enough, the only death sentence commuted during George W. Bush's watch as Governor of Texas was in the Lucas case. During Dubya's tenure, no less than one hundred and thirty death row inmates were executed. Oddly enough, Lucas's partner, Ottis Toole – convicted of murder in Florida – had his death sentence commuted by Dubya's brother, Jeb.

Supposedly responsible for several hundred murders, Toole and Lucas possessed a perverse penchant for rape, torture, necrophilia and cannibalism. As part of his Hand of Death indoctrination, Lucas alleged that he was trained in the finer aspects of abduction, arson and murder at a mobile paramilitary camp in the Florida Everglades. Tales of paramilitary camps training assassin-to-be is another murky area where rogue intelligence agency spooks merge with the shadowy world of cults – if indeed there is any substance to Lucas' claims. According to Lucas, the cult murders he performed were more than just random snuffs, and included hits on politicians and foreign diplomats. Stranger yet, Lucas claimed to have been friends with Jim Jones of People Temple's fame, another probable MK-ULTRA patsy. In this regard, Lucas accepted sole responsibility for delivering the cyanide used in the Guyana massacre.

To authorities, Lucas made reference to a cult-operated ranch in Juarez, Mexico, involved in drug distribution and Satanism and allegedly connected to a series of other ranches located throughout Mexico. Lucas' revelations were made several years before the Matamoros atrocities became public record. According to Lucas, cult members of the Juarez ranch included Mexican Federales, in addition to a member in high standing of Interpol.

Another area where MK-ULTRA and Satanism intersect is in the realm of multiple personality disorders (MPD'S). It has been alleged by certain sectors of the religious right that Satanic cults have mastered the ability to bury childhood memories of ritual victims via hypnosis. Then when these children become adults, they are re-contacted by the cult, and their memories reactivated. The victims are subsequently used for ritual ceremonies, then deactivated so as to retain no surface memories of the ritual abuse. To deal with the traumatic experience, victims compartmentalize these memories, such as rape or mental harassment. These compartmentalized memories, in turn, take the form of split, or multiple personalities. Psychotherapist Dr. Timothy Moss claimed that, for over thirty years, a "notorious psychiatrist" in Southern California was creating multiple personalities for Satanic cults.

Intelligence agencies, chiefly the CIA, have taken a keen interest in developing agents with multiple personalities, as documented in such books as *The Control of Candy Jones* by Donald Bain, *Operation Mind Control* by Walter Bowart, and *In Search of the Manchurian Candidate* by John Marks. *The Glasshouse Tapes* – a book chronicling the exploits of an *agent provocateur* named Louis Tackwood, who worked as an LAPD informer in the late 1960's – claimed that the LAPD had on its payroll a Pasadena-based Satanic cult, which was used to set up the Weather Underground, and other radical groups, in the sales of explosives. In the realms of intelligence work, strange bedfellows abound.

In 1992, further Process/Son of Sam revelations came to Maury Terry's attention in the form of an individual named Brother John, who in the 1960's was a friend and classmate of David Berkowitz. According to Brother John, "The Children" cult traced its roots back to the early 1950's, the offspring of a "nazi-sympathizing doctor" who formed "a ritual magic club that specialized in sex with children and drug dealing."

In 1961 – as a high school freshman – Brother John was recruited into the cult and described his initiation as a gang rape in Untermyer Park, followed by a ritual canine sacrifice. Afterwards, cult leaders turned Brother John into a teenage prostitute to big money interests, which included a consortium of judges, lawyers and doctors who specialized in sex with tots and teens. This group was allegedly in cahoots with a cabal of cops and politicians who helped cover up these deviant activities, which in time included ritual sacrifice of children. According to Brother John, this "ritual magic club" was taken over in the early 1970's by the Process Church. At that time, a heavy Satanic element was infused into the already existing organization.

According to Terry, the Process left New York shortly after Berkowitz's arrest. This, it appears, was their standard operating procedure: to leave to another locale after a fall guy had been fingered and apprehended for Process-related crimes. The Process next surfaced in Atlanta. Within a year after their arrival, a string of child murders occurred. The Process inner core (which Terry refers to as "the British faction") fled Georgia after Wayne Williams was arrested in the case. Although convicted of the slaying of two adults, Williams was never tried for the child murders. Nonetheless, authorities closed the case, pinning the entire string of slayings on Williams in the prototypical fall-guy fashion à la Oswald, Sirhan, etc. In 1998, some of Atlanta's top investigators from this period did an about-face, stating their belief on NBC's *Dateline* that Williams was innocent.

As to Brother John's allegations of child sex rings and satanic ritual sacrifices (conducted, no less, by a veritable Who's Who of rich, influential bigshots), later revelations of a similar nature surfaced during the late 1980's Franklin Committee investigations as documented in *The Franklin Cover-up*, authored by former Nebraska State Senator John Decamp. What at first appeared to be a late 1980's Savings and Loan scandal soon led Franklin investigators down many dark avenues and eventually to the highest levels of government. Drugs and child prostitution were at the core of the case, but mixed in with all of this was the Reagan Administration's involvement in Contra funding with laundered drug money, funneled through Franklin Savings and Loan. As the title of DeCamp's book suggests, the story was squelched by the powers-that-be, although anyone who has examined the case will see those all too familiar spectres lurking in the shadows, intermingling with intelligence agency spooks and closet Satanists lusting after little boys and girls.

CHAPTER 44
The Manson/Sirhan Connection

On June 5th, 1968, Senator Robert Kennedy – in the company of Roman Polanski and Sharon Tate – attended a dinner party at the Malibu home of John Frankenheimer, director of 1962's *The Manchurian Candidate*. After supper, Frankenheimer drove Kennedy to the Ambassador Hotel, where later he was allegedly gunned down by Sirhan Sirhan. Prior to RFK's assassination, witnesses observed Sirhan in the Ambassador Ballroom with an attractive, well proportioned young lady, wearing a polka-dotted dress, who handed him a cup of coffee – or some sort of murky beverage – from which he imbibed. Could the liquid substance Sirhan ingested have been spiked with a trance-inducing drug which set the ritual sacrifice in motion, *Manchurian Candidate*-style?

During his trial, Sirhan claimed he had no memory of the shooting, although he did recall the events leading up to, and immediately following it, as well as his encounter with The Girl in the Polka-Dot Dress. In a 1969 interview with NBC correspondent Jack Perkins, Sirhan was asked, "All right, after you poured coffee for the girl, then what happened?"

"Then, ah... I don't remember what happened after that," Sirhan replied. This suggests the possibility of hypnosis used in conjunction with psychoactive drugs employed to create a Manchurian Candidate, whose memory of the crime was erased to cover his handler's tracks.

Through revelations made public during 1970's congressional investigations, it was discovered that a post-hypnotic method known as "blocking" was used by MK-ULTRA practitioners. This technique enabled the programmer to lock away commands within the mind of the hypno-programmed subject which could be unlocked only through certain coded "triggers."

In hindsight, it appears the role of the Girl in the Polka-Dot Dress was that of a trigger, used to set off Sirhan's subsequent actions. If, in fact, Sirhan was programmed, it may have occurred in 1967 when he disappeared for three months, a period when his whereabouts were unknown to his family. When he did return, Sirhan had developed a sudden interest in the occult.

In the RFK assassination aftermath, LAPD created a unit named "Special Unit Senator" (SUS) to investigate the circumstances surrounding the assassination. SUS included in its ranks former CIA agents Manny Pena and Hank Hernandez, who are alleged to have destroyed crucial evidence related to the case, namely door jambs and ceiling panels containing multiple bullet holes, suggesting more than one shooter was involved in the crime. It was SUS who put together the evidence that later became the basis for the prosecution's case against Sirhan.

SUS found a book in Sirhan's possession, *Healing, the Divine Art* by Manly Palmer Hall, a hypnotist, spiritualist and founder of the Philosophical Research Society. Sources have alleged that

Sirhan attended Hall's Institute of Reflection in Los Angeles. Among Hall's clients was L.A. Mayor Sam Yorty, which provides another twist in this caper, as it was Yorty – following Sirhan's arrest – who branded Sirhan a commie influenced occultist who had been brainwashed by Leftist New Age propaganda.

During the investigation, Yorty visited LAPD's field command post set up near the Ambassador Hotel. Rooting around through the evidence on hand, Yorty discovered Rosicrucian literature and a pair of spiral notebooks filled with repetitive and disjointed scrawlings indicating that its alleged author, Sirhan, possessed occult affinities. Afterwards, Yorty informed the press that Sirhan was, "...a member of numerous Communist organizations, including the Rosicrucians." When it was pointed out to Yorty that the Rosicrucians were not Communists, he amended his miscue, stating: "It appears that Sirhan Sirhan was a sort of loner who harbored Communist inclinations, favored Communists of all types. He said the U.S. must fall. Indicated that RFK must be assassinated before June 5, 1968." Yorty received his intelligence on Sirhan from excerpted passages taken from the spiral notebooks, although it has never been established whether these notebooks were actually written by Sirhan. Added to this, the notebooks were seized from Sirhan's room at his family's Pasadena residence without proper search warrants. Shades of Lee Harvey Oswald a few years prior come to mind when the same tack was taken in a similar smear campaign, painting Oswald Marxist red.

As the years pass – and the true facts of JFK's assassination have slowly come to light – Lee Harvey Oswald's portrait becomes less distorted. Evidence now indicates that Oswald was most likely an intelligence agency asset, albeit a pawn in the grand schemes of things, and possibly even a product of MK-ULTRA. Like Sirhan, he left behind a diary that illustrated commie allegiances and an apparent psychological imbalance, although it's still in dispute whether Oswald actually authored the diary in question. Some suspect that the Oswald diary was the product of CIA disinformation, surreptitiously composed to frame him as a homicidal commie-symp.

Arthur Bremer – who shot George Wallace – left behind a similar incriminating diary, and was likewise branded a "lone nut." David Berkowitz also left behind an incriminating diary. So – as one can see – a familiar pattern has repeated itself.

‡

In *America Bewitched*, psychic Daniel Logan presented the theory that black magic cults were responsible for RFK's assassination, and that the cults in question were "100 percent white, hated the black race, and felt that the way world chaos could be ignited was to incite whites against blacks." According to Logan, members of "black-arts churches" were seen in full public view, black hoods and all, on the streets of Southern California right up until RFK's assassination. Afterwards, they suddenly vanished. Logan went on to list several "coincidences" pertaining to RFK's assassination:

1. Many black-art California-based cults such as Process Church of the Final Judgment teach the destruction of the United States through chaos and mass violence.

2. Members of these cults generally hate blacks.

3. Robert Kennedy worked for the advancement of blacks and was generally liked, trusted, and respected by them.

4. Black art cults are mainly localized in the Los Angeles area.

5. Robert Kennedy was assassinated in Los Angeles.

6. Sirhan Sirhan, the assassin of Robert Kennedy, had studied mysticism and was a devotee (albeit a misguided one) of Mme. Blavatsky, the woman who founded the Theosophical Society, and many of whose beliefs were not only mystically but politically inspired as well. (While living in India, she openly denounced the pacifist ways of Mahatma Gandhi, who was himself eventually assassinated!)

7. Charles Manson, while in prison in the nineteen-sixties, had also studied the occult teachings of Mme. Blavatsky, along with those of other mystical personalities.

8. The night before Robert Kennedy was murdered he had his last dinner with Sharon Tate

and her husband, Roman Polanski.

9. A few months later, Sharon Tate and her friends were killed by Charles Manson's family.

Ed Sanders, in *The Family*, brought up the possibility that the Process Church had "a baleful influence" on Sirhan. In the spring of 1968, Sirhan visited clubs in Hollywood on the same turf where the Process was then proselytizing their doom and gloom philosophy, and he spoke often, prior to Kennedy's death, of his desire to visit an occult group in London.

According to Sanders, a Process member named Lloyd worked as a Ambassador Hotel chef at the time of RFK's assassination and that Sirhan visited a friend in the Ambassador Hotel kitchen only a day before Kennedy was shot.

The evening following RFK's assassination, a Major Jose Antonio Duarte marched into LAPD headquarters with four companions, and stated that he and his men were "freedom fighters against Fidel Castro." On May 21st, Duarte claimed he had attended a leftist meeting where support for Castro was on the agenda, and – when he arose to deliver an anti-Castro harangue – he said a young Palestinian angrily accused him of being a C.I.A. agent, and that the two got into a jostling match. Duarte identified his young combatant as Sirhan Sirhan.

Later on, LAPD discredited Duarte's identification of Sirhan. Nonetheless, the whole affair raised the eyebrows of those in the conspiracy research community who had seen this scenario play out before in the JFK assassination, when Lee Harvey Oswald was a participant in a similar shoving match with anti-Castro Cuban, Carlos Bringuier, outside the New Orleans World Trade Mart.

As history instructs, Oswald was there that day handing out pro-Castro leaflets on the street. Bringuier – who supposedly just happened on scene – angrily confronted Oswald, inciting a shoving match, which a local news camera crew from WSDU-TV also *just happened* to capture on film. Not long after, WSDU's sister station, WSDU-AM, conducted a live radio debate between Oswald and Bringuier, which was "moderated" by another recurring character in Kennedy lore, Ed Butler.

In the JFK assassination aftermath, the Oswald/Bringuier radio debate was pressed to vinyl on the recording *Self Portrait In Red*, which presented posthumous evidence that Oswald was inspired to blow the proverbial crown from Camelot's head due to his Marxist affiliations. The organization that produced *Self Portrait In Red* was The Information Council of the Americas (INCA), with whom Ed Butler was associated. In retrospect, many now suspect that the Oswald/Bringuier confrontation was staged, the ultimate design of which was to build a false history around Oswald that could later be used against him.

Oswald, it appears, was but a patsy in a convoluted scheme, playing the role of commie agitator at the behest of his handlers. His mission was probably stated to him by his superiors as "intelligence gathering" as all the while he was being set up. Oswald was a double agent who got duped. Subsequently, Jack Ruby silenced him forever.

Following RFK's assassination, two researchers connected to the John Birch Society – Anthony Hilder and John Steinbacher – held a press conference, and afterwards appeared on several talk shows claiming that a Illuminati/Communist plot had orchestrated RFK's assassination and controlled Sirhan Sirhan's actions. Given these facts, it may seem odd that the previously mentioned Ed Butler – formerly of INCA – arranged the Steinbacher/ Hilder press conference. Butler, in my estimation, was likely performing the role of a disinformation agent, setting the stage for another sacrificial lamb, this time in the form of Sirhan Sirhan.

Hilder and Steinbacher possessed equally suspect backgrounds, as both had been protégés of Myron Fagan, a prominent player in the McCarthy Era Hollywood blacklisting brigade. Curiously, Hilder and a band of compatriots had been at the Ambassador Hotel the night before the assassination, passing out anti-Kennedy handbills. Following RFK's assassination, Hilder and his cohorts created considerable confusion by alleging that Sirhan was a Eugene McCarthy supporter. A year before, Hilder self-published *It Comes Up Murder*, which outlined a vast conspiracy theory of history starring Adam Weishaupt in the leading role, who in Bavaria in 1776 organized "the secret and evil cult of the Illuminati in order to wage Satan's war against Christian civilization." Eventually, according to Hilder, the Illuminati coalesced into the modern International Communist conspiracy, which, in turn, evolved into such evil New World Order fronts as the United Nations, and the Council of Foreign Relations.

In 1978's *The Assassination of Robert F. Kennedy*, authors William Turner and Jonn Christian suggested the Steinbacher/Hilder theory of the RFK assassination being a Communist Plot was a general theme that stuck in the public mind, whether accepted as fact or not. According to the authors, one effect of this Communist Plot disinformation campaign was that it permitted the LAPD to suppress evidence leading in the opposite direction, toward the far right.

In regards to Tate/LaBianca, Ed Butler wrote one the first articles on the murders in October of 1969 – prior to the arrest of Manson and his girls – entitled "Did Hate Kill Tate?" which appeared in a periodical published by Patrick Frawley, a far right winger and Nixon Presidential campaign. According to Mae Brussell, Butler performed the role of *agent provocateur* in penning this piece, in much the same manner that he was previously involved in JFK/RFK assassination disinformation.

Butler's article suggested that the Black Panthers had committed the Tate/LaBianca murders in association with communists, and that the rationale behind the killings was to spread terror among the masses. The Panthers – according to Butler's thesis – were doing this to "test the stomach" of America for future violence. Brussell suspected that Butler was trying to frame the Black Panthers, thus igniting a race war. In his own way, perhaps Manson was being manipulated into the same situation, ala Helter Skelter.

In his article, Butler presented clues supposedly left by the Panthers at the Polanski residence:

1) The white hood over Jay Sebring's head was a turn-about for the Klu Klux Klan.

2) The rope found around Jay and Sharon's bodies was an allusion to the lynching of blacks by white racists.

3) "Death to Pigs" scrawled on the wall in blood was a challenge to police. (Interestingly enough, Butler used the term "Blue Meanies" in the article when referring to the police. "Blue Meanies" was taken from the animated Beatle movie, *Yellow Submarine*, yet another Manson/Beatle connection.)

4) *Time* magazine quoted in an article that Jay Sebring was supposedly anti-black.

‡

In preparation for Sirhan Sirhan's trial, his attorneys put together a psychiatric team led by U.C. Berkeley's Dr. Bernard Diamond. Previously, Diamond had won acquittal for an Air Force Officer charged with mail bombing by putting him under hypnosis. Given this success, Diamond decided to employ similar tactics due to Sirhan's apparent amnesia regarding the RFK assassination.

When Diamond delivered his testimony, he presented the theory that Sirhan had been hypnotized at the time of the assassination. According to Diamond, Sirhan was a Grade-A hypnotic subject and, it appeared, had been hypnotized many times before. Sirhan admitted to Dr. Diamond that, upon occasion, he had put himself under by staring into a mirror. Sirhan's notebooks, Diamond concluded, were products of self-induced trances and, in fact, were "automatic writings" similar to those of mystics and seers who are able to channel "spirits" through spontaneous composition.

During Sirhan's trances he wrote "like a robot" which suggests he was functioning as an automaton, performing the esoteric bidding of some sinister force, which either emanated from his subconscious mind, or conversely, some external force.

A passage from Sirhan's notebook reads:

May 18, 9:45 a.m. –68. My determination to eliminate RFK is becoming more the more of an unshakable obsession... RFK must die – RFK must be killed Robert F. Kennedy must be assassinated RFK must be assassination ED RFK must be assassinated before 5 June 68 Robert F. Kennedy must be assassinated I have never heard please pay to the order of of of of of of of of this or that please pay to the order of..."

Dr. Diamond queried Sirhan about certain entries in his notebook while under hypnosis.

"Is this crazy writing," Diamond asked.

"YES YES YES," Sirhan responded in writing.

"Are you crazy?"

"NO NO."

"Well, why are you writing crazy?"

"PRACTICE PRACTICE PRACTICE."

"Practice for what."

"MIND CONTROL MIND CONTROL MIND CONTROL."

Dr. Diamond later surfaced as a principal defense witness in the John Lennon murder trial, examining Mark David Chapman as he had Sirhan thirteen years before. Mind control researchers have suggested that Chapman was originally programmed in the mid-1970's by MK-ULTRA handlers, then kept on hold until he was "activated" by J.D. Salinger's novel *The Catcher In The Rye*, in an identical manner that the Queen of Hearts was used as a post-hypnotic trigger in *The Manchurian Candidate*. When Chapman was apprehended at the Dakota Building – after shooting Lennon – he was sitting against a wall, reading a copy of *The Catcher In The Rye*.

The *Catcher In The Rye* was also found in the possession of Ronald Reagan's attempted assassin, John Hinkley, who could almost be considered a Chapman double. The use of doubles in assassination plots appears to be standard procedure in the framing of patsies, at least in the cases of such "lone nuts" as James Earl Ray and Lee Harvey Oswald. Reportedly, a man closely resembling Hinkley – waving a gun around and threatening to kill President Reagan – was apprehended by police on the New York subway prior to the assassination attempt on Reagan. Oddly enough, this "double" had an obsession for Jodie Foster, as well as an unnatural fondness for the *Catcher in the Rye*.

Another Hinkley/Chapman connection concerns the anti-Communist foundation World Vision headed by John Hinkley, Sr., an organization of which Chapman was a one time member. In this capacity, Chapman visited refugee camps that – according to researcher John Judge – doubled as recruiting grounds for intelligence operatives and would-be assassins.

During a nervous breakdown episode in Hawaii, Chapman was institutionalized at Castle Memorial Hospital, a medical facility allegedly involved in MK-ULTRA. Was it here that Chapman received his final programming? Ominously, when Chapman signed out on his last day of work in Hawaii, he signed the name John Lennon, then scratched it out, suggesting that this was the main focus in his mind, as if he had been triggered: a torpedo zeroing in and eventually destroying his target, a rock n' roll singer with heavy political leanings to the left.

When one examines the case histories of Oswald, Chapman, Hinkley, Sirhan, Arthur Bremer, et al, a common modus operandi, used to set up patsies, becomes evident, consisting of false trails, such as:

1) Planted weapons or ballistics implicating the alleged assassin to the crime;

2) Forged diaries portraying the assassin as psychologically unbalanced or treasonous;

3) A double (or impostor) assuming the identity of the alleged assassin, who – prior to the assassination – is engaged in activities aimed at further implicating the "patsy" to the crime;

4) Staged events prior to the assassination devised and performed to demonstrate that the "assassin" was a lone nut crazy.

In *The Assassination of Robert F. Kennedy,* authors Christian and Turner speculated that Sirhan's mind control handler might have been Hollywood hypnotist William Jennings Bryan, who had once worked as a technical adviser on the set of John Frankenheimer's *The Manchurian Candidate*. During their investigation, the authors came across a passage from Sirhan's diary that read: "God help me... please help me. Salvo Di Di Salvo Die S Salvo..." This reference was to Albert Di Salvo, the notorious Boston Strangler, a case that had been cracked by the aforementioned Dr. Bryan, who billed himself as the world's leading hypnosis expert. During the Korean War, Bryan had put his skills to use for the United States Air Force, and afterwards became a consultant for the MK-ULTRA program.

During the 1960's, Bryan set up a Sunset Strip practice, which he christened the American Institute of Hypnosis, using the locale for a variety of wide-ranging symposiums, including one called "Successful Treatments of Sexual Disorders."

"I enjoy variety and I like to get to know people on a deep emotional level," Bryan once told a magazine reporter. "One way of getting to know people is through intercourse." In 1969, the California Medical Examiners Board found Bryan guilty of sexually molesting four women patients under hypnosis. These improprieties notwithstanding, Bryan was a Christian fundamentalist and descendant of the original William Jennings Bryan, who was opposed to the teachings of evolution as argued in the Scopes "monkey trial."

Following RFK's assassination – before Sirhan had been identified as a suspect – Bryan appeared on Los Angeles radio station KNBC with host Ray Briem, and in an offhand comment stated that the assassin probably acted under posthypnotic suggestion. Later, when Sirhan was asked about the Di Salvo entry in his notebook, he drew a complete blank, admitting that the name was unknown to him. As stated before, Bryan was big on boasting about his involvement in the Boston Strangler case, and the authors suspected it might have been Bryan who actually placed Sirhan in a trance state prior to RFK's assassination.

For several years, Bryan had been dodging interview requests from Turner and Christian, but when a "disarmingly attractive" journalist, Betsy Langman, approached him in June 1974, Bryan consented.

"I am probably the leading expert in the world" Bryan triumphantly proclaimed, adding that he could, "hypnotize everybody in this office in less than five minutes." Bryan went on to detail his successes in the Boston Strangler and the Hollywood Strangler cases. But when Langman – who had been researching the possibility of assassination through mind control – asked, "Do you feel that Sirhan could have been self-hypnotized," Bryan went ballistic. "I'm not going to comment on that case," Bryan cut her off, "because I didn't hypnotize him...The interview is over!" Later, Langman met Dr. Bryan's secretary, who claimed that Bryan had received an emergency call from Maryland only minutes after George Wallace had been shot by Arthur Bremer, another purported mind-controlled puppet.

In the spring of 1977, Bryan was found dead in a Las Vegas motel room "from natural causes", although this statement was issued before an official autopsy was conducted. Afterwards, Turner and Christian were put in contact with two Hollywood call girls who claimed to have been servicing Bryan during his last year. According to the women, Bryan had become strung out on drugs, and his groin and thighs were pocked with needle mark bruises, although no mention of needle marks were mentioned in the coroner's report.

The call girls informed them that Dr. Bryan was constantly bragging about the famous people he'd hypnotized, among them Albert Di Salvo and, curiously enough, Sirhan Sirhan. The girls didn't suspect anything unusual in regards to the Sirhan reference, as Bryan had told them many times that he worked on murder cases with the LAPD . One of the girls thought they heard Bryan mention the name of James Earl Ray in a similar context. Bryan also confided to them that he was a C.I.A. agent involved in "top secret projects." After Bryan's death, his offices were sealed off from news reporters by his estate's probate lawyer, John Minder, who just happened to have prosecuted Sirhan Sirhan while a deputy district attorney.

As previously stated, Manson possessed an intense interest in hypnotism, which was initially spurred in prison, mainly through books, and from other inmates who possessed knowledge of the craft. Charlie maintained this interest after prison, as noted in his Sunset Strip visits with the manager of the Galaxy Club, who later opened the Hollywood Hypnotism Center, and on occasion discussed the finer points of hypnotism with Charlie. Dr. Bryan's offices were also located on Sunset Boulevard, as he was active there during the same period that Manson haunted the Strip.

Another possible Manson/Sirhan connection comes in the form of the late actor Sal Mineo, a frequent celebrity spectator during the Tate/LaBianca trials. In 1976, Mineo was slated to play the role of Sirhan Sirhan in an RFK assassination film, which featured in its plot conspiratorial themes of post-hypnotic programming and CIA involvement.

Unfortunately, Mineo was stabbed to death before the movie went into production. After his murder, *Newsweek* ran a story about "long-whispered reports of the actor's alleged bisexuality and fondness for sadomasochistic ritual quickly surrounded his murder."

CHAPTER 45
The Power Control Group

In the mid-1970's, another Tate/LaBianca/RFK assassination connection came to light when Vincent Bugliosi – then in private practice – defended Los Angeles TV station KCOP in a libel suit filed by Reverend Jerry Owen. Rev. Owen first came to the attention of authorities nine hours after RFK's assassination, when he informed police that he'd picked up a hitchhiker – a couple of days before – whom be believed was Sirhan Sirhan.

Owen had an alleged history of burning down churches and collecting the insurance money. He was implicated in six church arsons between 1939 and 1962, although no one was able to conclusively pin any of the crimes on him. An ex-boxer, Owen had other brushes with the law, often of a "strong arm" nature.

In 1968 – living in Santa Ana, California – Owen was known as the self-styled "Shepherd of the Hills" who visited shopping malls and gave free pony rides to children who promised to memorize bible verses. Owen subsidized his income by trading horses on the side, which is how he met Sirhan Sirhan – or so he claimed – when he picked up Sirhan hitchhiking in downtown Los Angeles prior to the RFK assassination.

According to a police report he filed, Owen encountered Sirhan standing on a street corner with some suspicious looking individuals; a man with long hair, wearing an occult symbol medallion, and another person whose description seemed similar to The Girl In The Polka-Dot Dress. Afterwards, Owen drove Sirhan to meet a friend who worked as a chef in a large building, the rear entrance of which was accessed by a cul-de-sac. While Sirhan went inside, Owen waited in his pickup. It was only later that he discovered this location was the Ambassador Hotel's rear entrance.

In 1969 – when Owen went on the airwaves with a program called "The Walking Bible" – Jonn Christian briefed KCOP management on Owen's background, which not only included his Sirhan Sirhan hitchhiking story, but as well the substantial sums Owen was able to raise to fund his show; money coming from an unrevealed source. Christian calculated that Owen committed to more than $130,000 a year, monetary peanuts compared to the likes of Oral Roberts or Billy Graham, but coming from a preacher with no visible means of income, this was a substantial sum. Even though Christian and Turner didn't come flat out and state as much in their book, it's my impression that they felt the money was a payoff from some unseen benefactor for Owen's role in the RFK assassination.

Leading up to the assassination, Sirhan was employed as an assistant manager at a horse breeding farm owned by Desi Arnaz of "I Love Lucy" fame. Arnaz, a staunch anti-Castro Cuban, was friends with mobster Mickey Cohen, who in turn was buddies with Alvin Creepy Carpis, Manson's prison mentor. Jerry Owen claimed that when he picked up Sirhan hitchhiking, the two discussed Sirhan buying a horse from him, which Owen allegedly agreed to deliver to the back entrance of the Ambassador hotel on the night of the assassination. William Turner believed that Owen's story about picking up Sirhan was fictitious, and that Owen had came up with it "...to put an innocent face on a pre-existing relationship with Sirhan." On the contrary, Turner and Christian's investigation verified that Owen and Sirhan at been seen together at the preacher's ranch on a pervious occasion, and that one of the witnesses reported that Owen said, "RFK had to be killed because he would stop the Vietnam War and God would be angry."

During the KCOP libel suit trial, Owen brought forward a devoted follower named, Gail Aiken, as a character witness. Vincent Bugliosi, primed by Turner and Christian, asked Owen if Aiken was Arthur Bremer's (George Wallace's attempted assassin) sister, which indeed was the case. Once this connection was discovered, as Turner recently noted, "...Aiden was hurriedly sent back to Florida where her brother, William Bremer Jr., had been convicted of fraud. William's attorney was Ellis Rubin, who represented the Miami Four in the Watergate prosecutions..."

In the end, a settlement was awarded to Owen in the libel suit. Nonetheless, the case opened up a Pandora's Box of conspiratorial connections, revealing Owen as someone who knew Sirhan well before he allegedly picked him up hitchhiking. It was this setting of a civil trial which Bugliosi used as a forum for attempting to reopen the RFK assassination investigation, and – although this gambit wasn't entirely successful – many new leads turned up as a result. However, it seems curious that Bugliosi associated himself with the Owen case, as he later served as prosecution for Lee Harvey Oswald's mock television trial of the late 1980's, and more recently has written a pro Warren Commission/JFK assassination book. Concurrently, Bugliosi supports a RFK assassination conspiracy theory, which seems incongruous, which is not to suggest that you can't discount one lone nut theory and not accept another. Just the same, it appears Bugliosi is playing both sides of the fence when it comes to the "lone nut" question.

If Mae Brussell were still alive, I'm sure she'd suspect Bugliosi of acting as a double agent in the Owen trial – and she stated as much in regards to the Tate/LaBianca trial: that Bugliosi offered up Charlie and the girls to the ritual alter of judicial sacrifice, while at the same time covering up certain aspects of the case connected to military intelligence and the Mob. Others that Brussell fingered as being part of this shadowy fraternity – the "Power Control Group" as she termed it – were Ed Butler, Paul Krassner, Larry Flynt, and Lawrence Schiller, as well as conspiracy researchers Dick Gregory and Mark Lane.

Attorney Mark Lane first came to fame when he represented Lee Harvey Oswald post-mortem, and was the first person to publish a book on the Kennedy assassination, *Rush To Judgment*. Lane followed this up in the mid-1970's with a book co-written with Dick Gregory on the Martin Luther King assassination, *Code Name Zorro*. Perhaps Lane's most curious relationship to the world of conspiracy theory was as lawyer for Jim Jones' People Temple, recounted in his1980 book, *The Strongest Poison*. Lane was at Jonestown when the "suicide pact" took place, escaping to the jungle during the siege. Such researchers as John Judge claim that Jonestown was a CIA mind control experiment gone awry.

Rumors that Lane is an intelligence agency asset have long circulated. Mae Brussell referred to Lane as a "vacuum"; an operative who sucks up info from conspiracy researchers then reports back his findings to the intelligence community. Another purpose of operatives such as these is to present certain "conspiracy theories", bolstered by a retinue of facts, then add to the mix a red herring or two, which in turn discredits the original theory, or distorts the known facts just enough to divert attention away from certain areas of inquiry. "Vacuums", it has been suggested, offer up alternative explanations and cover stories to conceal the true culprits.

According to Mae Brussell's theory, the Power Control Group exists on two levels; the first level consisting of those who engineer the hit teams, set up patsies and doctor the evidence, not only in the assassinations of JFK/RFK/MLK, but as well in such other "strategies of tension" as the

Tate/LaBianca murders, Jonestown massacre, Kent State, etc.

The second level engineered by the Power Control Group are the cover-ups, such as the Warren Commission Report, or the Tate/LaBianca trial. The Power Control Group – according to Brussell's hypothesis – consists of lawyers, politicians, and members of the media and entertainment industries, who have been co-opted by The Establishment.

Brussell's contended that certain Power Control Group members were selected to masquerade as legitimate researchers, as in the case of Dick Gregory and Mark Lane, respected "authorities" on the Kennedy assassination. In their appointed roles as conspiracy research spokespersons, such "authorities" disseminate only what the Power Control Group cast their covert stamp of approval on, and in this manner are better able to suppress more pertinent evidence, that those in control wish to remain concealed.

Perhaps the most colorful member of Brussell's "Power Control Group" was Larry Flynt. Brussell believed that her friend and frequent editor, Paul Krassner – who published Mae's articles in *The Realist* – had been wooed away and fallen victim to the Power Control Group when the broke and in debt publisher accepted a deal from Flynt to work for *Hustler* during this period. By manipulating Krassner, Mae theorized, the Power Control Group could better maintain a stranglehold on what she and other conspiracy researchers disseminated.

Upon assuming his position at *Hustler*, Krassner's first communiqué to Mae was a request for her to write a monthly column, with the disclaimer that he wasn't interested in anything pertaining to the JFK assassination. Mae found this odd, especially when – at the same time – Flynt had just added the *LA Free Press* to his publishing empire and, in its pages, had offered a one million dollar reward to anyone who could solve the JFK assassination. Some would cite reasons of petty envy, but Brussell felt her exclusion – as well as the exclusion of other JFK researchers from Flynt's *L.A. Free Press* – was a further example of the Power Control Group wielding its influence.

Another recurring character in Kennedy assassination research is Lawrence Schiller, who enticed Susan Atkins into selling the rights to her confession. In regards to the Kennedy assassination, Schiller was associated with Jack Ruby during his final days, once again playing a role, which – for all intents and purposes – appeared to be that of a disinformation agent. As has been well documented, Jack Ruby was a mass of contradictions. The rationale he first gave for killing Oswald was because he wanted to spare Jackie and her children the grief of a public trial. Later on, Ruby did an about face, claiming that a vast conspiracy was behind Kennedy's assassination. However, on his death-bed, Ruby recanted – in a confession captured on a Capitol Records album – stating that there was "absolutely no conspiracy." In the hospital room with Ruby at the time of this final confession was Lawrence Schiller. On January 4th, 1967 – two days later – Ruby died. It has been alleged that Ruby was the victim of a cancer-causing agent injected into him against his will. As previously noted, when Mae Brussell succumbed to cancer, there are those who alleged that she had been the recipient of a similar death-inducing agent. Schiller was the co-editor, in 1967, of a curious tome entitled *Scavengers and Critics of the Warren Report: The Endless Paradox*, an attack on Warren Report critics.

Another faction of Mae Brussell's perceived "Power Control Group" consisted of various lawyers overlapped in the Kennedy assassinations and Tate/LaBianca murders. Brussell claimed that Charlie met with a Beverly Hills law firm before his 1967 release from Terminal Island, and that this same law firm was later involved with Sirhan Sirhan. Brussell alleged that Tex Watson met with members of this same law firm immediately before the Tate/LaBianca murders. Another possible connecting point – in the Tate/LaBianca/Kennedy assassination nexus – is former Warren Commission member Joseph Bell, who met with Manson during the Tate/LaBianca proceedings, and was at one time a member of Sirhan Sirhan's defense team.

Mae Brussell suspected that famed lawyer Melvin Belli was another member of the "Power Control Group." Belli had been Jack Ruby's lawyer, and later represented the Rolling Stones and their involvement in the Altamont Rock Concert, which Brussell believed, in essence, was a similar "strategy of tension" on a par with the Kent State massacre; a tragedy orchestrated by the shadow government, whose main motive was to undermine the 1960's counterculture and peace movement.

Brussell's protégé, John Judge, is of the same opinion regarding Altamont, believing that the event was "set up to discredit Woodstock and to be the dark side of the coin with The Rolling Stones..." Following the Tate/LaBianca murders, as Judge has noted, it was a long time before any positive images of hippies or other members of the counterculture were seen on TV, or elsewhere in the media.

Is it possible that the fall of Camelot and the Manson Family murders have much more in common than most of us have ever realized?

CHAPTER 46
Home, Sweet Home

Convicted on seven counts of murder and sentenced to death, Manson was sent to San Quentin on April 22nd, 1972. After a California court decision overturned the death penalty, Charlie's sentence was reduced to life in prison, and he was transferred to the California Medical Facility at Vacaville. In an interview at the time, Manson described himself as a Christ-like prophet whose disciples got out of control.

On October 6th, 1972, Charlie was transferred to Folsom Prison. On October 24th – two weeks after his arrival – Charlie informed a guard that he'd dispatched a team of assassins to kill President Nixon.

In the fall of 1973, there were reports that Manson was regressing, and refusing to leave his cell. Charlie's fingernails grew long and curly, and he was reluctant to bathe. In the view of authorities, Manson's mental state was deteriorating. He was subsequently transferred back to Vacaville for psychiatric observation. It wasn't long, though, before Charlie was his old mischievous self, and – in the view of some prison officials – had merely feigned mental deterioration as a ploy to get off the Folsom main line.

Near the end of 1973, Inyo County Sheriffs and the U.S. Park Service were monitoring the activities of a band of Manson followers in Death Valley, which included T.J. Walleman, and an unidentified woman with an X carved on her forehead. A month after their arrival, someone attempted to rob a sporting goods store in Ridgecrest by crashing a hot-wired truck through the rear door. The Sheriff suspected the Manson gang of the attempted robbery, assuming that they were after the store's gun supply. However, authorities were unable to pin the crime on the group.

The Manson gang eventually settled at the Minnette Mine in Panamint Valley. While the gang was away one day, a nosy neighbor came snooping around and discovered a tunnel loaded with food and supplies. Other locals reported that the Manson girls were often heard giggling and whispering that Charlie's Family would be back at full strength by the end of 1974, implying that Charlie would rejoin them at that time.

Meanwhile, another group of Manson followers were renting a house in Stockton, California. This group included Nancy (Brenda) Pitman, Priscilla Cooper, Maria Theresa Alonzo (aka Crystal), and three Aryan Brotherhood bikers: Michael Lee Monfort, James (Spider) Craig, and William (Iceman/Chilly Willy) Goucher. Lauren and James Willett – who also lived at the house – were later murdered. Lauren's body was discovered buried in the basement of the Stockton house. Her husband, James, was found buried near the Russian River in Northern California. Monfort pled guilty to murder. Pitman, Cooper and Craig received accessory to murder convictions.

In October of 1974, Vacaville officers discovered escape plans outlined in a note written by Manson, which concluded by asking "if Rainbow was in the North and if the Queen of the South was out of jail?" Investigators suspected that "Rainbow" was a code name for Squeaky and the "Queen of the South" was Sandra Good.

On December 13th, two Manson associates – A.B. members Kenneth Como and Bobby Davis – nearly escaped from Folsom when guards discovered them using hacksaws to cut through the bars of their cells. A third inmate, Gerald Gallant, was also in on the escape. However, it is unknown whether Manson – back at Folsom during this period – intended to join them, as he and Como had had a falling out a year before. Apparently, Como was hot for Gypsy Share and when Charlie learned of their relationship, he tried to cut Como off by sending word to Squeaky, who passed on the gospel to Gypsy that she was to no longer to associate with Como. Like a good disciple, Gypsy obeyed, withholding her many charms, which led to a purported ass-kicking Charlie later received at the hands of Como in the Folsom exercise yard, ostensibly causing a rift between Charlie and the A.B. (Gypsy later went on to marry Como.)

In 1975, Manson maneuvered his way back to Vacaville, reportedly playing the prison psychiatrists like finely tuned instruments. An instance of Manson's purported chameleon-like trickster persona occurred one afternoon when Dr. Morton Felix was startled to discover an unknown inmate had crashed his group therapy session. Toothless – with a backward ball cap on his head – the mysterious stranger lectured the group about exterminating child molesters and Jews, and suffocating women who forced their husbands to work. To his shock, Dr. Felix later discovered that the inmate in question was Manson, who had altered his appearance by shaving his beard, getting a haircut, and removing his false teeth.

By the mid-70's, original Manson Family members had begun to splinter and, in 1975, Manson issued threats against Cappy Gillies, Ruth Ann Moorehouse, and Mary Brunner for leaving his Family. However, there were occasional new converts, such as a young lady named Misty Hay (aka Pat Gillum) who, in 1976, began corresponding with Manson. In due time, Hay was arrested and sentenced to five years in the federal pen for sending threatening letters through the U.S. Postal System. In September of that year, Hay sent a signed death threat to the president of the Sierra Club stating that "Charles Manson has people watching you now... so do your part to stop them from cutting down trees, or else you'll be chopped up yourselves. For every tree you let be cut down, you shall have your limbs cut off. Take heed of this mean letter or die!"

Another misguided soul known as the "Lady in White" – a middle-aged woman with glassy blue-gray eyes – appeared unannounced at Vacaville one day, sporting a flowing white gown, with matching white stockings and white shoes, reminding those who saw her of Betty Davis in *What Ever Happened to Baby Jane?* Despite her weird get-up, The Lady in White made it all the way to the Warden's office before her odd behavior drew enough attention to have her detained. Disturbed by her less than rational answers, guards searched the Lady in White and discovered a twenty-four inch-railroad spike hidden in the folds of her fancy dress.

"I've been sent by Charles Manson," The Lady in White announced. "Jesus was crucified with a spike. I'm going to use it to slay the demon who has possessed Manson's soul." Soon after, the Lady in White found herself in one of the many state-funded rubber rooms, courtesy of California tax-payers.

Not long after the "Lady in White" episode, a young man approached the Vacaville gate, demanding to see Manson. The disciple-in-waiting spun around in circles, screaming that his head was on fire, and that electricity was shooting between his ears. Manson, he said, was the only person on Earth who could relieve his inner torment. The police subsequently carted the young man off in a straight jacket.

As always, Charlie's fans and followers were constantly sending him things, including guitars and other musical instruments, which – Manson has claimed over the years – prison officials have unfairly restricted him from using. Edward George – in *Taming The Beast: Charles Manson's Life Behind Bars* – claims that Charlie was able, upon occasion, to receive some of these gifts, such as the guitars. Inevitably, Manson would play the instruments for a while, then in sudden fits of rage, destroy them. Whatever the case, Manson has continued making music over his years of confinement, producing several recordings, as well as other types of artwork. It is in prison, Charlie has stated, that he is at his most creative.

‡

In the mid 70's, neo-Nazi Perry "Red" Warthan began visiting Manson at Vacaville as an official liaison for the Ohio based Universal Order, an outfit led by former American Nazi Party member, James Mason. During this period, Mason glommed on to Charlie and propped him up as political avatar in the mold of a modern day Adolf Hitler at Pasewalk waiting to be released from prison to enlighten humanity. Mason touted Manson as "the primary living philosopher of revolution in the world today" and The Universal Order's "philosophical and ideological leader."

Warthan and Manson exchanged letters filled with plans of starting a Nazi/Manson training camp in the woods near Oroville, California, and Manson went so far as to send his second-in-command, Squeaky, to check out Warthan. Having passed the Squeaky-test, Warthan began face-to-face meetings with Manson, which came to an abrupt end in September 1982 after Warthan murdered a teenaged drifter named Joe Hoover. Authorities say the boy had been slain because he mouthed off to police about Warthan's Nazi group.

Manson was allowed back on the mainline in July 1980, which meant that he could wander Vacaville's main corridor and mingle with the general population. Along with Charlie's new-found freedom, he was awarded the chief clerk job at the prison chapel. Soon after, a white racist enclave had formed around him, which after awhile became even too much for Charlie to handle, as the constant parade of psychotic sycophants and autograph seekers began getting on his nerves. Prison officials, as well, grew wary of the situation when two inmates emerged one day zombie-like from the chapel with X's carved on their foreheads.

In October 1982, Manson lost his mainline privileges when a prison guard – attempting to get into the chapel – discovered the door had been bound from the inside by electrical wire. After gaining entry, a search of the clerk's office revealed a secret trap door, leading to the attic where a well-stocked cache was discovered, consisting of a glass vial containing a volatile white liquid, a piece of metal stock sharpened into a weapon, wirecutters, four bags of pot, one hundred feet of nylon cord, and a hot air balloon catalog. A search of Manson's cell later turned up a hacksaw, more marijuana, and a quantity of LSD. Evidently, Charlie had been planning a prison break. Although the attic in the clerk's office was enclosed, it connected to a series of air ducts, which would have eventually led to freedom and a hot air balloon trip on acid.

On September 24th, 1984, in the Vacaville hobby shop, another inmate, Jan Holmstrom – whose religious beliefs were at odds with Manson's – doused Charlie with paint thinner and set him on fire. Apparently, Manson had objected to Holmstrom chanting "Hare Krishna", which set off Holmstrom on a paint thinner throwing tirade. Other inmates extinguished the flames and rushed Manson to the prison hospital. Charlie suffered burns over 18 percent of his body, mainly to his face, hands and scalp, but the injuries sustained were minimal.

Manson was transferred to San Quentin prison in July 1985, and to Corcoran prison in March 1989.

CHAPTER 47

Where Have All The Buck Knives Gone?

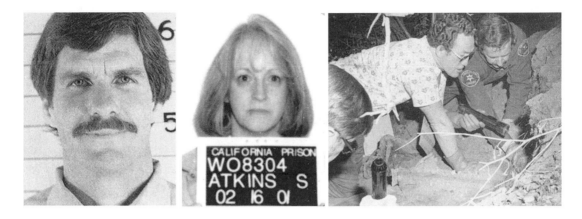

It's been forty years now since Charlie's Family left their indelible mark on American society. While the other convicted Tate/LaBianca murderers have renounced Charlie and undergone religious conversions, Manson has continued to hold his ground, refusing to recant or accept responsibility for the infamous murders attributed to his name.

During his imprisonment at the Men's Colony in San Luis Obispo, California, Tex Watson has become a successful jailhouse minister. His tax free organization – Abounding Love Ministries (ALMS) – reportedly brings in $1,500 a month. While in prison, Tex has fathered three children, all at the expense of California tax payers. It should come as no surprise that Tex is another adherent to Manson-as-Tate-LaBianca-murders-mastermind, which is the same position held by those former female Manson followers behind bars: Van Houten, Krenwinkel and Atkins.

As for the other former convicted Manson Family members, Susan Atkins now claims she never stabbed anyone, while Leslie Van Houten asserts that she only stabbed Rosemary LaBianca in the buttocks after she was dead. Tex Watson's position is that he was totally mind controlled by The Devil (i.e. Charlie) at the time, indicating that his involvement was due to demonic possession. Blame it on the Devil...

Of all those convicted for Tate/LaBianca, Krenwinkel has been the most quiet. It is reported that she has great feelings of guilt about her part in the murders and has yet to forgive herself. Like the others, her parole has been continually denied.

‡

When Susan Atkins was first taken into custody for the Hinman murder, she reveled in her memories of the Cielo Drive massacre, confessing to cellmates Ronnie Howard and Virginia Graham that it was the best sexual experience of her life. Atkins now denies having stabbed Tate, or any of the other victims. Following her jailhouse baptism, she turned her hands and palms upward, declaring: "I thank God that these two hands of mine have never taken a human life."

Like every other act in her life, Atkins' conversion to Christianity was done with grandiosity, as "the presence of the Lord came into (her) little cell like liquid waves of glory." From the instant she embraced Christ, Atkins let it be known that she considered herself a person endowed with great spiritual qualities. At the time, she put out a newsletter comparing herself to great biblical figures:

"Lately the Lord has been leading me in a very quiet walk with him. I am reminded how he led Moses into the wilderness for many years before He was able to use Moses; He did the same thing with Paul before Paul was placed once again before the people of God to minister unto them." (Newsletter, April '78)

In September 1978, Susan informed her readers that she would no longer be able to write her newsletter, and had this to add:

"...for I believe up until now these letters they have not been Susan's letters to you, but Words of encouragement and strength from God through the Holy Spirit through this vessel...I feel maybe in some small way, the way Paul the Apostle must of felt when he got on board the ship in the book of Acts, bound for Jerusalem."

From the above quote, it can be gathered that Atkins' possessed an inflated view of herself. This was the same Susan Atkins who once said: "To be big, that's the only thing that counts." Whether high on acid, Charlie, or the Lord, Atkins always made it a point of being the center of attention, be it dancing topless in swingin' 1960's go-go clubs, or bragging about her murders to jailhouse bunkmates.

While in prison, Atkins has been twice married. Her first marriage, in 1981, to Donald "Flash" Laisure, – who at 56 was 19 years her senior – was short-lived. On an episode of *Geraldo*, Laisure recounted an incident where Susan tried to stab him during a conjugal visit, pulling up his shirt to show a horizontal cut running across his stomach. According to Laisure, this attack occurred as he and Susan were watching television one evening and Laisure remarked about the good looks of a young lady on the tube. In response, Susan allegedly went ballistic, slicing Laisure. Just the same, Laisure comes across as a slick con man, who would no doubt spin a yarn for fun and profit. Nor was this his first marriage; at last count Laisure had been married 46 times. Atkins later remarried in 1987 to James Whitehouse, a law school graduate fifteen years her junior, to whom she is still married.

Recently, Atkins has fallen on hard times, and it appears doubtful she will live to see the Manson Family murders 40th anniversary. In July of 2008, officials at Corona Women's Prison made a compassionate release request due to Atkins' deteriorating condition, which included the loss of a leg and unsuccessful surgery for brain cancer. However, Atkins request was denied, a move supported by Governor Arnold Schwarzenegger. She is currently incarcerated at the Central California Women's Facility in Chowchilla, CA, in a skilled nursing unit.

‡

On January 26th, 1996, the Access Manson website was launched on the 25th anniversary of what webmaster George Stimson referred to as "Manson's illegal conviction for murder." Another mission of the site was to promote Manson's environmental organization, ATWA, which Sandra Good started in 1985. During that period, Good moved to Hanford, California, located in close proximity to Charlie at Corcoran State Prison.

ATWA is an acronym for Air, Trees, Water, and Animals. According to Access Manson: "ATWA is your survival on earth. It's a revolution against pollution. ATWA is ATWAR with pollution – a holy war. You are either working for ATWA – life – or you're working for death. Fix it and live or run from it and die."

In 2001, the site went offline. At that time, Good – and her boyfriend Stimson – left Hanford and have since issued no further statements in support of Manson or ATWA. Rumor has it Manson ended this relationship.

‡

Throughout his forty years in prison, Bobby Beausoleil – currently incarcerated at the Oregon State Penitentiary – has continued producing music. In 2004, Beausoleil's *Lucifer Rising* soundtrack was re-released. Other CD releases include, *Running With The White Wolf* (1998) and *Dreamways of the Mystic* (2006.)

In interviews, Beausoleil comes across as man who has made the best of an unfortunate situation, admitting fully his role in the Hinman murder.

‡

On December 23rd, 1987, Squeaky Fromme – serving a life sentence at West Virginia's Alderson prison – was reported missing, and a nationwide alert went out as security was stepped up for ex-President Gerald Ford. On Christmas Day, Squeaky was apprehended in the woods near Alderson. She was subsequently transferred to Lexington, Kentucky with fifteen months added to her sentence. Squeaky's escape was motivated by a false rumor that Charlie was dying of testicular cancer, which initiated her overwhelming desire to see her groovy little guru one last time.

Sara Jane Moore – that other failed Ford assassin and purported childhood friend of Manson's – was imprisoned at Alderson during the same period as Fromme. Like Squeaky, Moore escaped from Alderson in 1979, but was recaptured within 72 hours. A few years later, another failed presidential assassin, John Hinkley, Jr. – a resident of St Elizabeth's Hospital in Washington, DC – tried to obtain a day pass from the facility, but was subsequently denied when officials discovered letters he had written to Squeaky Fromme.

‡

In the late 1970's, Steve Grogan (aka Clem Scramblehead) cooperated with authorities by revealing the location of Shorty Shea's buried remains at Spahn Ranch. This disclosure helped Grogan secure his eventual parole. While serving time with Bobby Beausoleil at Tracy Prison in the mid 1970's, Grogan was among a group of inmates who performed on Beausoleil's *Lucifer Rising* soundtrack.

Although popular rumor has it Grogan worked for many years as a house painter in Southern California's San Fernando Valley, his involvement with the music industry has been ongoing, and at one time he reportedly toured with Hank Williams, Jr. Recently, Grogan has been using the stage name of Adam Gabriel, performing in two bands that have released albums: RhythmTown Jive and Christmas Jug Band. The latter provided a song used in a 2005 Christmas episode of the TV sitcom "My Name is Earl."

‡

Every few years, Manson and his former minions come up for parole, although there remains a dedicated group of victim's rights advocates who continue to speak out at these hearings. In recent times, certain Christian groups have mounted a vigorous campaign for the release of those former Manson Family members who have seemingly turned their lives around through the grace of the almighty: Watson, Atkins and Davis. Whatever eventually happens, one thing is certain: Manson will never get out, for no other reason than the media has portrayed him as the greatest madman murderer of all time, although it has never been proven that Charlie actually killed anyone.

In the late 1990's, FBI profiler John Douglas stated that if Manson were released, he would not consider him a violent threat to society, and that Charlie would probably go off into the desert and mind his own business – or maybe try to cash in on his celebrity status.

However, Douglas felt that the biggest threat Charlie posed would come from those misguided losers who would gravitate to him, and proclaim him their personal saviour.

Page 74. Left: Cathy Myers/Cappy Gillies. Right: Barker Ranch.

Page 78. Left: Barbara Hoyt. Centre: Kitty Lutesinger. Right: Family girls inside Charles Manson's customised dune buggy (photograph taken by Manson).

Page 84. Left: The Beatles, from *The White Album*. Centre: "Helter Scelter" [sic] door, found at Spahn Ranch. Right: The Dakota Building, New York, scene of Polanski's *Rosemary's Baby* and John Lennon's assassination.

Page 85. Left: Street execution in Vietnam, 1968; "snuff" footage broadcast on national US television. Centre: Danny DeCarlo. Right: Randy Starr.

Page 92. Left: Vern Plumlee. Centre left: T.J. Walleman. Centre right: Lawrence Bailey. Right: Poster for *Witchcraft 70* (1970), which advertises "The Sensual Ecstasies of Hippie 'Families'" and "Macabre Orgies of a Secret Sect of Evil" amongst its "unspeakable" delights.

Page 95. Left: Bernard Crowe. Centre: 6933 Franklin Avenue, Hollywood, the Rosina Kroner apartment where Charles Manson reputedly shot Bernard Crowe. Right: Black Panther leaders in 1968: armed, dangerous, and ready for race war?

Page 96. Left: Gary Hinman's house. Centre: Hinman's house with blood on the floor and "POLITICAL PIGGY" and panther pawprint on the wall. Right: Bobby Beausoleil, found guilty of murder.

Page 99. Left: Stephanie Schram. Centre: last known photograph of Sharon Tate alive, believed taken on the day of her murder, found inside Woytek Frykowski's camera. Right: Steve Parent, murder scene.

Page 102, top row. Left: Sharon Tate and Jay Sebring, murder scene. Right: Woytek Frykowski, murder scene.

Page 102, bottom row. Left: Abigail Folger, murder scene. Centre: "PIG" written in human blood on the door of 10050 Cielo Drive. Right: Roman Polanski returns from London to identify his wife's body.

Page 107, top row. Left: Sharon Tate, coroner's photo. Right: Jay Sebring, coroner's photo.

Page 107, bottom row. Left: Abigail Folger, coroner's photo. Right: Woytek Frykowski, coroner's photo.

Page 108. Left: Leno LaBianca. Centre: Rosemary LaBianca. Right: The LaBianca residence at 3301 Waverly Drive.

Page 110, top row. Left: Leno LaBianca, murder scene. Right: Rosemary LaBianca, murder scene.

Page 110, bottom row. Left: "RISE". Centre: "DEATH TO PIGS". Right: "HEALTER SKELTER". Manson catchphrases daubed in human blood at the LaBianca crime scene.

Page 112. Left: Rosemary LaBianca, coroner's photo. Right: Leno LaBianca, coroner's photo, showing "WAR" carved into the torso.

Page 113. Left: Charles Manson, pictured August 16th 1969, under arrest at Spahn Ranch. Centre: Frankie Carbo. Right: Frank Costello. Manson-Mob connections?

Page 115. Left: Charles Manson, summer of 1969. Right: Tex Watson, summer of 1969.

Page 116. Left: Sherry Cooper. Centre: Shorty Shea. Right: Raid on Spahn Ranch.

Page 118. Left: raid on Spahn ranch; Family members rounded up (plus Straight Satan Robert Rinehard, far right). Centre: Weapons cache recovered from Spahn Ranch. Right: Charles Manson, arrest photo August 22nd 1969.

Page 119. Left: Roman Polanski poses by the door of 10050 Cielo Drive. Right: Psychic Peter Hurkos crouches in the gore of the murder scene.

Page 121. Left: Gregg Jakobson, Manson demo-producer. Centre: Family "Creepy-Crawl" insignia. Right: One of the customised dune buggies used by the Family in Death Valley.

Page 124. Left: Fake graves at Barker Ranch were found to contain secret weapon and supply stashes. Centre: Barker Ranch interior. Right: Bedroom at Barker Ranch.

Page 126, top row. Left: The kitchen cupboard at Barker Ranch where Charles Manson was discovered. Right: Manson brought into custody at Inyo County jailhouse.

Page 126, bottom row. Left: Manson brought into custody at Inyo County jailhouse. Centre: Manson booked and photographed at Inyo County jailhouse. Right: Susan Bartell, also arrested.

Page 128. Left: Susan Atkins arrest photo. Centre: Virginia Graham. Right: Ronnie Howard.

Page 129. Left: Marina Habe, alleged Family murder victim. Centre left: Doreen Gaul, alleged Family murder victim. Centre right: Tex Watson under arrest. Right: The 10050 Cielo Drive murder weapon.

Page 131. Left and centre left: Posters for *Manson* (1973). Centre right: Front cover of the LIE album. Right: Nancy Pitman promoting the LIE album.

Page 133. Left: Scene from *Angels Wild Women* (1972). Right: Scene from *The Deathmaster* (1971). Early forays into the marketing of Manson.

Page 134. Left: *Life* magazine, December 1969. Centre left: Manson in court, December 24th 1969. Centre right: Manson talks to the press, June 1970. Right: Susan Atkins arrives at court, December 1969.

Page 135, top row. Left: Manson escorted to court, October 1970. Centre: Susan Atkins and Manson in court, October 1970. Right: Susan Atkins escorted to court, 1970.

Page 135, bottom row. Left: Manson – X'd out, 1970. Centre: Manson arriving at court, December 1970. Right: Susan Atkins in court, 1970.

Page 136. Left: *Rolling Stone*, June 1970. Centre: *Tuesday's Child*, Manson cover. Right: Dennis Hopper (himself arrested in 1975 after a naked, drink-and-drugs-fuelled rampage through Taos, New Mexico).

Page 137. Left: Linda Kasabian escorted from court by police. Centre: "Judas Day"; Family girls protest against "snitch" Kasabian. Right: Prosecutor Vincent Bugliosi presenting rope evidence from 10050 Cielo Drive.

Page 138. Left: The Jesus Christ "wanted" poster. Centre: Manson evincing messianic aura. Right: The Devil – "self-portrait" by Manson, made during his trial.

Page 140. Left: Leslie Van Houten, Susan Atkins, and Katie Krenwinkel on the police bus headed to court, 1970. Centre: Walking into court. Right: Manson walking to court, wearing ceremonial vest, flashing hand signals.

Page 141. Left: Catherine Share, Ruth Ann Moorehouse, and Lynette Fromme camped outside the courtroom. Right: Tex Watson under arrest, November 1971.

Page 143, top row. Left: Manson, March 1971. Centre: Manson, not long before receiving the death sentence. Right: Leslie, Susan and Katie with shaved heads after receiving the death sentence.

Page 143, bottom row. Left and centre: Family members on vigil, with shaved heads. Right: Manson in jail, December 1971.

Page 144. Left: Kenneth Como. Centre left: Dennis Rice. Centre right: Chuck Lovett. Right: Aftermath of the Hawthorne shooting.

Page 146. Left: SLA leader Donald DeFreeze and hostage-turned-terrorist Patty Hearst, San Francisco armed bank robbery. Right: Corpse of suicide cult leader Jim Jones.

Page 151. Left: L. Ron Hubbard, founder of Scientology, and renowned racist. Centre: Mae Brussell. Right: David Berkowitz, "Son of Sam".

Page 154. Left: Charles Manson's ATWA calling card. Right: Lynette Fromme and Sandy Good as Red and Blue; graveyard photoshoot.

Page 157. Left: Lynette Fromme and Sandy Good as Red and Blue; nude photoshoot. Right: Sandy Good as High Priestess of Mansonism.

Page 158. Left: Lynette Fromme arrested by President Ford's secret service agents. Centre: Leaving court on charges of attempted assasination. Right: *Time* magazine, September 1975.

Page 161. Left: William Mentzer. Centre: Ron Stark. Right: Robert DeGrimston, early Process Church meeting.

Page 167. Left: Unearthing human remains at Matamoros. Centre: Henry Lee Lucas. Right: Ottis Toole.

Page 168. Left: Sirhan Sirhan. Centre left: Mark Chapman. Centre right: John Hinkley Jr. Right: William Bryan.

Page 175. Left: Reverend Jerry Owen. Centre: Larry Flynt. Right: Altamont – death throes of the Love Generation.

Page 179. Left: Maria Theresa Alonzo. Centre: Charles Manson, 1978. Right: James Mason with Sandy Good.

Page 180. Left: Charles Manson, Vacaville, early 1980s. Centre: Charles Manson, *Live at San Quentin* album. Right: Charles Manson, 1985.

Page 183. Left: Tex Watson, prison photo 1987. Centre: Susan Atkins, prison photo 2001. Right: Sifting the bones of Shorty Shea, 1977.

Page 185. Left: Bobby Beausoleil in prison. Centre: *Lucifer Rising* CD, 2004. Right: Lynette Fromme prison escape, 1987.

Page 186. Left: "Helter Skelter" truck unearthed during Barker Ranch excavations, 2008. Centre: Charles Manson, prison photo 2006. Right: Charles Manson, prison photo 2009, aged seventy-four.

Access Manson Website, late 1990s

Anger, Kenneth; "Anger Rising: An Interview" by Dnyl of T.O.P.Y Chaos

Anonymous, *A Psychosexual History of the Manson Family*, Aes-Nihil Productions, date unknown

Atkins, Susan, with Slosser, Bob, *Child Of Satan, Child Of God* (Logos International, Plainfield, New Jersey, 1977)

Baddeley, Gavin, *Lucifer Rising: Sin, Devil Worship and Rock 'N' Roll* (Plexus Publishing Limited, 1999)

Bainbridge, William Sims, *Satan's Power: A Deviant Psychotherapy Cult* (University of California Press, 1978)

Barton, Blanche, *The Secret life of a Satanist: The Authorized Biography of Anton LaVey* (Feral House, Los Angeles, 1990)

BBC Interview with Bobby Beausoleil, conducted by Bill Murphy, 1994

Bishop, George, *Witness To Evil* (Nash Publishing, Los Angeles, 1971)

Black, David, *Acid: The Secret History of LSD* (Vision Paperbacks, London, 1998)

Blood, Linda, *The New Satanists* (Warner Books, New York, 1994)

Bluhm, Erik, "Charlie's Angels", *Great God Pan* magazine #6, Fall 1995

Bravin, Jess, *Squeaky - The Life And Times Of Lynette Alice Fromme* (St. Martin's Press, New York, 1997)

Bresler, Fenton, *Who Killed John Lennon?* (St. Martin's Press, New York, 1989)

Brussell, Mae, *Dialogue Conspiracy* radio program, 11/10/71, 1/15/78

Brussell, Mae, "Why Was Patricia Hearst Kidnapped?" *The Realist* magazine, 1974

Brussell, Mae, "World Watchers International", 11-16-84

Bugliosi, Vincent, with Gentry, Curt, *Helter Skelter* (W. W. Norton, New York, 1974)

Butler, Dougal, *Full Moon: The Amazing Rock and Roll Life of Keith Moon*

Cabot, Tracy, ed., *Inside The Cults* (Holloway House, Los Angeles, 1970)

Capote, Truman, *Music For Chameleons* (The New American Library, New York, 1980)

Conway, Flo and Siegelman, David, *Snapping, America's epidemic of sudden personality change* (J.B. Lippincott Company, Philadelphia and New York, 1978)

Constantine, Alex, "Operation CHAOS: Political murders and British Rock Musicians-An Annotated Guide", date unknown.

Cooper, David E., *The Manson Murders: A Philosophical Inquiry* (Schenkman Books, Inc., Rochester, Vermont, 1974)

Chaplain Ray, with Wagner, Walter, *God's Prison Gang* (Fleming H. Revell Co., 1977)

Day, Doris, with Hotchner, A. E., *Her Own Story* (William Morrow & Co., New York)

Douglas, John. with Olshaker, Mark, *Mind Hunter* (Pocket Books, New York, 1996)

Emmons, Nuel, *Manson In His Own Words* (Grove Press Inc., New York, 1986)

Felton, David, ed., *Mindfuckers* (Straight Arrow Publishers, Inc., San Francisco, 1972)

Freedland, Nat, *The Occult Explosion* (Putnam, New York, 1972)

Gaines, Steven, *Heroes And Villains, The True Story Of The Beach Boys* (New American Library, New York, 1986)

George, Edward, and Matera, Dary, *Charles Manson's Life Behind Bars: Taming The Beast* (St. Martin's Press, New York, 1998)

Gilmore, John, and Kenner, Ron, *The Garbage People* (Amok Books, Los Angeles, 1995)

Godwin, Jeff, *The Devil's Disciples: The Truth About Rock* (Chick Publications, Chino, CA, 1985)

Greene, Carol, *Test-Tube Murder: The Case of Charles Manson* (Germany, 1992)

Hall, Angus, *Strange Cult* (Aldus Books Limited, London, 1976)

Hanna, David, *Cults In America* (Tower Publications, New York, 1979)

Hidell, Al, "Who Killed John Lennon?", *Paranoia: The Conspiracy Reader*, issue 3, Winter 1994

Higham, Charles, and Moseley, Roy, *Cary Grant: The Lonely Heart* (Harcourt/Brace/Jovanovich, New York, 1989)

Judge, John, *Judge for Yourself: A Treasury of Writings and Speeches by John Judge* (Prevailing Winds Research, Santa Barbara, CA, undated)

Judge, John; personal correspondence, 1996

Judge, John, "Poolside with John Judge", *Prevailing Winds*, undated interview

Kaiser, Robert Blair, *"R.F.K. Must Die!"* (Grove Press, New York, 1970)

Kaufman, Phil and White, Colin, *Road Mangler Deluxe* (White-Bouke, Glendale, CA, 1993)

Keith, Jim, *Mind Control, World Control: The Encyclopedia of Mind Control* (Adventures Unlimited Press, Kempton, Illinois, 1997)

Keith, Jim; personal correspondence, late 1990's

Kerekes, David, and Slater, David, *Killing For Culture: An Illustrated History of Death Film from Mondo to Snuff* (Creation Books, London, 1995)

King, Greg, *Sharon Tate and the Manson Murders* (Barricade Books, New York, 2000)

Koenig, P.R., *Charles Manson and the Solar Lodge of the O.T.O.*

Krassner, Paul, *Confessions of a Raving, Unconfined Nut* (Simon & Schuster, New York, 1993)

Krassner, Paul: personnel correspondence, 1997

Landis, Bill, *Anger: The Unauthorized Biography* (Harper Collins, New York, 1995)

Lee, Martin A, and Shlain, Bruce, *Acid Dreams: The CIA, LSD and the Sixties Rebellion* (Grove Press, New York, 1985)

LeBlanc, Jerry and Davis, Ivor, *5 To Die* (Holloway House, Los Angeles, 1970)

Logan, Daniel, *America Bewitched: The Rise of Black Magic and Spiritism* (William Morrow and Co., New York, 1974)

Lyons, Arthur, *Satan Wants You* (Mysterious Press, New York, 1988)

Lyons, Arthur, *The Second Coming: Satanism In America* (Award Books, New York, 1970)

Manson, Charles: KALX radio interview, 2/27/85

Manson, Charles; Tom Snyder Interview

Marx, Samuel and Vanderveen, Joyce, *Deadly Illusions* (Random House, New York, 1990)

Mason, James, *Siege* (Storm Books, Denver, 1992)

McGowan, David, *There's Something About Henry, Part1: Sympathy for the Devil*, Disinformation.com, June 2000

Murphy, Bob, *Desert Shadows* (Falcon Press, Billings, Montana, 1986)

Nelson, Bill: Mansonmurders website, late 1990s

Nelson, Bill, *Manson Behind The Scenes* (Pen Power Publications, 1997)

Nelson, Bill, *Tex Watson, The Man, The Madness, The Manipulation* (Pen Power Publications, 1991)

Norris, Joel, *Serial Killers: The Growing Menace* (Doubleday, New York, 1988)

Parker, John, *Polanski* (Victor Gollancz, Great Britain, 1993)

Perry, Charles, *The Haight-Ashbury* (Rolling Stone Press, 1985)

Petros, George, "Ed Sanders: Fug and Family Man", *Seconds* magazine, interview with Ed Sanders

Phillips, John, with Jerome, Jim, *Papa John* (Doubleday & Co., Inc., New York)

Piccard, George, *Liquid Conspiracy: JFK, LSD, the CIA, Area 51 and UFOs* (Adventures Unlimited Press, Illinois, 1999)

Phillips, Michelle, *California Dreamin'* (Warner Books, New York, 1986)

Raschke, Carl A., *Painted Black* (Harper & Row Publishers, San Francisco, 1990)

Rubin, Jerry, *We Are Everywhere* (Harper & Row, New York, 1971)

Russell, J.D., *The Beautiful People* (Apollo Books, New York, 1970)

Sanders, Ed, *The Craw-Doo-Dah Gazette*, "Manson's Helter FBI Skelter" November, 1976

Sanders, Ed, *The Family: The Story of Charles Manson's Dune Buggy Attack Battalion* (E. P. Dutton & Co. Inc, New York, 1971)

Satan, Johnny; *Death Trip: The Story of Charles Manson and the Love and Terror Cult* (Death Valley Books, 1994)

Schreck, Nikolas, *The Manson File* (Amok Press, New York, 1988)

Shiva, Frater, *Inside Solar Lodge, Outside The Law: True Tales of Initiation and High Adventure* (The Teitan Press, ME, 2007)

St. Clair, David, *The Psychic World of California*, Doubleday, 1972

Tackwood, Louis E., *The Glass House Tapes*

Taylor, R.N., "The Process: The Final Judgment", *Esoterra* magazine

Terry, Maury, *The Ultimate Evil* (Doubleday & Co., Inc., New York, 1987)

The Family Jams, liner notes, Sandra Good and Charles Manson, Aoroa Records, 1997

Turner, William and Jonn Christian, *The Assassination of Robert F. Kennedy* (Random House,1978)

"Turning Point" ABC News with Diane Sawyer, Leslie Van Houten interview , 1994

Watkins, Paul, with Soledad, Guillermo, *My Life With Charles Manson* (Bantam Books, New York, 1979)

Watson, Charles, and Chaplain Ray, *Will You Die For Me?* (Cross Roads Publications,Inc., Dallas, Texas)

Wilson, Brian, and Gold, Todd, *Wouldn't It Be Nice, My Own Story* (Harper Collins Publishers, New York, 1991)

Wilson, Colin, and Seaman, Donald, *The Encyclopedia Of Modern Murder* (Crown Publishers, Inc., New York, 1983)

Wizinski, Sy, *Charles Manson, Love Letters To A Secret Disciple* (Moonmad Press, Terre Haute, Indiana, 1976)

Zaehner, R. C., *Our Savage God* (Universal Press Syndicate, New York, 1974)